and That's the Way It Was

IN JACKSON'S HOLE

by Jack Huyler

A Jackson Holer since 1926

•

with Foreword

by Clifford P. Hansen

Former Governor of Wyoming and U.S. Senator

Jackson Hole Historical Society and Museum

Jackson, Wyoming

2003

Second edition, revised
Jackson Hole, Wyoming

•

Published by
Jackson Hole Historical Society and Museum
P.O. Box 1005, Jackson, Wyoming 83001
(307) 733-9605

•

Cover and book design: Tracy Lamb
Editorial review: Sigrid Asmus
Front cover photo credits: Upper left and right, Collection of the Jackson Hole Historical Society and Museum; Lower left, Collection of the Huyler Family;
Lower right and center, Collection of the Jackson Hole Historical Society and Museum.
Back cover photograph: Elizabeth McCabe, Collection of the Huyler Family.

•

ISBN 1-886402-04-3

Library of Congress Cataloging-in-Publication Data

Huyler, John S., 1920-
And that's the way it was in Jackson's Hole / by Jack Huyler; with foreword by Clifford P. Hansen.—2nd ed.
p. cm.
ISBN 1-886402-04-3 (alk. paper)
1. Jackson Hole (Wyo.)—Social life and customs—Anecdotes. 2. Ranch life—Wyoming—Jackson Hole—Anecdotes. 3. Frontier and pioneer life—Wyoming—Jackson Hole—Anecdotes. 4. Huyler, John S., 1920-—Anecdotes. 5. Jackson Hole (Wyo.)—Biography—Anecdotes. 6. Oral history. 7. Folklore—Wyoming—Jackson Hole. I. Jackson Hole Historical Society and Museum. II. Title.

F767.T28H89 2003
978.7'55—dc21

2003044647

Wyoming State Historical Society Award to Jack Huyler's book
and That's the Way It Was . . . in Jackson's Hole
2001

Award: Publications Award - Books - Non-fiction

General: One of two awards in this category

Nominated by: Ed Cheramy, Member of the Board of Directors, Jackson Hole Historical Society and Museum

Purpose of award program:
"To recognize an author or authors who have contributed significantly to the history of Wyoming through a book or pamphlet/brochure/calendar."

Purpose of the non-fiction award:
"Publications - Books - Non-fiction, on a Wyoming subject, locale of which is Wyoming or an adjacent area. Note: Two awards in this category are given each year.

Award Certificate says the following:

Wyoming State Historical Society
Historical Award

Jack Huyler
Rocking H Ranch, Wilson

Has received the award given by the Society for the year 2001
in recognition of accomplishments in the promotion and preservation
of Wyoming history in the field of Publications Awards—Books
for his book, *and That's the Way It Was . . . in Jackson's Hole.*

FIRST EDITION DONORS

The publication of the first edition of this book
was made possible through the generosity of:

Ed and Shirley Cheramy

Whit and Betty Clayton

Ted and Addie Donnan

Keeping History Alive for Future Generations of Teton County
The Halpin Family—Lost Creek Ranch, Moose, Wyoming

Jackson Hole Stock Agency

Jack's Neighbors at the Snake River Ranch

Tracy Lamb

Dean and Carol Lewis

Gloria McCourt

Art and Sally Peters

Tom and Birdie Rossetter

John and Marge Ryan

Bob and Barbara Shervin

Mike Wardell

SECOND EDITION DONORS

Publication of the second, revised edition of this book was made possible through the generosity of:

An Anonymous Gift

Keeping History Alive for Future Generations of Teton County
The Halpin Family—Lost Creek Ranch, Moose, Wyoming

Jackson Hole Stock Agency

Carole and Norm Hofley

Tracy Lamb

OTHER TITLES

published by the
Jackson Hole Historical Society and Museum

Jackson Hole: Crossroads of the Western Fur Trade, 1807-1840
by Merill J. Mattes

•

David E. Jackson, Field Captain of the Rocky Mountain Fur Trade
by Vivian Linford Talbot

•

Landmarks of the Rocky Mountain Fur Trade:
Two One-Day Self-Guided Tours from Jackson, Wyoming
by Pierce Olson

EXPLANATION OF USAGE

Dudine, the feminine counterpart of *Dude*, was in general use throughout the heyday of dude ranching. For reasons unknown, it has virtually disappeared.

Gradually, after World War II, *Jackson's Hole* evolved into *Jackson Hole.* I use the former to designate the Old Days.

Opinions expressed in the chapters that follow are mine and are not necessarily shared by the Jackson Hole Historical Society and Museum.

—J. H.

PHOTOGRAPHS

CONTENTS

FOREWORD

Jackson Hole, Wyoming, was one of the last valleys in the western frontier to be settled. The most formidable deterrent was lack of easy access. Steep canyon walls and high timbered mountain passes stopped wagons until late in the nineteenth century. The first settlers were single men; families came later.

Despite the area's relative inaccessibility, its resources, as they became increasingly well known, brought more residents. Early on, trapping, hunting, guiding, raising livestock, and mining were important. But one characteristic was dominant—its sheer, unique, incomparable beauty. With Yellowstone just to the north, visitors coming to spend the summer made guiding an important source of income. Inevitably dude ranching followed. Our author, Jack Huyler, has spent at least part of each year in Jackson Hole since he was just a boy. While no one can do justice in recording the lives and activities of all the settlers, Jack has done a masterful job in preserving a wide swath of the lives of many.

In 1898, one year after he first spent a summer in Jackson Hole, my father, Pete Hansen, homesteaded south of present-day Teton village. After a few years he sold that property, moved east of the Snake River, and continued cattle ranching in the Zenith area. The Huylers, on the west side of the Snake, were dude ranchers. Our families have known each other for a long time.

For those interested in learning about the Old West as it really was, Jack Huyler has captured that time in Jackson Hole in the memories and stories he presents in this work. He lived in Jackson Hole when ranching was paramount and when the valley was a microcosm of the early American West. In recounting his stories and tales, Jack recreates the early days of the valley. He reminds us that Jackson Hole attracted people of very diverse backgrounds and interests. Through his stories he chronicles the old-time residents and the colorful personalities that made the valley special, from pioneers and horse traders to cowboys and dude wranglers.

For over fifty years Jack has collected tales and stories that document the folk traditions of this exquisite valley nestled beneath the Teton Range. He learned many of his tales at his Rocking H Ranch while the old-timers, and a few young'ns too, gathered around the campfire after a potluck supper served up on a hay wagon. Old-timers recounted their stories of days gone by and reminisced about "Them What's Gone."

Jack knows the folk history of Jackson Hole as few others do. He has done a marvelous job of recounting the folk stories and tales of old Jackson Hole. His descriptions bring to life the early settlers and the original characters who inhabited the wilderness beneath the majestic Tetons. The lure and significance of his collection of memories is the portrait of human life that they illuminate and the way that life meshes with the wildness of the valley and its stunning natural beauty.

The author has watched the development and changes that have taken place in the valley during his many years here. He was most aware of the impact that the splendor of this area would have on its ultimate destiny. In setting down his tales and memories, he memorializes the traditions that have been passed down orally about the Huyler family and this very special community. It is important, then, that he has taken the time to capture the past and to record it for the future.

Clifford P. Hansen
Former Governor of Wyoming and U.S. Senator
Jackson Hole, Wyoming, 2000

ACKNOWLEDGMENTS

I am indebted to the following for reading sections of this opus in rough draft and for verifying, adding to, or correcting my accounts: Joe Albright; Steve Bartek; Jo Anne Byrd; Lawrence Cheney; Ed Cheremy; Glenn Exum; Barbara Gray; Joan Grever; Cliff and Martha Hansen; Karly Johnson; Larry Kummer; Tom and Cile Lamb; Lokey Lytjen; Lee Lundy; Danny Mayer; Bob and Claire McConaughy; Pierce Olson; Jack Richards; John Richards; Charlotte Robertson; John Ryan, Jr.; John "Tommy" Waldron; Mike Wardell; Jackie Richards Williams; Michael Johnson, Cultural Resources Specialist of Grand Teton National Park; and the Jackson Hole Historical Society and Museum.*

As this list testifies, I have made sincere attempts to corroborate my memories of the old days; nonetheless, I suppose some errors of fact (dates and the like) may persist. For those I apologize, yet even though the date may be in error, the tales are true as I witnessed them or heard them from my father or other reliable oral historians.

I also gratefully acknowledge the infinite patience and good humor and seemingly infinite knowledge of my computer "gurus," Cliff Kirkpatrick and Jerry Holden, who somehow solved my problems—usually by phone—whenever my computer "did me wrong."

I am indebted to Bob Lucas, and to his sister Jennifer Flannagan and brother-in-law Wes, who saw to it that a particular pitchfork of historic importance was returned to our Rocking H Ranch after an absence of 66 years.

I cannot close these acknowledgments without thanking my younger son, the highly successful author Stephen P. Huyler, for carefully reading every page of this typescript and making useful and constructive suggestions.

Above all, I am indebted to my beloved wife, Margaret, who, as with all my writings, read every word aloud to me so that I could hear it as well as see it. That is no easy job!

* For 73 years I have wished that I had been born in Jackson's Hole. As a non-native, one of my lifetime ambitions was to become President of the Teton County Historical Society (as it was known before its merger with the Jackson Hole Museum). My election to that position was one of the proudest honors of a long life. The cadre of that group are the true elite of the Valley. They were kind enough to listen to the reading of most of this book, contributing additions, explanations, and corrections.

PREAMBLE

I write this book to make certain that my children and grandchildren will hear these stories and pass them on exactly as I heard or witnessed them.

DEDICATION

To the members of the Jackson Hole Historical Society and Museum,

fine folk preserving those things of true worth in the valley we love.

Thank God for them and for memories.

Map of Jackson's Hole
Showing Principal Dude Ranches

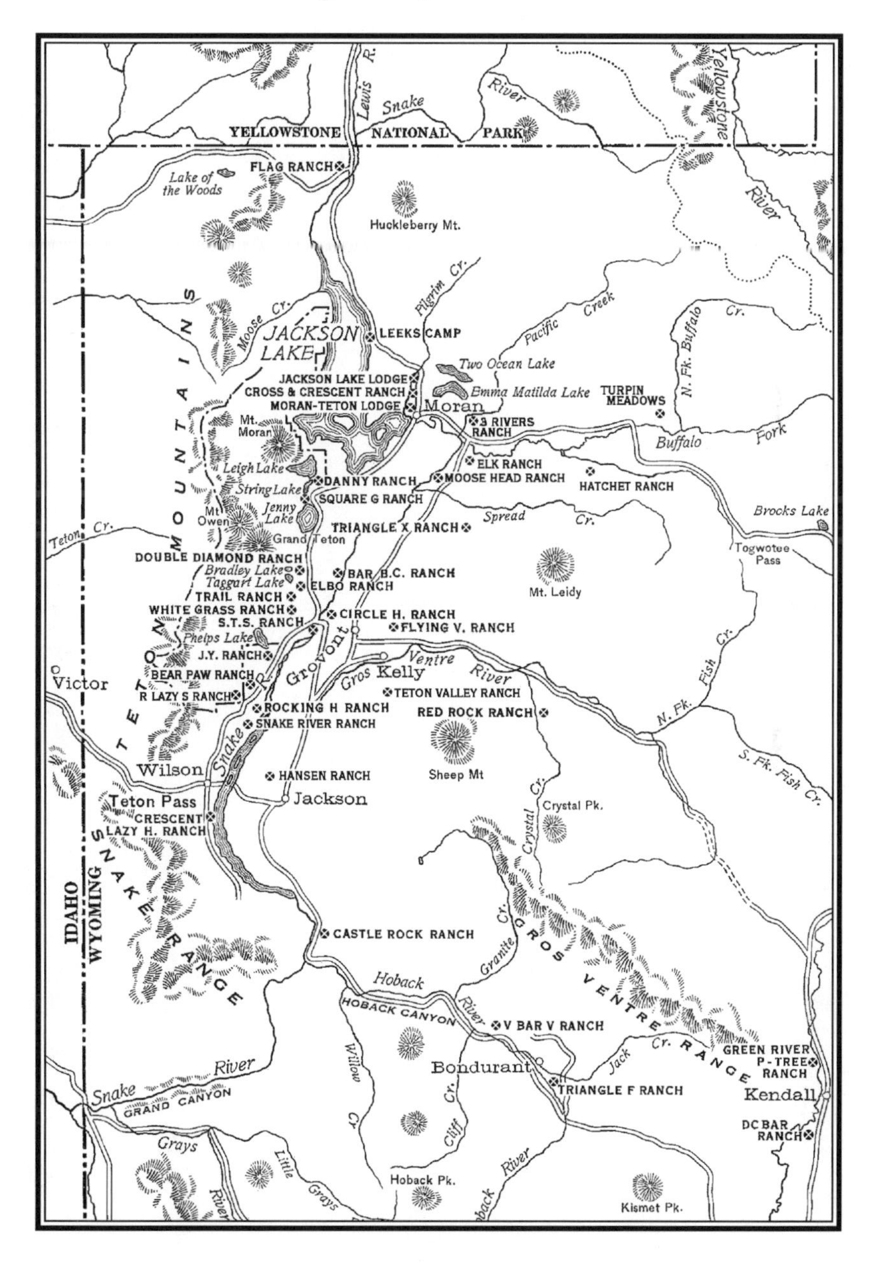

The above map has been altered from its 1928 original, and is used here with permission of the Union Pacific Railroad Museum.

CHAPTER ONE

The Old Man

The Old Man deserves to be first in this book because he was the most unforgettable "character" of all the "characters" I have known throughout a long life.

He (1867-1933) didn't like neighbors; and since it was generally accepted that he had killed three or more men in Jackson's Hole before the Law became well established, land adjacent to his sold cheap.

Why this aversion to neighbors? Was it just personal? Probably, it was more than a desire for privacy. The old homesteaders hoped neighboring land would stand unoccupied until their children or grandchildren became old enough to homestead it, thereby doubling, tripling, or quadrupling the original holding; so not infrequently they "discouraged" neighbors. With the Old Man, however, it was more than that.

Photo courtesy of Danny Mayer. Original photo scanned and enlarged by Ted Holden

"Mr. Huyler, there ain't a man in Jackson's Hole that would lift that tarp.", c. 1930s.

Henry and Rube Winslow, from "over the Hill," (Idaho) tried to homestead next door to the Old Man. One morning, when Henry stepped outdoors to relieve himself, a bullet cut his activity short. Hearing the shot, Rube went out to see what it was all about. That was the last sight he saw. The killer dragged both men into the cabin and set fire to it. In Wilson they saw the smoke, and hurried to investigate. The whole thing might have been passed off as an accident, except that the sod roof and ridge log had fallen across one of the bodies, protecting part of one corpse from burning. When the fire was out, someone moved that unconsumed ridge log, and there was Henry's torso with a bullet hole in it. The chimney of their cabin can be seen yet from Fall Creek Road.

Bill, one of the Old Man's sons, confessed to the killing. He was sentenced to from 12 to 20 years in the State Penitentiary in Rawlins, but was let out early because every one was sure he hadn't done it in the first place. They were sure that it had been the Old Man, who didn't like neighbors. In prison, Bill was quoted as saying, "I confessed to keep my Dad from being lynched."

Is it any wonder that Judd, another neighbor, built his cabin with windows eight feet above the ground so that he couldn't be bushwhacked while at home, yet, by standing on a box, he could shoot out.

Speaking of bushwhacking, those who knew said that whenever the Old Man drove his wagon to Jackson, or even up to Wilson, he took one of his womenfolk with him on the wagon seat as protection from bushwhackers.

The Old Man was reputed to have killed Paul Morris. Accepted rumor had it that a prominent citizen of the Valley hired the Old Man to kill him because Morris was working against the National Forest. The killing was supposed to look like an accident. At the time of his death Morris had his shoes off irrigating and was found covered with mud; however, the weapon found in his hand was not muddy; therefore, it was a murder, not an accident. Our friend Ollie Van Winkle found him and made the deduction.

"Wild Cat" Johnson was convicted of killing two trappers whom Bill Menor had ferried across the river and of burning their buggy so completely that only the metal remained; but one of those who found the remains tripped on a log and fell, ending up eyeballing a 25-30 Winchester stuffed under that very log. Justice of the Peace Lorenzo Waterman sent the serial number to Winchester, who furnished him the name of the store in Montana to which they had shipped the rifle. Waterman wrote the storekeeper, who gave Johnson's name. "Wild Cat" was convicted on circumstantial evidence and died in Rawlins; but there are those who think that the Old Man did the killing.

The next man to move onto the property next door to the Old Man came to town after a month or so offering to sell out. "Why?" people wanted to know.

"Because every morning when I come out of my tent, straighten up, and stretch in the morning sun, I see something gleam in the bushes. It's the sunlight off that Old Man's rifle barrel. He's always a-watchin' me."

"He hasn't shot at you, has he?"

"No, and he's not gonna get another chance."

Coulter D. Huyler, my Dad, bought that neighboring quarter-section on Butler Creek for, I believe, a dollar an acre. A quarter-section, 160 acres, was the homestead acreage available under the Homestead Act. It was down Fall Creek, 20 miles south of the Bear Paw, where we lived, but Dad envisioned it as the site of a hunting cabin.

He hired a couple of log men to build a cabin and contracted for a load of logs to be delivered for that purpose. We plus Jack and Bernice Neal (Bear Paw foreman and wife) rode with pack string and camping equipment from the Bear Paw to the newly acquired ranch. "We" consisted of Mother, Dad, Coulter, Charles and Gwyn Grant (Coulter's and my foster brother and sister), and me. Family movies lead me to believe that I was about eight years old, in which case, the year was 1928.

I believe it was the afternoon of the day after our arrival that Jack Neal looked up and announced quietly, "Here comes the Old Man."

The county road descended a hill just west of the site selected by Dad and Mother for the new cabin. Down that hill came a team and wagon driven by the white-haired Old Man. We moved to the edge of the road. Though only a youngster, I well knew that this was my first gunman and I feared it might be my last. Standing beside Mother, I tried to hold onto the leg of her Levis. I failed; no slack to grab.

As the Old Man drew alongside, Jack Neal introduced him by name to Dad. The Old Man's first utterance other than a quiet "Whoa" to his team was his gracious, "I don't like neighbors."

Dad was ready for that one. "I don't like neighbors either, unless they're good neighbors; but I'm prepared to be a good neighbor if you are. For example, the bridge between your place and mine needs repair. I'll pay for the materials if you'll furnish the labor." In those long ago days materials were more expensive than labor.

"That sounds fair enough. Mr. Huyler, would you like a quarter of elk?"

I was too small to see the blood stained tarp which the others had noted covering something in the back of the wagon. The day was early August, weeks before the opening of hunting season. The Old Man swung around on the wagon seat, flipped back the tarp, and handed down a forequarter of elk. It was then that Dad made what—so far as I know—was the only mistake he ever made with the Old Man. "I'd think you'd be afraid to drive right down the middle of the county road in the middle of Summer with that elk in your wagon."

"Mr. Huyler, there ain't a man in Jackson's Hole would lift that tarp."

Point made. End of conversation.

Despite the fact that we bought milk daily from the Old Man and that he often walked down with his pretty blonde daughter, Helen, "Honey," of an evening when she came over to deliver it, the betting in town was that when we returned East that Fall, there would be another mysterious fire and the new cabin would go up in flames. The odds makers underestimated Dad.

The day before we packed up to ride back up Valley to the Bear Paw, a couple of weeks prior to returning to Connecticut for the Winter, Dad stopped in at the Old Man's ranch.

Collection of the Jackson Hole Historical Society and Museum.

The real article, c. 1920s.

"My family and I are returning East for the Winter. Here's the key to the padlock on our cabin. I don't want to put you out, but any time you're going past, I'd appreciate it if you'd look in on things."

I suppose nobody had ever appealed to the Old Man before.

"Mr. Huyler, you just noise it around the Valley that I'm keepin' an eye on your place and nobody will trouble nothin'."

Nobody ever did.

In fact, Dad and the Old Man became good friends as well as good neighbors; they always addressed each other as "Mister" in a time and a place when most people didn't. The Old Man was reported by Jack Neal to have said, "Mr. Huyler is the only man in Jackson's Hole that's in my class." Dad took it as a compliment.

My brother, Coulter, dubbed our place the Bar Nothing; Dad liked the name, and it stuck as long as he owned it, though the brand was never registered.

It was the following Fall that a pair of young Rembrandts took on the Old Man's snow-white goats. The Old Man loved animals and, in addition to horses and cattle, kept pigeons, chickens, and those two snow-white goats.

One day my buddy Clyde Hinesley, Gwyn, and I came riding through the Old Man's spread on our way home. No one was there.

Have you ever understood why women decide to apply lipstick when they do? I have not. Anyway, Gwyn, ten years my senior, pulled out a bright red lipstick and began to apply it. Inspiration struck: There were those goats; there was that lipstick. Clyde and I borrowed the red, while Gwyn beat a sensible retreat to the Bar Nothing next door.

No artist ever approached a virgin canvas with more enthusiasm than we did those goats. A red circle around one eye, red tips to white ears, a red mustache, red horn tips. Lipstick failed before inspiration. Tossing the empty tube into the Old Man's trash, we crawled back onto our horses and took off for "home" well pleased with ourselves.

I guess Dad and the Old Man got a good chuckle over our escapade when next they met; but that wasn't the way we boys heard it.

When he saw us, Dad reported, "I have a message for you boys from our neighbor. He doesn't like what you did to his goats. He said to tell you that next time he sees you boys, he's going to cut off your ears and nail them to his barn door."

That was the message, and that was the way it was delivered, without even a hint of a smile.

You can well imagine how Clyde and I avoided that ranch and what a sharp lookout we kept for the Old Man.

There isn't much that a couple of boys can contribute to the running of a hunting camp. Our contribution was to ride to Wilson for the mail twice each week. For the next couple of trips we gave the Old Man's spread wide berth.

It was an 18-mile round trip, that ride for the mail; and it added a mile to go around the Old Man's place. After a couple of rides, Clyde and I decided that although we didn't dare ride the road, which passed right near his buildings, we could cut across his hayfields. It was Fall; the hay had been cut and stacked. We rode down through the trees at the edge of a hay field. We examined that meadow carefully; then, assured that we were safe, we over-and-undered our ponies and charged across, determined to make the crossing in the shortest possible time.

When a field is mowed, it cannot be mowed along the ditch berms. As a result, a man working on a headgate cannot be seen. He was, and we didn't. He must have heard the drumming of hooves, for he straightened up to see. We were headed directly for him.

"Whoa!" He was always quiet spoken. We hauled our cayuses to a stop.

"Did yer Dad give you my message?"

I can feel them now: my ears getting hot and growing huge as I contemplated losing them. I suppose nobody ever saw two more frightened boys. After all, this was the Old Man! He killed folks!

"Y-y-y-es, sir," we managed.

He must have seen that we were frightened almost out of our wits. He smiled his slow smile.

"You boys mustn't be givin' my goats high-falutin notions. I can't afford to keep 'em in lipstick."

Did he truly believe he was invincible, or was he trying to perpetuate his myth for self-protection?

Ed and Fred lived on the Crescent Lazy H Ranch, a few miles up the road. They were young; they were reckless; they were dead shots with a pistol. In fact, they waited until snow fell for easier tracking and stalking; then they shot their elk with six-guns.

One day, Dad asked the Old Man what he thought of the brothers.

"Them boys are itchin' to have a showdown with me, but I ain't got the heart to kill the only two men in Jackson's Hole with enough nerve to stand up to me."

Did he really think he could "take" them? Together? Singly? I have wondered for years. Only he knew.

Possibly the best of Dad's stories about the Old Man occurred following the death of a prominent, but controversial, citizen.

"You probably knew So-and-So about as long as anyone else," commented Dad. "Some people say he was a crook; some people say he was an honest man. What do you think?"

The Old Man looked reflective. "I killed a man on his account oncet. He called him a crook; I called him a liar; he was quick tempered, and I had to kill him. [Paul Morris?] But I've often thought I'd like to meet up with that feller agin and tell him I think he was right."

That about covered it, didn't it? Enough said.

In 1933 the Old Man died of pneumonia. It was his custom when Snake River was low to drive his team and wagon across the river to and from Jackson, rather than adding extra miles by driving up to the Wilson bridge. One cold Winter's day a wagon wheel lurched into an underwater pothole. Thrown from his seat, the Old Man got thoroughly wet. When he had been younger, it probably wouldn't have bothered him; but he was old: Sixty-six was old in those days.

I missed him. He had always been kind to me. I relished the few occasions when I had come across him in Jackson, for he loved chocolate sodas; and if I had 30 cents, I'd buy us each a soda. What I enjoyed most was that, like the gunslingers of fiction, he always sat with his back to the wall, tolerating nobody directly behind him. Also like them, he always wore his gun to town.

Today the Bar Nothing is a hillside full of homes, and the Old Man's homestead is part of the 9,000-acre Snake River Ranch. Was it irony or fate that Toll Chapman, who bought the Bar Nothing from Dad in the 1950s, was half-brother of "Wildcat" Johnson, the moonshiner who died in State Prison because he confessed to killing a man everybody thought the Old Man had gunned down?

"There were some wild ones in here in the old days," quoth one Old-Timer recently. There certainly were.

CHAPTER TWO

Harry

The first night Dad ever spent in Jackson's Hole was at the Circle H, a dude ranch owned and operated by Harry and Ethel Harrison near Moose. They remained close friends, and may be yet.

Harry was tall, lean, ramrod straight, hawk-featured, poker-faced, and, without any question, the best dressed man in the Hole. Ethel was petite and also impeccably dressed. No one would have thought of referring to Harry as a dude, but he certainly did dress!

At a time when most of the dude ranchers in Jackson's Hole had come in from the East, the Harrisons were "the genuine article." As an Old-Timer said to me recently, "Harry was nobody to monkey around with."

Harry was one of the finest silversmiths whose work I have ever seen. His was every bit as good as that of Edward H. Bohlin, who made a fortune in Hollywood selling silver-mounted chaps, belts, spurs, bits, and saddles. I have a pair of spurs which Harry made for Dad—to me the most beautiful pair of spurs I have ever beheld—and a belt buckle featuring a bronc rider and bronc, and for Mother a lovely pair of chaps with six gracefully engraved large silver conchos and twelve small. In addition to working silver, Harry occasionally engraved steel barrels on six-guns. His own were extremely handsome.

I never knew of Harry's selling any of his silver work; he gave it to friends, a saddle for Bob Crisp, the chaps for Mother, the spurs for Dad. How could he afford to do that? Where did he get all that silver? Ethel owned a silver mine in the Paradise Valley outside Las Vegas.

Harry, himself, always wore gabardine riders, rather than jeans, tucked into the tops of his boots, a Stetson of fine quality creased with four dents and held in place with a finely braided leather stampede string. He was the only man I remember in these parts in those days who wore a stampede string, although nowadays they are quite common. Around the hat was a fully stamped leather hatband, with handsome silver buckle, keeper, and tip—all engraved and sporting his brand. Through his belt loops ran a hand-tooled belt whose tip, keeper, and buckle matched those of the hatband. His gun belt—and he never seemed to go off the home ranch without it—matched, of course; the Colt .44 Peacemaker with ivory grips was, likewise, immaculate; the brass cartridges in the belt shone. His tailored riders were invariably sharply creased and tucked into a pair of Blucher boots. In those days cowboy boots stood on two-inch or two-and-a-half inch undershot heels. Although he was tall, Harry's were two-and-a-half-inch heels to emphasize that he was a rider, not a walker. Many old-time cowboys prided themselves upon small feet for the same reason. I suppose Harry's made-to-order boots were sixes.

For special occasions in his later years Harry made for himself and wore a solid gold belt buckle, keeper, and tip, and gold buckles on watchband and hatband with gold keepers and tips. He was something to see!

A dude? Hardly. He "packed lead." Once, when I was a "button"—Yes, I once was—Harry showed me a shadow in the fleshy part of his thigh; the shadow was a bullet. He told me that it had never become infected and didn't bother him; so why go through the pain—I think he called it "trouble"—of having it removed. Even at seven or eight years old, I hadn't the nerve to ask him how it got there; and he never told me.

The Mountain Men rode large horses, while the Plainsmen rode little mustangs. Harry rode sixteen-hand geldings, yet he carried the rawhide riata of the Plainsman in a country where nobody else did.

His horses wore the most beautiful saddles imaginable, for Harry had good taste: He didn't clutter up the beautiful tooling with too much silver: just a tastefully engraved plate on each swell, a nameplate on the cantle, and, perhaps, a horn cap. Such a saddle he made for his old friend and former employee Bob Crisp. Some years later, when I heard that Bob was going to sell his saddle, I rode for the better part of two days from hunting camp on Lower Granite Creek to try to buy it. "J. R." Williamson beat me to it; but I recall the price he paid: $125!

Under the porch of the main cabin of the Circle H lived Ming. Ming was not a cat, nor a skunk, nor a chiseler, nor what else you might imagine. Ming was a pet black bear. In the Summers when the dudes were around the place, Ming wore a collar and chain, and came out to be fed at anyone's call.

Today's purists would have known that Ming was being mistreated, but Ming didn't know it. She quite liked the easy life, as was proved by the fact that, let loose every Fall to hibernate, she returned every Spring to her den under the porch.

Ming liked the kids in the area, and she especially liked their sandwiches;

however, their horses didn't like Ming. In the Fall when school started, the children converged toward the little one-room schoolhouse which stood 250 yards below the dugway on the west side of Snake River which still leads from the bench down to Moose. Ming would follow whining piteously, begging for honey or jam. The horses would panic at the bear ambling along behind them making peculiar sounds. Something had to be done. Ming had to be chained until the estimated moment of hibernation.

One Spring, when the snow seemed to hang around even longer and deeper than usual, Ethel Harrison worried about her pet. It had been a long hibernation; Ming would be extraordinarily hungry. Ethel fried up a pound of bacon and set out, calling from time to time. Of course, she could not know where Ming had dug in, but she presumed it would be somewhere on the ranch. "Ming! Oh, Ming! Come, Ming!"

Suddenly, the softened snow gave way under Ethel; and she fell three or four feet into a snow cave, ending up beside a startled, newly awakened bear. Was it Ming?

Tentatively, "Here, Ming, here's some nice bacon for you." The fire went out of the eyes; it was Ming.

Rusty and Nora were a pair of Irish Terriers belonging to Ethel. Wherever she went, they went. They were well trimmed and groomed, well behaved, and so disciplined that they helped her with her fishing. Ethel tied her own dry flies, preferring 14s and 16s. She would take her four-ounce split-bamboo rod, a creel, two or three of her flies, and the dogs down to the river. No net, yet small flies and light gut leaders. Did she Catch-and-Release? No one caught and released in those days unless the catch was too small to keep. In fact, we were told by the experts that if we so much as touched a live trout it was doomed, for our hands, even wet, would remove enough of the slime which protects a trout that it would become vulnerable to parasites and would surely die.

Ethel fished from the banks, with Rusty and Nora beside her, one on each side, trembling in anticipation, but sitting.

In those days before the pressure put upon it by the plethora of today's fishermen, the Snake was one of the premier fishing streams of the nation; and Ethel could lay those little flies of hers down so gently and realistically that they were sometimes seized by dragonflies before trout could get them.

When Ethel hooked a fish, the dogs began to whine eagerly, but they stayed in place. By the time she had played the trout sufficiently to bring it in, the terriers were beside themselves with excitement, yet still in position. As she angled her fish near the bank, Ethel quietly spoke one word, "Rusty" or "Nora;" and that dog only sprang into action: into the water and out with the trout.

I've enjoyed a rather long life frequently associated with trout and fly fishermen. Rusty and Nora were the only Trout Retrievers I have seen or heard of.

I mentioned that Ethel fished from the banks of the Snake. Until the dikes were built in the mid-fifties, the Snake River was one of the nation's finest fishing streams. The dikes and thousands of eager fishermen and guides changed that. The Snake River is the eastern boundary of our property. We, our children, and grandchildren own to the "thread of the river," that is, to the center. During the Summers nowadays, it is rare that we can go on our dike without seeing one or several rubber boats bringing fishermen to our favorite fishing holes. What to do about it? I stopped fishing. The fun is gone.

In the days before the dikes, we quite often fished from horseback. Cold water is good for horses' legs and bad for the joints of humans. Furthermore, it is much easier for a horse to stand in the swift current than for a man. I have old family movies of Dad and Jack Neal a-horseback with trout on their lines. Today a horse would surely be injured trying to make his way to the water over the sharp granite boulders of the dikes.

If we were mounted on green horses, we would ride to a nearby gravel bar

Collection of the Huyler Family.

A bumper catch, c. 1930s.

and dismount to net the trout; however, the horses soon became accustomed to the splashing of fish and the singing of reels, and stood quietly as we brought the trout to the net. One stallion, Frolic, a palomino, actually seemed to enjoy the play. He would watch, ears pricked forward, as I reeled in and would turn his head to watch as I lifted the fish from the water, from my net, whacked it with my "priest," and slid it into my creel.

On the other hand, even with Frolic one had to take care not to let the trout come in close on the upstream side. No horse, no matter how sophisticated, likes a line between its legs—especially a line with an active trout on one end.

Ah, the banks of the Snake in the old days! I rarely fished out of sight of our cabins and rarely failed to catch my limit, which in the old days was 14, then eight, then six. If 20 minutes passed without a strike, I was discouraged. Half an hour, and I probably went home deflated. Catch-and-Release? Only small ones. Catch-and-Eat! The fresher, the better. As mentioned previously, we were told by ichthyologists such as Harold Hagen that a touched trout was a dead trout; that even a wet hand removed enough of the trout's protective slime to render it susceptible to attack by parasites. I wonder how many of today's much-handled trout survive. According to his brother John, he still maintains that a handled trout is a dead trout.

My greatest thrill on the Snake? In early August 1952 my fishing buddy Art Peters dropped into Hardy's in London, purchased a tiny fan-winged fly such as I had never seen and mailed it to me in an ordinary envelope. The clerk assured him that it was a successful fly in England. Would it work on

Collection of the Huyler Family.

Author on Frolic fishing a side channel, 1952.

Fish Creek or the Snake?

The afternoon after I received it, a heavy thunderstorm halted our haying. I came in from the fields, took down my four and a half ounce split bamboo, Phillipson rod, and headed for the riverbank. As I walked upstream, I noted a sizeable log across a side channel from me. Stripping line as I walked and false cast, I managed to drop those little white fan wings onto that log. A moment later the current took up the slack and the little fly dropped into the eddy below. WHAM! And the fight was on. The trout was big; the fly and tippet, tiny. What a glorious fight it was! The odds were only slightly in my favor. Eventually, I netted a 22-inch cutthroat which weighed five pounds. The evidence is on one of the doors of our Kids' Cabin.

The secret of my success? That unnamed English fly and the little verse which I have recited since childhood when fishing:

Fishy, fishy in the brook
Come and bite my tiny hook.
Mama fry him in a pan;
Jackie eat him like a man.

There! Use it with luck.

Harry and Ethel sold the Circle H to a family from the East and bought and moved onto what they called the Crystal Springs Ranch, now Teton Village. That spot had an unusual distinction: It had the honor of being the

Collection of the Huyler Family.

A good catch, 1952.

very worst spot for mosquitoes in our part of the Valley and, perhaps, in the entire Hole.

Today, thanks to years of a Mosquito Abatement Program, the mosquitoes we do have are tolerable. In those days and until sometime in the seventies, they were intolerable. Nowadays when the mosquitoes are bad, there may be 20 or 30 around a person or a horse. In those days, there were clouds.

Yes, from late June until the hay was mowed in early August, Crystal Springs was worst; the Aspen Ranch—now R Lazy S—was not far behind, and our Lower Ranch, the Rocking H, was a close third. It's difficult to imagine how bad they were: They followed irrigators and riders like the cloud which cartoonists draw over heads to indicate a funk. From ten in the morning until after dark one kept one's favorite horses in the barn except when in use. Fortunately, most of our nights were sufficiently cool that our sleep was not troubled by that damned, merciless "mmmmmmmm." The livestock, too, got a break at night.

Mosquitoes did, in fact, kill horses, the very young, the very old, the weak. We called it "Swamp Fever." It was really pernicious anemia caused in weaker animals by an extended loss of blood to mosquitoes. Truly, all of us ranchers who lived in swampy or irrigated areas annually lost horses to "Swamp Fever." From time to time, mosquitoes also brought equine encephalitis, "Sleeping Sickness." In 1942, we Huylers lost several of our best young colts to equine encephalitis.

Small children were helpless against the clouds of mosquitoes. Margaret recalls with horror hearing our daughter, Ruth, aged two or three, screaming. Ruth was not given to screaming then or later. Margaret went outdoors, and there was the little girl sitting down in the tall grass with a cloud of the damned insects over her head and on every bit of her chubby tender skin they could find. She could not slap them fast enough, had just given up, and had sunk into the grass in despair. What would have happened to the dear little girl had not Margaret heard her? I was out in the hay meadows; Margaret was working in the house; we suppose Ruth had been tagging after her six-year-old brother on some quest or other.

Cows, and even calves, seemed not greatly bothered; but the horses we hauled down to California in the Fall and back in the Summer looked, during mosquito season, as if they had hives. Oddly, those same horses if they had wintered on the ranch, though they would be covered with biting mosquitoes come Summer, did not show the bumps. Similarly, those of us who worked in the fields developed a degree of immunity or tolerance. The bites itched; but if we didn't scratch, they went away shortly. In fact, mosquitoes seemed to prefer "fresh blood" to that of those of us who worked among them.

Jerry Vogt, one of Dad's foremen, stoutly maintained that he had acquired total immunity to mosquitoes, an immunity that was available to any willing (spelled *foolhardy*) soul. Required were a friend, two fifths of whiskey, and plenty of willingness. One dawn, the subject arose and swigged a big dram of booze. With breakfast he took more until he had consumed half of the first bottle. By then, of course, he was totally "plastered."

Enter the friend, who took his buddy out to the meadow and, stripping him, left him there in the warm sunlight with the second bottle.

Every time the drunk awoke, he was to drink until he went back to sleep. So the day passed.

At sunset his friend returned, dressed him—for ranch hands were a modest lot—and brought him back to the bunkhouse, where the remaining half of the first bottle was used to taper him off slowly.

The next day, he had a terrible hangover, but was immune. Jerry swore by it; and I must admit that I never saw a mosquito bite him; they would alight on him, sniff around a bit, then fly off to some likelier soul, or even to a cow. Jerry would stand there smug and superior.

Mosquitoes were an adversary not to be taken lightly! Those who decry the use of insecticides will find an ally in me; but those purists who protest even the use of larvacides should have spent a day or two at Crystal Springs

Collection of the Huyler Family.

Rocking H colts, 1940. These four died of equine encephalitis.

Ranch or the Rocking H in the old days. In those days it never entered my mind that someday I would happily spend every July here. Such foolishness was inconceivable before Teton County's Mosquito Abatement Program.

Ranches with fast-running streams and without beaver ponds or flood irrigation had no mosquito problems. On the Bear Paw, mosquitoes were rare at the same time that they were abominable two miles away. Had mosquitoes on the Bear Paw been comparable to those on the Rocking H, we'd have had no dude ranch. The season was short enough as was. Lose five weeks of July, and a dude rancher couldn't make it in Jackson's Hole.

Rufus Wesson was a great friend of the Huylers and of the Harrisons. He promised Harry one of the first production Smith & Wesson .357 magnums, which were the first of the now-proliferated magnums. This was in the late 1930s, just prior to World War II, 1938 or '39.

We had seen a prototype demonstrated: Its accuracy was closer to that of a rifle than of other handguns; its penetration, startling. In the demonstration we observed, an armor-piercing bullet was fired into the back of an old sedan. It penetrated the metal body, the back of the back seat, the back of the front seat, the fire wall, and split the engine block. We were impressed; Harry wanted one. Not that he had any dramatic use in mind, but that he liked fine tools. He would get a standard model, would decorate and engrave it. He would wear it with pride—and he would wear it wherever he went. He wanted it badly.

The order was placed at the first opportunity. Mr. Wesson, himself, assured Harry that he would see that the order was expedited. Harry's would be one of the very first production models to be delivered.

Although he had too much pride and self-discipline to complain, time must have dragged for Harry. Days became weeks; weeks became months; months became a year. The gun arrived.

Smiling to himself behind that poker face, Harry grabbed the box of cartridges he had acquired in anticipation, and drove to town to show his acquisition to his closest friend, Jim Francis. Jim, the Sheriff of Teton County, was presiding in the Log Cabin Saloon as was his wont. A conversation much like the following must have followed their first shot of red eye:

"Look here, Jim. It's come! The best handgun ever built. (Barkeep, bring us a drink.)"

"Hell, Harry, you know there never was and never will be a better handgun than the old Peacemaker. (Another shot, please, bartender.)"

"Jim, I know how you feel; but we have to accept progress, and this right here in my hand is the latest and best. (Bartender, just leave that bottle.)"

"Harry, there have already been later models, but none better than the Peacemaker or anywhere near as good for that matter."

"Well, let's go out and see."

They took a fresh bottle, left the Log Cabin, and sat down in the town square.

The following morning Harry came riding over the ridge from his Crystal Springs Ranch. I was fooling around the saddle house as he rode up on a big dapple gray.

"Good morning, Jack."

"Good morning, Mr. Harrison." To his face I never called him Harry.

"Is your Dad around?"

"Yes, sir, I think he's reading in the main cabin."

I mentioned some time ago that Harry Harrison was a romantic figure to me; so I hopped on Dreamy bareback and followed him up to the hitch rail in front of the main cabin. By the time I had turned Dreamy loose to run back down to the corral, he had dismounted, deliberately as always, easing himself to the ground, and made his customary three wraps with the reins around the hitch rail. He was a deliberate man, was Harry Harrison. He moved and thought deliberately—well, almost always.

I held the screen door for him as he entered the cabin.

Immediately after greeting Dad, Harry drew his new magnum, showed it to Dad, and inquired improbably,

Collection of the Jackson Hole Historical Society and Museum.

Jim Francis, Sheriff of Teton County, 1950.

"Coulter, would you like to buy that gun?"

Dad was surprised. He knew how long and how eagerly Harry had awaited that very gun. He did not know what had happened in Jackson the previous night.

"Harry, you don't want to sell that gun."

"Yes, Coulter, I'm going to sell it; and knowing how interested you have been in its development, I thought you might like to buy it."

"Are you sure you want to sell it?"

"Absolutely."

Dad didn't know what had brought this change of heart to his old friend, but he realized that there must be a story behind Harry's offer. He later said that he figured that if he bought it, he could sell it back to Harry someday; whereas, if someone else bought it, it might disappear from the market forever. So he bought it.

Later that day, returning from town, Jack Neal divulged the reason:

Harry and Jim Francis, by then having each downed more than a few good "belts," had taken their pistols—and the bottle to keep them company—to the far side of the town square, where after making themselves comfortable and settling any dust they might have stirred up, they had commenced to test the .357 against the .44. Their target? The doorknob of an empty store across the street—yes, across one of the town's main thoroughfares!

Frank Bessette, chief deputy sheriff, tried to reason with his boss, who by then was enjoying the contest, the evening, and the booze. "Hell, Frank! Nobody lives downstairs," quoth the Law of Teton County. And they kept at it until they ran out of ammunition.

The next morning, sober and contrite, Harry determined to punish himself by selling "the gun that caused all the trouble."

He never would buy it back, though Dad offered it to him repeatedly.

A few years later, during World War II, about to ship to the China-Burma-India Theater, I discovered to my consternation my weapon of choice—not my choice but the Army's—to be a .45 Colt semi-automatic. Because I had been raised by Dad, who was a fine shot with both rifle and pistol, I had managed to qualify Expert with every Army handgun except that Colt .45. With it I barely qualified as Marksman, yet that was to be my sidearm. I felt threatened; I wrote Dad and requested the loan of Harry's magnum for the duration. I mounted it on a GI webbed combat belt to which, in India, I had cartridge loops stitched. I hadn't the class of a

Harrison or a Patton, but it went with me everywhere and served me well, or I might not be here to write this.

It was Mike Yokel, World's Champion Middleweight Wrestler prior to World War I, who in 1908 had homesteaded 160 acres, which included the site of what became the Stagecoach Bar and the land up to Nate Davis's (site of the Trail Creek Ranch today). With the help of "Uncle Nick" Wilson, for whom the town is named, he built a cabin there; however, he was busy defending his title around the world and did not move to Wilson to stay until 1925, so he sold the cabin to Nick McCoy. A number of years later, Mike became the Valley's first realtor; but this was his first real estate deal. He died in the St. John's Hospital Nursing Home, a highly respected citizen with his wits about him at 102 years of age.

Nick McCoy was one of the McCoys of the Hatfields and McCoys of feuding fame. Although the origin of the feud is unknown, it attracted national attention in the 1880s and 1890s.

Both families lived on Tug Fork, a stream that divided Logan County, West Virginia, from Pike County, Kentucky. The West Virginian Hatfields had been Confederates; the Kentuckian McCoys, Unionists. Although the families had never been neighborly, the *Encyclopaedia Britannica* informs me that "the first major bloodletting did not occur until 1882, when Ellison Hatfield was mortally shot in a brawl with the McCoys; and in revenge, the Hatfields kidnapped and executed three McCoy brothers [Nick's brothers Phamer, Randolph, and Tolbert]."

Collection of the Jackson Hole Historical Society and Museum.

Mike Yokel, World's Champion, c.1920.

Thereafter, the Hatfields and McCoys frequently ambushed and killed each other." Probably the feud was ignited by a Romeo and Juliet love affair between Johnse Hatfield and Rose Ann McCoy—an affair which was broken up by the McCoys.

The encyclopedia goes on to point out that whenever McCoys or Hatfields were arrested in their home county, they were invariably acquitted and released. Such blatant perversion of the law inevitably raised the heat of the feud.

The feuding gradually abated and ended in the 1920s.

Isn't it remarkable that one of those notorious McCoys should live his latter years in Wilson, Wyoming?

Those who knew said that Nick had fled Kentucky after having killed two peace officers who had killed one of his brothers. Nick had drifted to Nevada, where, we are told, he panned enough gold to buy an interest in a Reno bawdy house.

One day, he and the owner of a similar establishment met on the street and engaged in a heated argument. Nick was mounted; it is unclear whether the other man was on horseback or afoot. Infuriated by something the other man said, McCoy took down his rope, roped the man, and dragged him down the street to his death. It is probable that Nick meant only to cow his opponent rather than to kill him—at least that is what he always said. He had, nonetheless, killed another man. Thinking it advisable to leave town quickly, McCoy gathered such valuables as he could carry in his saddlebags, abandoned his investment, and rode eastward, ending up in Wilson. There he bought Mike Yokel's cabin, transformed it into a bar, and remained in Wilson until the very end of his life.

Mike Yokel, of German extraction, could—and did—sing German songs. There was much anti-German sentiment in the U.S.A. during and shortly after World War I. An Old-Timer informed me that Mike returned from defending his championship in Australia to be told by his wife that Nick McCoy was spreading gossip that Mike was a German sympathizer.

Mike knew, continued the Old-Timer, that McCoy kept a pair of .45s under his bar; so when he marched in for a confrontation and stopped directly across the bar from the proprietor, the first thing he said to McCoy was, "Keep both hands on the bar." Mike had lightning reflexes. As the Old-Timer said of him, "He was easygoing, but he could move so fast you couldn't see him." Had McCoy reached for a gun, Mike would have had him across that bar before he could have fired a shot. Mike explained to McCoy in no uncertain terms that although he was of German extraction, he was 100 percent American, and he did not want to hear any more allegations about treasonous leanings. The rumors stopped.

Shooting up the town of Jackson may have been Harry's most notorious escapade of his later years, but it was not his only escapade involving "shooting irons." He left his mark on Wilson, too.

According to neighbors, in order to beat Winter boredom, Nick McCoy, Jim Francis, Harry Harrison, and cronies Pete Karpi and Joe Bodan, would from time to time gather at the Stagecoach to consume some of the fine moonshine made by McCoy, and to "let off a little steam; but they never got so drunk that they couldn't take care of themselves."

Jim Francis was wont to proclaim, "I'd sooner be in a den of rattlesnakes than around a bunch of drunks." He knew whereof he spoke.

In daytime the cronies would shoot at the heads of Nick McCoy's chickens and turkeys pecking for food in the road. A dead chicken or turkey called for a donation of $1 to the owner, unless it was killed by a head shot. Such a kill was "on the house."

The mothers of Wilson would quickly call their children home when the shooting began.

Collection of the Jackson Hole Historical Society and Museum.

Drinking and shooting buddies, c. 1940s.

The favorite indoor game of those sharpshooters was to stick a candle sconce with lit candle into the chinking between the logs of the Stagecoach, and to shoot at it. Anyone hitting the candle had to buy drinks for the house, but anyone shooting out the flame won drinks on the house. No mean feat! Try it in your cabin, not mine.

It is told that on one such night, when he was feeling no pain, Nick announced that he had such faith in the shooting of his friend Jim Francis that he would let Jim shoot a one-ounce shot glass off his head.

"Naw, you wouldn't!"

"Yes, I would."

"Well then, let's see him do it."

"Yeah, I sure would admire to see that!"

"All right."

Witnesses say that Jim looked a bit unsteady as he drew bead on the jigger on Nick's head; but Nick never wavered. "BANG!" Nick dropped to the floor as if he had been pole-axed. Jim's bullet had grazed his scalp as it smashed the glass. Perhaps for a moment Nick thought he had been killed; but it was barely a crease. As he helped his friend to his feet, Jim was heard to mutter, "I always told you you had a peaked head."

Lest the reader conclude that behavior such as the above was unique to Wilson, I quote about an incident in nearby Pine Bluffs:

> Other cowboys soon appeared, and, without the formality of a formal introduction, immediately became intimately friendly. Then followed beer. This was succeeded by more beer and in turn by beer. Then followed some beer, which was succeeded by quite a lot of beer. Then came beer. . .
>
> For eight mortal hours the pale air was laden with disjointed chunks of revelry. It was a scene of the wildest and most extravagant carousel set down in the quiet midst of the bleak prairie, and one which would give life and reality to an early-day border romance. **—from the *Cheyenne Democratic Leader*, September 27, 1884**

Would Harry, Jim, Joe, Pete, or Nick have felt out of place in that scene?

As age and throat cancer began to take their toll on McCoy, he sold his bar to Billy and Blanche Thompson, who tore down the old cabin and built the nucleus of the present building. Blanche ran the restaurant; Billy, the bar. Each kept the money made by his or her part of the establishment.

Lee Lundy and Charley Brown, the blacksmith, were the next proprietors, who, in turn, sold to Walt Callahan. It was the first owner, Mike Yokel, who chose the name which lasts until this day—the Stagecoach Bar. The name was most appropriate because for years Harry Scott or Clay "Rawhide" Seaton stopped the stagecoach there, at the foot of Teton Pass, to pick up or discharge passengers.

Nick McCoy died of throat cancer; but in his last weeks it was his friend Mel Annis, the man who built our Rocking H barn, the D Triangle barn, the Snake River Ranch barn, the Hardeman barn, and several others around the Valley, who took Nick back to Kentucky to die where he had been born. As Mel said to him, "What can they do to you now?"

The Hatfields and McCoys! Who would have suspected a connection with the little town of Wilson in Jackson's Hole, Wyoming?

Harry and Ethel sold Crystal Springs Ranch to Chester Simpson and moved into the Louis Fleming homestead cabin in the very mouth of Granite Canyon. What a romantic spot that was, a little clearing among huge trees, with the creek dashing at their doorstep. For some years after the Harrisons departed it, Margaret and I found it a favorite place to "smooch."

I can imagine that the only drawbacks to that site from Harry's viewpoint might have been that because of the roar of that creek and the prevailing breeze out of the canyon, anyone could have sneaked up on them undetected even by the dogs, and that up there in the mouth of that narrow canyon the Winter snows piled ten feet deep. For several Summers he and Ethel lived with the noise of the creek, but commenced spending their Winters in Las Vegas, where he must have cut quite a figure! Did he—could he—wear his six-gun there? I'm confident that he wore a high quality Stetson with the four creases, and his tailored riders sharply pressed and tucked into fine, well-polished Blucher boots.

Harry and Ethel's last years were spent in Las Vegas around the Horseshoe Club, where, I would imagine, he was a shill, for his appearance alone would have drawn people to the place just to see "the genuine article"—and Ethel had shilled in Jackson during their last years here.

I suppose his friends there got that gold belt buckle, the engraved six-shooters, gun belts, belts, hatbands, wristwatch bands, spurs, and probably even a saddle, bridle, and chaps. When I heard of Harry's death, I made some unsuccessful phone calls. I'd have happily gone into hock for some of those things.

Nonetheless, Harry Harrison's Smith & Wesson .357 magnum, one of the last two guns to shoot up the Town of Jackson, hangs on the wall of Margaret's and my living room today. I hope it always will. There also are the chaps, belt buckle, and spurs that Harry made and gave to my family as tokens of friendship.

CHAPTER THREE

Jack

It was Harry Harrison who brought Dad and Jack Neal together. As a result, Jack was Foreman of the Bear Paw and the Rocking H from 1927 until 1943. From Jack I learned always to carry a sharp knife and matches, which I do today, even in suit or tuxedo in a big city.

On the subject of clothing, it is important for the reader to visualize almost all old-time cowboys as wearing vests. Sometimes the vests were leather or tanned calfskin with or without the hair; but more often they were old suit vests. Their function was to furnish extra pockets. There is an old compliment, "Friend, you're as handy as an extra pocket." Except for a few devout Mormons, I cannot recall an old-timer who neither smoked nor chewed. Those extra pockets came in handy—like a friend.

I learned much of value from Jack Neal. Although lazy, he could do anything, build anything, take over leadership of almost any group of men after a few minutes. Clyde and I followed Jack around like a pair of puppies. Whatever Jack did, we did. If he hunkered, we hunkered. If he whittled, we whittled.

He was a quiet man. As we whittled, from time to time he would hold out his hand for our knives. He would check their edges. All this without a word. If they were razor-sharp, he would return them with a smile

Photo by Harrison R. Crandall. Collection of the Huyler Family.

Jack Neal, c. 1937.

and a grunt of approval; if one was a bit dull, he would ruin what edge it had on any handy rock before returning it to its owner without comment. A big sharpening job lay ahead of that kid, and it had better be soon.

Until 1936 Jack smoked—a lot. Clyde and I were bearers of his matches. Whenever he wanted to light up, he would hold out his hand, palm up, and one of us was expected to put just one match into it. Jack had never had the opportunity to be a Boy Scout, yet he was a one-match man, snapping it into flame one handed with his thumbnail. Try it.

I must have been about 11 the day Clyde and I were following Jack up to the Circle H. As we rode down the hill past Wister Draw, we noted Jack was rolling a cigarette. We began to pat our pockets: empty. Jack didn't look around, but that hand, palm up, came up beside his shoulder. We had nothing to give. He glanced around to be certain that we had seen him; then he rode over to the shade of a tree, dismounted, and sat down. Still no word spoken. We turned and loped for the Bear Paw, perhaps four miles away—and back again.

When Jack was an old man, a bit younger than I am now, I reminded him of the incident. His eyes crinkled, and he chuckled that quiet chuckle of his. He remembered all right.

"You had matches, didn't you? You probably smoked a sack of Bull Durham while we went for your matches, didn't you?"

"Why, sure I had matches. I was no greenhorn."

One day when I was perhaps 18, Jack and I were driving home from the Lower Ranch. In those days, we never referred to it by its formal name, the Rocking H, but always as the Lower Ranch. At any rate, on this particular occasion we got a flat tire on the stretch between the Rocking H gate and the front gate of the Aspen Ranch. Groaning, I went to the trunk for the jack and was considerably annoyed to see Jack Neal abandoning me to my labors. About the time I put the jack on its base, however, he arrived with a fence rail. Searching briefly for a sizable rock to use as a fulcrum, he put one end of the rail under the axle and lifted the car by the simple expedient of standing on the other end of his pole while I changed the tire. Far easier than jacking up one of those old-fashioned mechanical jacks. Hydraulic car jacks had yet to be invented.

That was ingenuity of the same caliber as that of Jackson Hole's first surveyor, Billy Owen, who, having to work without a chain man, measured his surveys by tying a rag to a spoke on his wagon and counting the rotations of his wagon wheel.

Early settler Ben Garton showed perhaps even greater ingenuity, when he surveyed an eight-mile ditch from Flat Creek to Dry Hollow without a transit. He used a carpenter's level and a kitchen match. That kitchen match under one end of the level gave him all the slope he needed to get the water to flow.

Ben would set the level on a sawhorse, dig under the legs until the level was even; then add his match and sight along the level to his next point. Ingenuity amounting almost to genius.

Jack knew horses, how to select a good piece of horseflesh in the first place, then how to "make" a horse. Any horse he rode for very long reined well; and he and his three brothers could teach any horse to running walk. I have always wished to be able to do that. The secret was patience. A popular race frequently connected with pre-World War II rodeos was the Novelty Race, wherein each rider walked a quarter or half mile, trotted the next, and ran the last. Jack and Ike's Honah and Euchre were strong competition for each other, but no other horse pressed them over a period of perhaps ten years. They built up huge leads at the walk, trotted like moose, and raced each other home. Part of the Neals' secret was that when they started a colt, they only let it walk for the first three months. They kept pressing and checking any break of gait. I never had sufficient patience to find out whether I had the skill.

Jack was one of the few horsemen I have known who could "rib" a horse. Most horsemen can tell a horse's age from the condition of its teeth and mouth. Very, very few from the ribs.

I had a great little gelding named Jeep, whose mouth belied his age. When he was 14, his mouth stated that he had just turned 9. Jack had never seen the horse until the day I asked him to guess his age. To my surprise, instead of opening Jeep's mouth, he just ran one hand up under the light sheet I had on the gelding and declared, "Fourteen." Amazed, I inquired how he knew that. He told me and he showed me—the last thing he taught me before he died. It's the spacing between the ribs. When a horse is young, the ribs lie practically against each other. As he ages, the cartilage between the last two ribs enlarges or sags and spreads them a bit. The next year it is the corresponding rib on the other side, and so on. Extremely few horsemen know that technique and most who do treat the knowledge like some sworn secret and will not even talk about it.

Jack was also an extraordinary dog trainer: stock dog, sled dog, or canine companion. He always spoke quietly to his dogs, barely above a whisper. He pointed out that dogs have very sensitive ears, that when we shout at them, they must try to get away to protect those sensitive ears from pain. In doing so, they close their ears and don't listen. He wanted his dogs to listen—and listen they did. It was amazing how far they could hear that soft voice.

Jack taught his dogs to pull the rawhide latchstring and open the kitchen door when he approached it with an armload of wood, and to rear up to close the door with its paws after he came through. Just prior to any thunderstorm, Fleur, a German Shepherd and dam of our first sled dogs, would open the door, go into the cabin, close the door, and hide under the couch until the storm passed; and since she, like most dogs, sensed an approaching storm before we did, we often knew when to don jackets or run for cover before the storm hit. She could not, however, raise the bar to let herself out when the sky cleared.

I have often wondered whether my three children were better horsemen at given ages than I had been at the same age. Honestly, I know they were. I certainly rode more in the Summertime, as there was nothing else to do. All of our games and play began with the horse: Cops and Robbers, Kick the Can, Hide and Seek, riding Uncle John Dodge's calves, playing with the Resor kids. No matter what our plan, we had to get there; the horse was the only transportation. It never occurred to us to walk; it wouldn't have occurred to our parents or to the Neals to drive us. There were no bicycles; we rode all day every day.

Most of our riding was unsupervised, however. We kids clambered onto our mounts and took off in any direction to do whatever we had in mind for that day. I recall this independence when I was no more than eight years old.

Pack trips, hunting trips, fishing expeditions, moving cattle involved adults and, therefore, adult supervision, that is instruction. We didn't mind that instruction. We took it for granted; we knew that we didn't know. In the end, we rode well, but we were riders rather than horsemen. We rode only from June into October. Although Dad, Mother, and Coulter contributed to my horse education, it was Jack Neal with whom I spent most time and who taught me most. He was a good teacher, patient but demanding.

I am happy that he lived to see me with one of my two or three truly fine horses. I hope he felt that his training was responsible. Largely it was, though when the time came, I learned more useful horsemanship from Monte Foreman than from all the rest put together. Monte took me from fairly accomplished rider to, I hope, accomplished horseman. I have learned something useful from every horse clinic I have ever attended, be the instructor Jess Kahle, Ray Hunt, James Gough, Cam Schryver, Bill Culbertson, Susan Baker, Susie Hauge, or Buck Branaman; however, I learned more of use to me from Monte. I like to work horses at speed; he, Cam, and Suzy Baker were good at that. I have never seen the others work at higher speed than a lope.

Monte frequently "laid over" on the Rocking H between clinics. What a ball I had with him and Suzy Baker galloping across mowed hayfields: jumping irrigation ditches and hay bales, rolling back, doing flying changes of lead, 360s, and sliding stops as we played tag! I have never had more fun.

Margaret's and my kids, on the other hand, rode year-round and usually rode with us, with Jess Kahle, with the boys of the Thacher School: on the gymkhana field, on pack trips. They rode in clinics. A lot of instruction took place. I don't know whether they liked it or resented it. It seemed natural to me to give it unasked, and the same was true from Jess or the boys. Our children took care of their own horses on a daily basis from the time they were, perhaps, six years old. Can a preteen be a horseman? Seems to me that the two who loved it were. By the time they were 12, I'd have been happy to have either of them ride any horse of mine anywhere—and they could have.

Dad's definition of a horseman was, "A horseman improves every horse he rides. It's as simple as that." Our John and Ruth began to do that early on. Although our youngest, Steve, rode a lot, his interests lay in other directions; and his friends weren't riding. He rode for transportation.

When they were, I suppose, 11 and 14, John and Ruth put an ad in the Jackson papers, "Will teach your horse new performances or cure bad habits for $5 per performance or bad habit." "New performances" were such as neck reining, ground tying, opening and closing gates from either side, permitting mounting from either side or the donning of a slicker without dismounting, carrying double, flying changes of lead. "Bad habits" were such as pulling back when tied, moving away as the rider mounted, shying at a cowhide, nipping while being cinched. Pulling back was by far the most common, and the kids had a cure which was usually successful:

If a horse pulls back suddenly, he can frequently break a halter snap. If he pulls back against a rope, it doesn't fight back. On the other hand, John and Ruth had a couple of old automobile inner tubes, each tied with many wraps of a soft rope to a large cottonwood tree. To one of their inner tubes the kids would tie a pullback horse. When it pulled back now, the inner tube pulled equally hard in the opposite direction. The horse could not lean against it; the rubber fought back. Soon the horse's muscles would begin to quiver; and sooner or later he would come back, up to the tree. One of the kids would "spook him" with a gunny sack or slicker, until he would no longer go back against the rope. A five-dollar investment saved owners quite a few tie ropes. Five dollars purchased a lot in those days; and for two youngsters, John and Ruth made good money that Summer, while various friends and neighbors had better horses as a result of their training.

Jack Neal was one of two men I have known who could examine a horse's hooves, go to another location, shape a set of shoes, bring them back, and after trimming the hooves, nail them on without alteration.

He would examine the feet up at the Bear Paw, drive down to the Lower Ranch, where there was a blacksmith shop; fire up the forge, shape the shoes from a bar, turn heel calks, punch the holes, cool the shoes, and bring them back to the Bear Paw for Ike or Slats to nail on.

Speaking of Slats and Ike brings up another of Jack Neal's talents—and a most valuable talent it was: He could find good men and hire them.

Walter "Slats" Helm, for example, drifted into Jackson's Hole from Texas in the Summer of '35 or '36. He thought he might like to spend Summers in a cooler climate than that of the Texas Panhandle.

In his Model A Ford coupe he drove out to the Rocking H one early Spring day looking for employment. Slats earned his name: tall, long-waisted, slim, slow of movement and slow of speech. He came to us from Texas. You could tell that as far as you could hear him. That drawl was pure Texican.

Shortly after he and Jack struck up a conversation, the telephone rang inside the cabin outside of which they were standing. A moment later Jack stuck his head out. "Slats, this is going to take a few minutes. Grab that sledgehammer there and break a few of those rocks we're gonna use for a chimney." Jack wanted to find out whether Slats would do work disassociated with horses and cattle.

Slats, albeit unhappily, recognized the challenge, picked up the sledgehammer, and went to work. He noted that its head seemed a bit loose on the haft, but it wasn't his sledge, and it didn't matter to him until a few minutes later Jack arrived unheard behind the spot where Slats was working. At almost the same moment the loose hammer flew off its handle and struck Jack in the head, knocking him down and out. It might well have killed him, but it didn't.

The first thing Jack said to the lanky cowboy who had just poured a pitcher of water on him was, "You're hired."

Was revenge foremost in Jack's mind the next morning when Slats reported for work and dragged his well-worn saddle out of his Model A Ford "Whoopee"?

Into the round corral next to the barn Jack had put Baldy, a big, black, bald-faced, white-stockinged four-year-old gelding. Slats confessed later that when he saw that big horse already in a corral by himself, he knew that here was hardly an ordinary colt and that this was a test.

He did not know that Dee Goodrick, the Neals, Coulter, and I had given him up, that he had been taken to Cecil, an old-time "bronc stomper," who could ride him, but could not train him. It was a bronc ride every time. Cecil had brought him back a more effective bucker because of the practice he had had.

Dad and Jack did not want to get rid of the big gelding because he was beautifully put together, and so extraordinarily handsome. You may see a lot of blacks with good conformation, but you don't see many with that much white on them.

Slats recognized his challenge, but was up to it. He entered the corral, caught the horse, put on him a headstall with a snaffle bit, saddled him. For all of that Baldy stood quiet. He had put up with that a good many times. We specta-

Collection of the Huyler Family.

Slats Helm and Ike Neal on Baldy, c. 1938.

tors gave no significance to the fact that there was a raw cowhide drying on the corral fence just next to the spot where the horse was standing. As he gathered the reins, cheeked the horse, and drawled, "Easy, son!" Baldy, no doubt, thought, "I've been here before." He hadn't.

It required only one fluid motion from the ground to the saddle *and* to pull that cowhide off the fence by its tail. Here was something unanticipated by spectators or horse. Bucking immediately became the least of Baldy's concerns as he fled that hide which flew out behind him in his speed like some gigantic kite. Around and around that corral Baldy raced without bucking a jump. Finally, exhausted and heaving, the gelding stopped, the whites of his eyes rolling at that damned thing. The rider on his back, drawling soothingly, eased the hide to the horse's shoulder. He quivered, but did not bolt. He was too tired. Putting the hide gently back onto the fence, Slats added rubbing to his soothing talk. A series of pats became louder and more firm as the horse stopped flinching from them; then Slats eased from the saddle as smoothly as he had mounted; and Lesson Number One was over.

Slats stayed with us until after World War II and loved to say, "If I could pick up that cabin, old Baldy would carry it." Dad and Slats sorta shared the big, black, bald-faced gelding until his death.

We never saw a better dude wrangler than Jack Neal's brother Ike. There were Ed, Jack, Ike, Marguerite, and Tom Neal. Ike was the best dude wrangler.

On a steep and narrow trail, two or four of the dude kids—or perhaps an adult or two—would be nurturing acrophobia. Ike would point out a crack running diagonally across a granite face up ahead. "See that? There's the trail! Runs right across that cliff." Attention of the acrophobes would focus on that crack until we got so close that they could see that Ike had been "pulling their legs." Meanwhile, they would have crossed the narrowest, most precipitous section of the day's trail while they were focused on that crack.

It was inevitable that youngsters who idolized the cowboys would, when they returned from "jingling" the horses with the wranglers, want to breakfast with their heroes. It was also inevitable that those same "heroes" needed a break from the infatuated kids. Yet, the cowboys did not wish to offend the dude kids. Ike Neal had the perfect solution.

"Sure, Jenny. Come in the kitchen and have breakfast with us. Cookie, serve up an extra plate. Would you like some coffee? Sugar in it?"

What youngster drinks black, unsweetened coffee? Ike would pour a shot of cream into the youngster's cup and his own to cool it, would grab a handful of sugar, let some fall into his own cup and some into the kid's. He would stick his big, work-gnarled finger into his own cup and quickly give it a stir. Then, withdrawing his finger he would lick it clean before reaching over to stir the coffee of his young friend. That always did it. I never saw one of those kids drink that coffee, and few of them returned to the kitchen for breakfast. Ike had accomplished his mission: assured himself a break and defused a bit the infatuation—and all without uttering an unkind word.

Ike also drove six horses in the Bear Paw stagecoach. Quite a few men could drive a four-horse hitch, but not many, six. It is a fine art. The difference between a four-horse and a six-horse hitch is somewhat the same as the difference between an 18-wheel truck and semi-trailer and one of those with another big trailer attached behind. Turning required experience not to let the swing team turn when the leaders turned, but to keep them and the wheelers in line until they reached the same exact spot where the driver had turned the leaders. That way, the stagecoach tracked the leaders, whereas if the swing and wheel teams cut the corners so did the stage, which could result in a wreck. A driver of six has a handful of "ribbons," as drivers termed the reins.

There are few sights more impressive than to see a good driver bring a stagecoach in at a gallop. Ike did that every Summer Sunday at the Chapel of the Transfiguration in Moose.

Collection of the Huyler Family.

Ike Neal driving, c. 1936.

Few readers of this little book can recall the days when horseback riders rode the streets of Jackson. As late as the 1950s Ike Neal operated a horse trading and livery stable on a lot just off Pearl Street, where the back rooms of the 49er Motel now stand. The streets were dirt, and cowboys and cowgirls—as well as would-be cowboys and cowgirls—roamed the town.

Ike had gone full-time into the horse selling and leasing business after the Bear Paw Ranch sold to John D. Rockefeller, Jr. Ike had a most unusual mind-set: If he couldn't sell a horse for $150 one week, he raised the price to $175 the next and $200 the week after.

"Ike," I protested, "if he won't bring $150 today, how do you expect him to bring $200 next week?"

"I got that much more feed in him, so I gotta charge more every week to break even." Frequently he got away with it.

One day a greenhorn who had purchased a horse from a local horse trader returned in high dudgeon. "That horse you sold me is as blind as a bat! I want my money back!"

"Naw, sir," responded the seller all unperturbed, "I told you he was a good horse, but he didn't look good."

Was that horse trader Ike Neal? Ask Charlie Petersen. It sounds like the kind of stunt Ike would have enjoyed pulling.

Collection of the Jackson Hole Historical Society and Museum.

"She's worth twice what I'm askin' for her." (Ike Neal, Sheriff Olin Emery, and John Wort), c.1948.

When young, Fred Crandall had been a stagecoach driver. It was he who taught Ike to hitch and handle three teams together. Backing a wagon with one team is not easy; with two it is a skill; with three it is a rarefied art.

In appearance Fred reminded me of the legendary Yavapai Pete:

A face like a hatchet, a head made to match it.
A nose like a pelican's beak.
He'd seen so much weather, his skin was like leather;
his hands was all horny and rough.
You could tell by his stride he was just made to ride
and no bronc for him was too tough.

A bachelor like so many old cowboys, Fred's only vanity was a wisp of still-brown hair and a well-groomed handlebar mustache. Before coming into the kitchen to eat, he habitually paused before the little mirror by the pump to comb that wisp of hair and to wax the ends of that magnificent mustache. His only weakness was booze. Following monthly payday, Fred would drive to town and get "plastered." He would stay until all his money was gone. Any hand from the Bear Paw or Rocking H would try to borrow money from him so that "Old Fred" would have something left at the end of his binge. Fred knew what we were up to, but he was kind-hearted and found it difficult to turn down a friend. "I know what you're a-doin'; so I'm jest gonna lend you five so you won't go home dry."

"Fifty dollars and found," that was a good cowboy's wage in those days. If his friends were successful, Fred might have $15 or $20 "fer smokes" returned to him come Monday morning.

Like Slats, Fred rarely smoked "tailor mades," preferring to save money by "rolling his own" from a sack of Bull Durham and papers. Like Slats or Jack, he could roll a good one one-handed while the other hand was occupied with reins.

Unlike Slats and Ike, Fred, though friendly, was something of a loner; and that nature plus his weakness for alcohol kept him from being a "dude wrangler." He was an irrigator who summered in the Foreman's Cabin at the Rocking H. His company was animals: horses, a milk cow, and Pete.

Pete was a tough little Boston Bulldog belonging to Jack and Bernice Neal. He was tough because he had to be. The very evening of the day Jack brought the little puppy home, Pete stuck his nose into a mousetrap under the bed. His nose being snub and thick, the trap got no hold, and Pete escaped. Jack fished the trap from under the bed, reset it, and urged the puppy, "Get it,

Pete! Sick 'em!" Responding to the urging, although frightened, the little fellow crept toward the trap on his belly. Getting close, he quickly stuck out one paw and as quickly withdrew it. Nothing happened. Crawling closer, he repeated his tentative reach. "Snap!"—but the paw was already making its fast retreat. All of us cheered Pete, and Jack reset the trap. The pup repeated his approach. Again success and cheers.

From that time forward, on his own Pete would spring every mousetrap he found. He even learned to spring them with his nose as well as his paw: in and out as quick as a flash.

Next came rat traps, which Neal purchased just to test his dog. Finally, gopher traps and even coyote traps. Pete would whine for us to set them for him to spring; but hanging on a pine tree near the front door of the Main Cabin of the Bear Paw was a bear trap. Each of its jaws, with teeth the size of a crocodile's, was longer than Pete. He would look up at that trap and whine. Of course, no one ever set it for him, for it was so big that although the jaws might have snapped together harmlessly above him, they could have cut him in two had they grabbed him.

As is mentioned in Chapter Ten and indicated above, cowboys tend to be practical jokers. Pete had been brought up in the School of Hard Knocks. He wore a little harness, which had a ring on it for a leash. If one of the hands could make a quick enough grab, he just might hang Pete on a nail on the saddle house wall. When that happened, the little dog erupted into a paroxysm of anger which prevented even his friends from taking him down until he cooled off.

And though Pete was everywhere on the ranch, he knew who his friends were. Pity any of the hay hands who struck a match close behind him or tried to pick him up by that harness.

Being a bulldog, Pete liked to grab the end of a rope held in his direction and hang on, growling happily, while one of us spun him around and around as fast as we could, or swung him in shoulder-high circles until we, not he, were dizzy. I never saw him lose one of those contests.

Because of all this daily exercise, Pete was extremely muscular and was heavier than most Boston Bulldogs.

He could not resist porcupines or skunks. Encountering either, he would bark for help; but if help did not arrive shortly, Pete would dive in. With a nose full of quills, he would trot to one of us he trusted seeking help. I wonder how many quills I pulled from his little pug nose while he sat in front of me without restraint as I performed the painful task. Tears rolled down his cheeks and mine.

But, when Pete was sprayed by a skunk, he knew from experience that no one on the Bear Paw wanted him and he would not be permitted inside any cabin—that is no cabin on the Bear Paw. There was, however, one cabin on the Rocking H which did not seem to mind. Fred Crandall would take him in.

The little dog would take off alone, trotting the five miles between ranches and staying there until something told him that he was no longer redolent. Then he trotted home. Fred hated to see him leave.

I'll not forget one ride on the box of the stagecoach between the Jackson Rodeo Grounds and the Rocking H. I suppose it was about 1935 and I was about 15. Fred was in a hurry to get the horses to the ranch, unharnessed and turned out, so that he could return to town for some serious drinking. As a sort of warmup, I suppose, he had a case of beer at our feet. It's only 13 miles. Did he really finish 24 bottles? Hindsight makes that seem unlikely, if not impossible. They did, however, make him cheerful and a bit reckless. About the Nethercotts' place he began to sing. I had never before heard Fred sing. I learned a few things from his version of "Little Red Wing." The farther we went, the louder he sang and the more joyous he became. "You want to see how fast these fellers can run?" he queried as we turned off the county road into the Snake River Ranch. Not waiting for an answer, he took the six-horse whip out of its socket, cracked it above the horses, and shouted, "Yaaaaaaaaaaah!"

That was all very fine and great fun until we approached the wooden

Collection of the Huyler Family.

The Bear Paw stagecoach moving out, c. 1936.

bridge over Lake Creek. The road bends a bit to meet it at right angles, then resumes its former direction on the other side. For a few minutes I felt as if I were riding with one of the legendary stagedrivers of the past. Perhaps I was. I'd swear we crossed that bridge on two wheels and that a third was hanging over the water. I was hanging on with both hands—one on the low side rail by my left thigh; the other on the baggage rail which ran around the top of every stagecoach.

Pleased with what he had done and had shown me—and possibly once more thirsty—Fred eased the six horses to a lope, then a trot, then a walk for the last mile home. "That's called drivin', Jackson," he told me happily as he bit the cap from another bottle. It sure was!

None of us ever knew anything about Fred Crandall's past, but occasional glimpses led us to speculate. The possibilities seemed many.

Jack Neal loved to trade horses with Joe Bodan, a horse trader from Pinedale mentioned earlier in connection with the Stagecoach shooting matches. They were forever trying to "job" each other. Each kept one eye open for some nag he might pass off on the other. One day after each had acquired an animal he considered worthy of the other, they agreed to trade "sight unseen." Jack's horse was old, thin, lame, had a horrible fistula, and was blind in one eye. Common decency demanded that the old nag be put out of its misery as soon as the trade was completed. We all thought Jack must have the better of Joe at last.

Joe had his horse brought from behind his barn; it arrived on a sled; it was already dead. Both men, hugely pleased with themselves and with each other, laughed until they were breathless.

Another time I saw Jack Neal bested was incidental. In the Rocky Mountains in those days they used the word *stout* to mean *strong.* Jack was looking through the Sears Roebuck catalogue for some "long-handled" underwear. It was listed in four sizes: small, medium, large, and stout. "I'm pretty stout," thought Jack, using the adjective as he usually did; and he ordered two pairs of stout man's "Long Johns." When they came, he could, and did, grasp the center buttons at the waist and pull them all the way around to the middle of his back. When he realized the joke which he had accidentally played on himself, no one was more amused than he; and he recounted his gaffe to any and all who would listen.

CHAPTER FOUR

Eliza

It had been from Eliza Hubbard Waterman Seaton—Mrs. Jack Seaton—that Dad had bought the Bear Paw in the Fall of 1926. I heard him tell the tale a hundred times.

Dad had seen the Tetons in 1898 from the rise above Yellowstone Lake and had not forgotten them.

In 1925 he again came west, this time with Ed Pouch and Prent Gray, to hunt elk from Ernest Miller's Elk Horn Ranch in the Gallatin Gateway. The three were trophy hunters.

Although he had been west only as a boy, Dad was an experienced hunter and an excellent shot. He bagged his bull the first day. He then informed his companions that he planned to rent a car from Ernest Miller and go see Jackson's Hole. These were successful, young, New York City businessmen; the word *Depression*, as in *The Great Depression of 1929*, had yet to become something to reckon with. The men sent Dad off with, "If you see anything good, count us in on it."

Collection of the Jackson Hole Historical Society and Museum.

Eliza Hubbard Waterman Seaton, 1926.

Ernest and Grace Miller knew Harry and Ethel Harrison and recommended them and their Circle H Ranch to Dad, who stopped there throughout his three days in the Hole. He asked the Harrisons if they knew of any properties that would make good Summer homes. Harry replied that there was a pretty quarter-section near the mouth of Granite Canyon that had so many rocks and boulders on it that it wouldn't be worthwhile to farm, but should make a jim-dandy Summer place. "The old lady, Mrs. Seaton, lives there alone. Her husband left her some time ago, and her daughter just recently married and moved out. She's gettin' pretty long in the tooth and might sell." Dad headed down the Moose-Wilson road to find out. His only directions were, "You'll come to a big boulder on the right side of the road, with a wagon track just shy of it leading uphill to her place."

That Moose-Wilson Road, itself, in those days was little more than a wagon track. The road into the ranch was as described, a mile-long wagon track up a steep hill. Dad was driving an old touring car. For those too young to remember what that means, it means a soft top, no windows, two bench seats.

As he drove into the ranch clearing, the old lady was chopping wood. He said the wind was blowing from her to him. She was a bit deaf; she didn't hear him until he was, perhaps, a hundred feet away. She sank the ax into the block, put her hand to her sacroiliac, and straightened up slowly. By then, the car was right next to her. Dad reached over, turned off the ignition, and said, "If you were to sell me this place, you'd never have to do that again."

"Well, I just might," she responded; so he got out of the car.

The place, itself, was, of course, 160 acres—a quarter-section—the usual homestead in Teton County. On it there were two log buildings: a two-story cabin, consisting of two rooms downstairs with a loft above, and a one-story, one-room cabin with sod roof and dirt floor, which she used as a shop and sometime stable.

Collection of the Huyler Family.

Eliza "Ma" Seaton's homestead cabin in winter, c. 1920s.

Granite Creek in all its glory rushed through the place and fed its one irrigation ditch.

Dad and Eliza Seaton agreed on a price. Dad stated that he was returning to the East for the Winter and asked that she have the proper papers drawn ready to sign—and that she be moved out—by the following July 1. She said she would; they shook hands; Dad wrote her a check for the amount in full. That handshake was the only contract or receipt he ever had. It was sufficient. The Huylers took possession in July, 1926.

As her grandson Rex Ross told me the story: In 1882 Eliza Hubbard and Lorenzo C. Waterman had married in Minnesota. They moved to Oklahoma, then via two covered wagons to the Teton Basin in Idaho, where they joined her father—six-foot-four, wild, mean, hard-drinking, fighter Bill "Scot" Hubbard, who lived in Tetonia.

En route in the wagons to join her father, Eliza frustrated a holdup attempt. Because they felt threatened, they had stopped near a homestead and, finding no one home, had put their mules inside the homesteader's empty barn. Despite the danger, Waterman could not stay awake. "Get in the wagon and sleep, then," said Eliza; and she sat up all night under one of the wagons with a shotgun.

Next morning Lorenzo was fearful of being bushwhacked when he went to the barn to get their mules; but they were snorty types, suspicious of everybody, let alone strangers; so when he found them standing quietly, he knew no one was there.

Shortly after they had hooked up and pulled out, two riders showed up alongside the wagons. Waterman, who only had a handgun, got down onto the wagon tongue between the mules for protection; but Eliza reached back, grabbed her double-barreled, muzzle-loading shotgun, pointed it at one of the men, and said, "You sons-a-bitches better get out of here before you get more lead than you can swallow." They skedaddled.

One evening a few years later, the entire family, including the Hubbards, was camped across the river from the town of Green River. Big Bill decided to cross to town for a drink and a fight.

When half the night had passed and he wasn't back, they decided someone should go after him. None of the men would; but Eliza, declaring, "I'll get him," caught and saddled a horse, crossed the river alone in the middle of the night, walked into the saloon, grabbed her gigantic dad by the ear [literally], and led him out. "She was the only one who could have got away with it—or got him outa there for that matter," added her grandson.

In 1903, Eliza's daughter "Georgie" Waterman, later to become "Georgie" Ross and the mother of my chief informant, Rex, "came across the Hill" to Jackson's Hole. Near the mouth of Granite Canyon she discovered the beginnings of a cabin, but nobody working on it; so she moved in, completed the one room, sod roofed cabin, and made herself at home on John Mangum's claim. When Mangum returned from his trip and found a woman on his claim, he abandoned it.

When it was that her mother, Eliza, left Waterman in Idaho and came to live with Georgie, I do not know; however, in 1910, Eliza Hubbard Waterman married Jack Seaton in Butte, Montana, where both were visiting relatives—she, her sister. He was 40; she, 58. Everyone said the marriage wouldn't last because of the age difference, and it didn't. Of course, they were childless.

Jack was no relation to the many Seatons who today live in the Hole, and in later years Eliza was wont to refer to him as "That Irish son-of-a-bitch." In due course, she left him and took over the Bear Paw when Georgie left to marry, proving up on the claim her daughter had entered, grubbing the sagebrush with a hoe, and putting in 15 acres of grain north of where Dad later built the pond. Her grandson thought that she probably had Wesley Bircher build the two-story cabin in the teens.

Jack Seaton owned a place near the Snake River which Dad later bought in putting together the Rocking H, and subsequently sold to Mr. Resor in 1930. Meanwhile Eliza's first husband, Lorenzo Waterman, had come to the Hole, and homesteaded practically next door to husband Number Two on property that also became part of the Rocking H and eventually of the Lake Creek Ranch. Lorenzo became the Justice of the Peace who, as detailed in Chapter One, tracked down the rifle in one of the killings ascribed to the Old Man.

So there they were: Eliza and both of her former husbands, in the big, wide, wild West living within five miles of each other. After Eliza sold out to Dad and moved in with Georgie, they all lived within two miles of each other.

Eliza carried her sack of Bull Durham and a package of papers in the top of her stocking. Because I was a kid, in my presence she didn't hesitate to hike up her skirt to fetch her "makings" or return them.

At 78 she fell and broke her hip in Jackson, where she was hospitalized and never released. When Rex heard about her fall and went to see her, he found her in a coma. She was buried in the Teton Community Cemetery in 1930 with Watermans, Rosses, Flemings, and Mangums.

That cemetery, just north and east of Teton Village, in which her wooden headstone may still be found by the careful searcher, was the result of the diphtheria epidemic of 1900 and of the flu epidemic of 1917. Altogether, three dozen men, women, and children are buried there. It was there that Pete Hansen, father of Senator and Governor Cliff, lost his eye. Pete was helping bury those who had died of diphtheria when a piece of gravel flew up from his pick into his eye, which started bleeding. Pete just put his bandanna over it and kept on working. A few days later, infection set in, and his eye had to be removed right there on the ranch. There was no resident physician in Jackson's Hole in 1900.

To the Huylers, however, Eliza Hubbard Waterman Seaton's true memorial is not the stone in that cemetery. That handshake in 1926 is her true memorial. Several thousand dollars, 160 acres, and two cabins transferred on a handshake, the handshake of two strangers, one of whom sensed intuitively that the other's word was her bond.

We Huylers rarely go into that cemetery, but we honor that woman of integrity several times each year as we tell of her handshake, which was as good as a notarized contract.

As death approached, Eliza Seaton announced, "I want the tallest men on this side to be my pallbearers, and I don't want no preacher a-preachin' over me. I'd like Doc Huff to say a few words at my funeral—and that's it."

And so it was.

CHAPTER FIVE

"Uncle John"

In her interesting and informative book, *This Was Jackson's Hole*, Fern K. Nelson writes of John Dodge. I wish to add here our family's perspective of that remarkable man, that truly tragic figure in the history of Jackson's Hole.

Why tragic? As Fern points out, he had been born into wealth in Council Bluffs, Iowa, and as a Remittance Man, supported by a monthly allowance or remittance from home, he never had to worry about his daily bread. He had to worry about his mind. The tragedy was that he knew he was "crazy." He had some lucid days, but they were few, and he would say to Dad or Mother, "Margaret (or Coulter) you'll have to excuse me; this is one of my sick days."

How had it happened?

Evidently, John L. Dodge had been a truly brilliant young man. In Harvard Law School he had been Number Two in his class. He had been selected by Chief Justice Oliver Wendell Holmes to be one of his Summer law clerks. He had a right to be proud; his parents should have been proud; however, if he was proud, his father did not show it. He kept pushing: "John, you can be first in your class instead of second! John, you can be first!" So John pushed and pushed and snapped. My mother told me that story one day early on when I was making fun of the old man, of his shaking, of the odd things he did.

Fern recounts the tale of his plowing the field. That story may have come from Dad or it may have happened more than once; however, I was with Dad one day as we drove down the lane between the Wilderness Ranch (John Dodge's place) and Mose Giltner's place.

"Uncle John" was riding along on a sulky plow drawn by his two hump-backed mules, Hobo and Bobo. Yes, he had two pair of mules which were truly hump-backed: Hobo and Bobo, and Lobo and Bess. I have never seen another hump-backed mule—or horse for that matter. This odd-looking team, naturally, added to the ridicule which was too often directed his way.

The lines were lying at his feet. He was reading what proved to be *Variety*. Dad stopped the car for a visit as the mules wandered our way. Looking up, the old man saw us and put down his paper. Beginning at the ends, he gathered his reins and halted. After chatting a bit about the weather, mosquitoes, cattle prices, and the hay crop—the usual topics of neighborly discussion, Dad brought up the subject of the unusual plowing procedure.

"Mr. Dodge, don't you think it would go faster if you drove your mules in a straight line?"

"Yes, Coulter, it probably would; but that way I wouldn't get my reading done. This way, if I keep them moving, I guess they'll get to it all sooner or later."

He clucked at Hobo and Bobo, and drove off. Who was crazy?

I came home mocking the old nontraditionalist. Mother told me of his breakdown, how in our day he could probably have been treated and restored to soundness of mind; but that in his time not enough was known about the mind, and he got no help. She demanded respect for "Uncle John." Understanding the situation, we kids gave him our sympathy, if not the respect he deserved.

Why did he call his place "the Wilderness Ranch"? Its location, being directly opposite the confluence of the Snake and Gros Ventre Rivers, it must have been flooded from time to time since the end of the Ice Age. It certainly was flooded when the first Jackson Lake Dam went out in 1908. I don't recall what "Uncle John's" place looked like before the Kelly Flood; however, when it came along in 1927 his place took a direct hit. Not only was it inundated, it became the receptacle for tons of river rock. By the time I remember the property, it was aptly named.

"Uncle John's" cattle were hardy rather than fat. He didn't seem to care if we kids rode his calves. We rarely if ever saw him riding his pastures anyway; so we felt quite safe in cornering a bunch, roping a calf or two, and trying to ride them. We'd get a rope on one, and a couple or three kids on the rope. Then one of the older kids, probably Stan Resor or Clyde Hinesley, would grab the calf's head and get him stopped until the others could get the catch rope off him and a short riding rope on him. Then in some sort of informal rotation one of us would climb aboard and grunt, "Let 'er go!" We rarely lasted more than a half-dozen jumps.

I know why "Uncle John's" calves were never fat; but we kids saw to it that they developed plenty of muscle; and, after all, muscle weighs more than fat, and cattle are sold by weight.

Had he caught us, the old man would probably have laughed and encouraged us because he loved kids and he was a bronc rider himself; nonetheless, we were frightened of being caught.

"Uncle John" loved and raised bucking horses. Two in particular come to mind: Mary Miles Minter and Desert King.

If any reader is older than I am, he or she may remember a star of the silent films, a platinum blonde whose real, or film, name was Mary Miles Minter. She had first come to Jackson's Hole to play opposite Tom Mix in *The Cowboy and the Lady.*

Recall the copy of *Variety* the old man was reading while he plowed? He was stagestruck, and in the mid-1920s was focused on Miss Minter. She for her part was flattered by his letters and by his invitation to visit on "The Wilderness Ranch." She probably did a bit of sleuthing and discovered that John L. Dodge was the scion of a wealthy family. Hmm! She'd investigate. For the sake of propriety, she arrived with a "companion."

"Uncle John" was, of course, delighted. He desired to put on a wild west show for the two ladies. This he couldn't quite handle all by himself; so hitching Bobo and Hobo to his fringed surrey (yes, he had a surrey with a fringe on top long before *Oklahoma!* and the song), he assisted the ladies into it, tied the white mare behind, and drove up to the Bear Paw Ranch.

Dad knew a good photo opportunity when he saw one and filmed what followed: the hump-backed Bobo and Hobo, Mary Miles Minter, the actress; Mary Miles Minter, the bucking horse; "Uncle John"; and the rest of our family, who were spectators.

Jack Neal eared down Mary Miles Minter the mare, while "Uncle John" saddled her. The stars in the surrey oohed and aahed as suspense built and the old man eased

Collection of the Jackson Hole Historical Society and Museum.

John Dodge, c. 1927.

aboard. "Fanning" a bronc with a ten-gallon hat was the way it was done in the old days; so he took off his hat before crying, "Let 'er buck!" Jack stepped back out of harm's way. To our consternation and "Uncle John's" chagrin, the white mare bucked two or three jumps straight ahead, then broke into a gallop. Around the ranch clearing she swooped while Dodge fanned and spurred. The mare had taken off straight ahead; but the old man had the halter rope in his left hand and was fanning with his right; so she gradually circled as she ran. By the time they had looped the clearing, horse and rider were winded. She ran up to the familiar surrey and stopped. "Uncle John" sometime earlier had sold Dad two young mares, Nip and Tuck. Now, he dismounted and offered the halter rope to Dad with, "Coulter, as you can see, she doesn't buck; can't make her; she's well on her way to being a good saddle horse. Why don't you buy her for your family?"

Dad declined, and "Uncle John" took both Mary Miles Minters back to the Wilderness Ranch. Presumably, the movie star, noticing how John lived, concluded rightly that although he was a scion of a wealthy family, he was a remittance man without access to family treasure. She and her companion returned to Hollywood, never to be seen again in Jackson's Hole except on the silver screen. Loyally, "Uncle John" attended every one of her movies that appeared at The Club, where movies were shown in those days.

The Club still stands on the Square, the tallest roof on the east side.

Desert King was a buckskin gelding, a saddle bronc who was popular at the rodeos because he could be counted upon to pull out every trick in his bag: swap ends, high dive, sunfish, spin, and bawl and beller the entire time.

When Desert King was put into a chute, "Uncle John" could be seen behind that chute extracting oats from a pocket of his duster and reaching it through the slats to his horse. In fact, he slipped treats to all of his broncs. He owned several.

He not only owned them, he rode them. His or anybody else's. It was quite a sight to see him coming out of a chute on a saddle bronc with that ubiquitous duster snapping behind him in the breeze created by his passage! One time he hit on the idea that it would add to the fun and general excitement if he distributed eggs to the kids at the rodeo to throw at him as he rode. Was that incident the source of the slang expression *to egg someone on*? It was surprising that no kid threw an egg at another kid, that all of us held them to throw at "Old Dodge." The only good to come from that one-time incident was that his friends and neighbors put a stop to it that first time.

They protected him from his own indignity. They thought too highly of him, of what he had been, of what he might have been, to let him ridicule himself or be publicly ridiculed by others. Moreover, John L. Dodge was 60 years old by then, and bronc riding is a young man's game, to say the least. It was time he stopped. When asked why he kept riding, he responded, "The glory of a thousand eyes on me."

Fern writes of John Dodge's eliminating the necessity for chopping firewood by running one end of an old fence rail into his stove no matter where the other end might rest. It was a bit like plowing that field: it would all get burned in the long run. I saw it a dozen times myself: sometimes the end of the rail was outside his door, as his cabin wasn't very large; sometimes it was in the middle of the floor. Either way it had to be stepped over and around. In any case, since the stove door could not be closed, the cabin had a layer of wood smoke from the ceiling to about four feet above the floor. It was a good idea to sit down as soon as possible to get some air. In fact, during "Uncle John's" last years, which he spent in his "town house" in Wilson, some children one day stuck their heads into his smoky doorway and saw him stretched out on the floor, apparently dead. They spread the alarm; help rushed to the cabin and dragged him out of the smoke to examine him. Indeed, the problem was the smoke: carbon monoxide had overcome the old man. Had the kids not found him and rescuers dragged him out into the air, he would surely have died.

Grant "Tiny" Hagen loved to tell of the time he and another Boy Scout visited "Uncle John" to enlist his support for some project or other. The stove was smoking; "Uncle John" was mixing some flapjack batter. He invited the boys for breakfast. They sat down as quickly as possible to get out of the smoke, only a moment before two chipmunks came chasing each other up the fence rail. As they saw the people and the fire, they leapt from the rail to one of the purlins. One didn't quite make it and fell. He fell right into the pot of batter which the old man had just set aside. Boys and man watched intently as the little fellow scrambled up the wooden spoon, shook himself, and dashed off. "Uncle John" picked up the batter and resumed his mixing. "Well, I guess he took all he touched." The boys weren't so sure.

I don't know whether or not this story is apocryphal, but it certainly circulated in our valley.

John Dodge decided to have a boat built. He would try Winters on the sea in warm latitudes. He had read that the hardest wood in the world was ironwood from South America. Perhaps he had not read that it is also the heaviest. Or perhaps he reasoned that if there were steel ships, there was no reason not to have an ironwood boat. I suppose it didn't occur to him that a hull of ironwood must be considerably thicker than a hull of steel.

At any rate, so the story went, ignoring the advice of experts and amateurs, he commissioned the construction of his boat. When launching day arrived, and it was slid down the ways, it promptly sank.

Another Dodge story, which I believe was probably true, had to do with his Wild West Show. This occurred, if it did, some years before we Huylers came to Jackson's Hole.

At the time, Buffalo Bill's Wild West Show was touring Europe, and young John Dodge had met and talked with Cody himself. The Wild West Show had repeatedly toured the United States to packed tents. John Dodge, lover of theater and admirer of Buffalo Bill, felt that here was a stage upon which to exhibit his talents. Was he not by now the genuine article?

The Wild West Shows of the old days were not rodeos; they were exhibitions; the cowboys were not contestants; they were paid performers. John L. Dodge's name and its association with wealth attracted professionals. He signed on cowboys and Indians. The grand opening would take place in Omaha. Renting a site took all of John's allowance; he asked his fellow performers to be patient. He would pay them from the receipts of the first performance.

Patience ran out. Grub and firewater were expensive. Surely the Dodge family would bail him out. Surely they would not. His men delivered an ultimatum: "Pay us what you owe us and we'll go on. Otherwise . . ."

What to do? Surely the crowds would come if the show opened. But how could he open without his cowboys and Indians? He would put on a one-man wild west show for one evening, collect his ticket money, pay his performers, and everything would then go smoothly.

That first night Dodge, himself, was in the ticket booth selling such tickets as were sold. He then put three broncs into the chutes, took the megaphone and announced, "John Dodge coming out of chute number one on Broken Bones." Laying aside the megaphone, he climbed onto Broken Bones and was bucked off.

Dusting himself off, he grabbed his megaphone. "Next rider, J. L. D. coming out of chute number two on Widow Maker." And out he came.

This time he completed his ride, but without pickup men, had to bail off as best he could.

"Jackson Hole John coming out of chute number three on Appendicitis."

Then it was time for the calf roping, and the same "three contestants" roped three calves. And so it went, but, of course, slowly. So slowly that most of the spectators left. Fortunately, in those days they did not have brahma bulls and bull riding, or "Uncle John" might have died right then and there. As it was, he paid off his "hands" as best he could and, discouraged, dragged himself home to his Wilderness Ranch near Wilson.

In his classic, *Diary of a Dude Wrangler,* Struthers Burt describes John Dodge's wrestling a black bear that had followed its nose into his wagon when it had smelled his grub sack. John had not looked in back until he was under way and heard the bear. His mules had stampeded; and John had let them go while he concentrated on the job at hand, throwing the bear out. This man was an athlete of undaunted courage.

The old man loved animals, but never had a dog or cat. He came close, however, when he located a coyote's den and brought two pups home as pets and companions. They needed to eat; so the old man hired young Lawrence Cheney to bring them a dead jackrabbit or two dead ground squirrels daily. Lawrence told me that even though he had to buy shells for his .22 and walk four miles round trip to deliver his kills, the 20 cents Dodge paid him per day was more than he could earn at any other job available to him at his age. In late November, "Uncle John" went home to Nebraska for the Winter and had the coyotes shipped there. Lawrence wondered what they ate that Winter and what finally became of them. They did not return in the Spring with John Dodge. Not many jackrabbits in Omaha, and most rodents hibernate.

Have you ever seen a jackrabbit in Jackson Hole? Unless you were here before 1939, you have not. Before that time there were jillions; however, a plague wiped out all the jackrabbits in Jackson Hole and in Montana that year. Although there are plenty of them a hundred miles east of Jackson Hole, they have never made a comeback here.

A man who had worked briefly on the Wilderness Ranch concluded after a couple of drinks in Jackson that "Old Dodge" had treated him shabbily and announced that he was going back across the river and "whip that old man." He disappeared headed for the Wilson bridge.

When word spread from the saloon to some of the town's more responsible citizens about the threat to their old, "crazy" friend, several headed out in their cars to protect him.

It happened to be one of "Uncle John's" lucid days. When his former hand, more than slightly inebriated, confronted him, John recalled the skills he had learned as a member of Harvard's boxing team. Added to that skill was considerable hard muscle gained by riding broncs, wrestling bears, and picking rocks on the ranch.

When his would-be defenders arrived, they found their friend contentedly tending a badly beaten man. Jackson Hole was delighted. The story was widely told. There was no more talk of "whipping that old man."

It seemed that there was always a new John Dodge story circulating our valley, which would remind folks of old John Dodge stories.

For various odd reasons, most of "Uncle John's" employees did not stay long. He was, after all, more than a wee bit odd. One man in particular had good reason for quitting.

It was Winter when he drew his pay and stopped in Jackson on his way out. He was asked why he was quitting so soon. "That old man," he responded, "is too much for me. Every morning he jumps out of bed, runs to the river, jumps in, then comes running back to the cabin and jumps in bed with me to get warm."

No one blamed him for leaving.

In his later years, "Uncle John" was even more pathetic than he had been earlier. Stooped and leaning heavily on a stick, he was rarely clean shaven or combed; his pajamas always protruded above the waist of his filthy tweed trousers and frequently through the open fly. Above the waist he wore a shirt, with buttoned collar much too large for his now scrawny neck; a cardigan sweater, which didn't get cleaned very often; a filthy old tweed jacket. Atop his tousled head perched a felt hat—not the cowboy hat one might have expected, but a fedora, which once may have been jaunty, but now was battered and worn askew. In fact, if one judged from the hat alone, one could not be sure in precisely which direction "Uncle John" was traveling.

One day at the Blackfoot Fair John Dodge met Bear Face Dodge. The latter had acquired his name after a bear attacked him, leaving his face horribly scarred. The day the two Dodges met was one of John's "good" days.

He walked up and accosted the stranger. "You must be Bear Face Dodge."
"How did you know?"
"Well, I'd heard your story, and there are all those scars on your face."
"Well, and you must be John Dodge."
"How do you know?"
"Because your fly is open and your pajamas are sticking out of it."

Had it not been for Fransje Schofield, Clarence "Stearny" Stearns, his wife Dodie, their partner John Schwartz, and for his tenants, the Shinkle family, all of whom did what they could for him, his plight would have been tragic rather than merely pathetic. Dodie washed the old man's linen when she could get hold of it, and all joined in keeping an eye on his safety.

As had been the case his entire life in Jackson's Hole, children did not understand John Dodge and deviled the stooped old man. How old was he? No one seems to know; but at the end, he was ancient.

John Dodge loved watermelon and during the Summers, before returning to his cabin a quarter-mile away, would frequently buy one from Clarence or Dodie. Invariably some youngster would volunteer to carry it home for the oldster. En route, inevitably, the watermelon would be dropped, breaking, of course. The end result? The kids got most of the melon.

Another prank they played was to sneak into his cabin early of a morning and steal his watch. Missing it, the old man would hurry excitedly down to Hungry Jack's and telephone the sheriff. Shortly thereafter, the thief would show up with the watch and "sell it back to Old Dodge."

He spent most of his daylight hours sitting on a soda fountain chair on the porch of Hungry Jack's General Store. There he would call for a sarsaparilla (a type of soda pop), visiting with such as would stop and talk—and on "good" days, recalling famous trials of years gone by.

In Jackson on October 27, 1933, while a jury deliberated the fate of Vick Henrie, who had shot and killed Ed Nichols in the first stall of our Rocking H barn, quite a group had gathered around John Dodge, who declared that since the defense was temporary insanity, the jury must either hang Vick or set him free. There could be no in between. He cited legal precedents with names and dates. His hearers were greatly impressed. It was one of his "good" days.

"Uncle John" had siblings: Nell; Carrie; and Bob, who was a noted flutist.

Hunter Scott, his nephew, frequently visited the old man on the Wilderness Ranch. We saw a lot of Hunter during those visits because he was a most attractive young man and my foster sister, Gwyn, was just plain beautiful.

When his Uncle John died, leaving his ranch to Hunter, the latter gave acreage to the State of Wyoming for the C Bar V School for the Handicapped. How appropriate! "Uncle John" would be pleased that on that land there is also a riding arena for the Jackson Hole Therapeutic Riding Association.

He would, however, have been astounded to learn that the remainder of the Wilderness Ranch has been subdivided and developed rocks and all.

The John Dodge Subdivision has become an upbeat, stylish neighborhood. I can imagine the old man shaking his grizzled head in disbelief. None of the rest of us living then could have imagined it either.

A nice postscript to the chapter is that one of the residents, Lisbeth Beise, is dedicated to the idea of restoring John Dodge's homestead cabin as a memorial to a fine old man, a good citizen who deserved better of life than he received.

CHAPTER SIX

"Dad"

What an amazing shot he was! Old as he was, he rarely missed. When he took aim, hand, eye, intent, and tobacco juice came together as a team. It was his custom to remove the smallest ring from a lid of the wood stove in their kitchen before rearing back in his chair to chaw. Rear back he would, and let 'er rip he did. Rarely was there even a sizzle.

I suppose I called him "Dad" because he was Clyde's dad; but quite a few people called him that because of his years and pleasant nature. His real name was Jim Hinesley.

His family had crossed the plains and mountains in a covered wagon when he was a small boy. He had spent most of his life in Bellevue, Idaho, coming with his wife to Jackson's Hole well along in years because his daughter, Bernice Neal, and son, Clyde, already lived and worked here.

The heart of Wilson was not then the Stagecoach Bar nor Hungry Jack's Store. In fact, it was about a quarter-mile north of them, where Fish Creek Road starts north, where the Owens live, and where Lundy's Store and Post Office and Yokels' Hotel stood.

"Dad" bought a log building on that corner and converted it into "Jim's Place," a bar and pool hall. Young and old had lots of fun in Jim's Place. I wish I were a good pool player. I am not. I suppose there was my opportunity; however, it was perhaps ten miles from the Bear Paw; and by the time I got there on any given day, the cues were in use and it was almost time to start the ten-mile ride home.

It was in that bar that I was most thoroughly put into my place. "Dad" was 84; I was a brash 16. I intended to compliment him. He was a bit hard of hearing and had a high-pitched voice.

"Dad," I shouted, "I hope I'm as good a man as you are when I'm your age."

He fixed me with a watery eye, turned to locate the nearest brass spittoon, scored a bull's eye on it then another on me: "How the hell could you be? You're not now." Hmm.

Ordinarily a quiet place, Jim's Place was on one occasion the focus of considerable excitement. A transient hay hand had suggested after a drink or six that he might "knock off that little place in Wilson." The word got around, and Dad's friends rallied to protect him and to "Get that son-of-a-bitch if he so much as tries."

The most unusual of those vigilantes was Jack Dempsey—yes, the former Heavyweight Boxing Champion of the World. When he, himself, had been Middleweight Wrestling Champion of the World, Mike Yokel had "discovered" Dempsey and helped him start his climb to Heavyweight Boxing Champion of the World. From time to time, Dempsey came to visit his old friend and mentor. The most famous heavyweight wrestler who ever lived, "Strangler" Ed Lewis, was another sometime visitor to Mike.

The holdup threat must have been issued about 1935. Jack Dempsey was long retired, but what a hunk he was! Overweight, but all of his avoirdupois seemed to be muscle. He had nothing to hide, and didn't. Almost invariably he wore a polo shirt, which exposed those gigantic arms, huge shoulders, and broad chest. "Dad" must have felt safer when the two giants, Jack and Mike, showed up to defend him.

Darkness fell, the vigilantes, well armed, tried to stay quiet and out of sight in the back of the darkened pool hall. They wanted the holdup man to come. They were ready for him. No one was quite sure which transient worker had made the threat. What did he look like? They must await his move. They stayed out of sight all right, but hardly silent.

Did he come by, sneak up in the dark, sense the reception awaiting him, and move on, or was the threat idle talk in the first place?

No resident of Wilson will ever know. Around midnight "Dad" gratefully locked up and said good night to his friends. Gosh! The holdup at Jim's Place might have been the "Manassa Mauler's" greatest fight.

My father rode East on the train with Jack Dempsey that Fall. As they were boarding the Twentieth Century Limited in Chicago, a stranger reached over and hit Dempsey hard on the arm. Jack scowled the scowl that had intimidated many a fighter and rubbed his arm. Dad was appalled. "How does anybody dare hit you?"

"It happens all the time, Mr. Huyler. Seems like everybody wants to be able to say, 'I hit Jack Dempsey.' They know I can't hit them back. But how I would like to sometimes!"

The *American Heritage Dictionary* describes Jack Dempsey as the "American prizefighter who won the world heavyweight title in 1919 but lost it to Gene Tunney in 1926. He brought new popularity to the sport of boxing in the United States." He certainly was a hero in Wilson, Wyoming!

Dempsey's nemesis, Gene Tunney, also showed up in Wilson, population 100. There, on Betty Woolsey's Trail Creek Ranch, he and the equally legendary Paul Petzoldt got into such a heated argument that blows seemed likely. What a fight that would have been! Had I been there, I would have egged them on rather than moderated. Ask Muggs Schultz to tell you the story some time.

"Dad" Hinesley is no more; nor are his store-bar-poolroom or the spittoons. Mike Yokel, Strangler Lewis, Jack Dempsey, and Gene Tunney are gone. So are Louis Fleming, Orson Cheney, and Betty Woolsey and Earl Hardeman. Wilson is the less for those losses, yet Virginia Huidekoper is still there; and although it has been a long time since Ginny followed her Jim headlong through the panes of closed windows into snowdrifts, amazing happenings still occur in the Stagecoach. In truth, my home town, Wilson, Wyoming 83014, is an unusual place, though "civilization" is crowding and harassing it. I am glad that my address is not Teton Village, the Aspens, or even Moose. How long can Wilson keep its identity? Hang in there Ginny!

CHAPTER SEVEN

Homer

Homer was "deef." Of that there could be no doubt. Nor was there doubt in anybody's mind that Homer was an original. Even before his deafness, there had been no doubt about that.

Until I watched Homer as his deafness and consequent social isolation increased, I had thought that total blindness would be harder to bear than total deafness. Homer was, at the end, about as deaf as a person could be; and it isolated him. Despite his best efforts and those of his legion of friends, it isolated him. We really could not carry on a conversation of more than a sentence or two with him.

And, of course, deafness altered his voice. It became harsh and unmodulated, invasive. You could hear him coming a block away, yet Homer was not by nature an intrusive man. Curious, yes; invasive, no.

Collection of the Jackson Hole Historical Society and Museum.

Homer on Homer Richards Day, c. 1980.

When Mayor Sam Clark declared Homer Richards Day, Homer commented with justifiable pride, "There ain't a thing in this town—*nothin'*—that I haven't had anything to do with." Some double negatives there, but it sorts out to what he meant. The *Jackson Hole Guide* editorialized, "That's a pretty broad claim, but Homer's record proves the brag."

When he was a City Councilman, Homer borrowed money from the bank to purchase the rodeo grounds from Cleo Karns. The town wanted to purchase it, but hadn't the requisite funds; Homer volunteered, "By golly, I'll borrow it, and the city can repay me when they get the money." His son, Jack, recalls that Homer even had to make one or two of the interest and amortization payments himself when the town was broke.

Homer was at one time substitute mayor when Doctor Huff had to go East on family business.

There was no more generous man in Jackson! Homer commissioned and had built at his own expense the beautiful war memorial in the center of the Square. All of us whose names appear upon it are proud to be there and are grateful to Homer. It was typical and appropriate that Homer selected that particular cowboy and that particular bucking horse to crown the monument: Guy Holt on Steamboat. He had admired them on Wyoming license plates for decades.

Dick Moore, who was chairman of the committee to raise funds to build the Festival Hall out at Teton Village, reports that Homer was the only one of the many donors who did not wait to be asked; he came to Dick and brought his contribution.

With his sons, John and Jack, Homer owned and operated the Ideal Lodge, which he later renamed The Flame Motel.

Whenever Homer learned that a tenant at the motel was there to attend a funeral, he refused payment. "You've got enough troubles without my addin' to 'em."

For a wedding or a christening, charging was fine.

Although the conditions are rare, one can still get

Collection of the Jackson Hole Historical Society and Museum.

Homer with his war memorial, 1976.

"snowed in" in Jackson Hole and be unable to leave for days. In the Winter of 1949, all roads leading into and out of the Valley were closed by snow for more than three weeks, three weeks during which the recently inaugurated airport was shut down also.

One Winter when a bunch of us got "snowed in" in Jackson, and a weekend became a week, Homer knocked on each door the morning the original reservation expired, "It ain't your fault that you cain't leave; so it won't cost you nothing till you kin."

Homer's longtime close friend Slim Lawrence had devoted a lifetime to collecting local historical memorabilia. He had nowhere to exhibit his collection. Homer owned quite a few buildings in his part of town. He offered Slim a 99-year fixed-price lease on one of his buildings if Slim would convert that building into a museum and move into it his thousands of artifacts. In 1958 the fascinating and informative little Jackson Hole Museum opened its doors. Since Homer's and Slim's deaths, Jack and John, in typical Richards style, continue to honor their father's agreement.

Homer always carried a pocketful of Tootsie Rolls "fer the little childern." He always put the welfare of "the little childern" ahead of any others. "They're our future, y'know." He distributed Tootsie Rolls to some of his favorite big kids, too. I still carry a petrified one in a pocket of one of my jackets, where feeling it reminds me of him.

Homer had been born in Ellanorah, Missouri, on September 12, 1895. He had married Eliza ("Mother") on October 14 of 1920. Homer had been a barber and hairdresser in Missouri, a fine trade because it was in demand everywhere. They came to Jackson in a roundabout way in 1924. He and Eliza had tired of Missouri mud. "There was too much mud in Missoura in 1923. We had to take sticks and poke the mud out from between the spokes of our Model T (Ford) afore it could move. I jist got sick and tired of that mud, and Mother and I decided to move to Californi." They set forth on August 9, Homer, Eliza, and a baby, Jim.

En route to the Golden State, they stopped with relatives in St. Joseph, Missouri. One of those relatives owned a red Durant automobile, which Homer coveted on sight. Away went their Model T. Away went their savings! Eventually, the red Durant became the first, and perhaps the last, Durant to make it to Jackson's Hole. Homer had his car, but precious little money remained for their journey; so out came the barber's shears, clippers, and curlers; and one might say he cut and curled his way from St. Joe to Salt Lake City.

In Salt Lake City Homer and Eliza were warned against crossing the dusty, hot, Salt Lake Flats and the Nevada or California deserts with the baby. There would be few facilities; gasoline and even water would be hard to find. They turned northward toward Portland, Oregon, where they spent the Winter of 1923-24 and Homer rebuilt their savings by barbering. After working in the shop of someone else for awhile, he bought his own and hung out his own shingle.

Tired of Missouri's mud, by Spring they had also tired of Oregon's "eternal drizzles."

"Mother and I had promised ourselves that we'd visit Yellowstone Park; so we set out to see her in Summer of nineteen and twenty-four on our way back to Missoura—or so we thought." It took them 11 years to reach that Park. Tire trouble halted them in Shelby, Idaho. While dickering for a new tire, "We began visiting with the man who ran the place. He suggested we go to the Park through Jackson's Hole rather than West Yellowstone; so we headed for Victor. We camped on the Pass side of town near Bircher's sawmill, an' I looked up at them mountains. We didn't have no mountains like them in Missoura, y'know; an' I kinda worried about that Durant, loaded down the way it was. The sawmill feller warned us that there was still lotsa snow up there on what he called 'The Hill.' Some hill!"

Quinn Riggan, Garl's brother, expressed the opinion that the Durant could not make it and offered to haul them across with his team. Offer accepted.

Collection of the Jackson Hole Historical Society and Museum.

"Some Hill!" c. 1920s.

In Jackson's Hole at last and thinking to be here for only a few days, the Richards family camped first on Fish Creek at the foot of Teton Pass before starting north toward the south entrance of their goal, Yellowstone Park.

Struck by the beauty of Jenny Lake, they stopped "fer a few days" at that predecessor of motels and bed and breakfasts, a tent camp, where the proprietress served meals.

It was there that Homer and Bill Scott began a long business relationship and enduring friendship. There was no Teton Park, but Bill ran a boat and horse concession at the lake. Bill asked Homer to stay the Summer and help him with both. Homer received a percentage of the take.

"I give Bill Scott credit for everything we've got," said Homer. "He got us to stay here, y'see."

"The longer I stayed, the better I liked Jackson's Hole. I finally found out that there were homesteads open near Jenny Lake; so I tried to file on 640 acres that included the lake. That sure woulda been dandy; but they told me that the lake was in the reclamation survey; so I filed on a quarter-section. Later I found out that more was available; so I filed on another 160 which stretched out to Timbered Island, where there was lots more logs fer building. I figgered I'd build cabins fer tourists. I spent all Summer snakin' logs with a team I borried from Ans Harthorn of Kelly; an' yu know what? I used that team the whole Summer an' Ans wouldn't take a penny fer it. That's neighborin'!"

A second baby was due that Winter; so they went back to Missouri and barbering, returning to Jackson's Hole the following Summer with Jim and John. As they drove up the Hoback Canyon, they heard a great, distant roar. It proved to be the Gros Ventre slide.

By Winter 1925, Homer's six, two-room cabins had been framed and a Post Office constructed on his homestead, but Jenny Lake was remote for a mother with two infants; so they spent the Winter in Kelly, where Homer joined his friend and Jenny Lake neighbor, Albert Gabbey of the Square G, and both men kept busy building furniture for their Jenny Lake cabins.

When the snow left in 1926, Lida Gabbey was appointed the first Postmistress of Jenny Lake. The Post Office was the little building constructed on Homer's land alongside the dirt and gravel highway. Alongside it, Homer erected a small grocery store that included one gas pump and, naturally, a barbershop.

In February 1927, a third son, Jack, was born to complete the family. Jack was the only one born in Jackson's Hole, and it is typical of Homer's enthusiasm and loyalty that Jack's full name is Jackson Hole Homer Richards. Tragically,

Jim was killed in World War II, but John and Jack, following in their father's footsteps (no one could fill his shoes), became pillars of the community and active in good works. Homer's granddaughter, Jackie Williams, moved into his old home and operated it as a small bed and breakfast.

"People laughed at me for wanting that homestead," Homer recalled in a 1978 *Jackson Hole Guide* interview. "They said the soil was too rocky to raise anything. But I knew what I was a-doin'."

"I could see the Park a-comin'," the *Guide* quotes Homer as saying, "and I felt it was a good thing. If the Park wasn't made, then the road between Yellowstone Park and Jackson would be lined with junk and people wouldn't be able to enjoy the mountains at all."

In 1929, when the first, small Teton Park was dedicated, embracing only the major peaks and a few lakes at their base, Homer and Eliza sold out to John D. Rockefeller Jr.'s Snake River Land Company. He used that money to purchase the location of the present Sundance Inn, "Jackson's Inn-town Inn." Some of those Jenny Lake cabins were moved to Moran and thence to Colter Bay; others were moved into Jackson, where two on East Kelly are so totally encased that no one could ever see that the basic structure is log. One of those was for some years the home of Max May. A third cabin was moved onto the corner of East Kelly Street facing Willow. It became the home of author and newspaper editor Floy Tonkin. That cabin recently made another move. It can now be found on Second Street in Wilson. Homer built well.

Never one to waste time, as soon as Homer had purchased his Jackson site at 135 West Broadway, a block-and-a-half from the town square, he set to work constructing the Ideal Lodge, a series of 25 small stucco cabins, which were ready for tourists when the season opened in 1930.

In 1935 Homer and his family finally made it to Yellowstone Park.

At the time, there were two hotels in Jackson, but nothing specifically designed to accommodate people with cars. The cabins served the tourists and the Richards family well and were sold and removed in 1954 to make room for The Flame Motel, solidly and beautifully constructed of sandstone. (I often wondered why Homer thought The Flame a better name. Was it because of the sign he envisioned?)

At any rate, to advertise the new name for his motel, Homer went off to Las Vegas and purchased a big, revolving, multicolored, neon sign featuring flickering flames. He was ecstatic when he returned to Jackson. "Jack, jist you wait till you see it. It's the most beautiful sign you ever seen." It arrived; and it was, indeed, something to see! Not only did the neon flames flicker realistically, but the entire sign rotated like a weather vane.

A few years later the Town Council passed an ordinance against moving signs. Homer appeared before the Council to request that his sign be grandfathered. With a wink to the audience, he appealed to the Councilmen, "Can't take it down, you know. I use it to pump my water."

The family's home he constructed in matching materials and style off the last unit to the northwest. As he accumulated funds, he bought property stretching north until he owned several blocks. "It looked like good business property to me." How right he was! A look at a photograph of the town at that time will impress one with his vision and acumen.

The Richards home is impressive. It is much more expansive inside than it appears from the outside; at first glance it becomes clear that here is a building that was built to last—if not forever, for at least a couple of centuries. Fire, earthquake, riot, and flood might do their worst: here is a fortress that could and would withstand any or all. Supporting that sandstone is heavy construction steel trucked into the Valley for that building.

Jackson's first Recreation Center was the Richards basement. Down there on AstroTurf he had a croquet course permanently set up, as well as ping-pong and pool tables. As can be imagined, Homer was a skilled croquet player; but I don't recall his playing ping-pong or pool. Many a long midwinter's evening was shortened by that basement and by singing around the electric organ, which neither he nor "Mother" played, but which he bought and kept for others to enjoy.

In one corner of the basement rec hall was an artificial Christmas tree fully decorated year-round so that all he had to do was to carry it upstairs when the season rolled around. Homer was very proud of that. "Saves trees, an' it saves trouble."

Collection of the Jackson Hole Historical Society and Museum.

Homer and his Jenny Lake gasoline pump, c. 1925.

It was Homer's expressed hope that his basement would become a recreational center for the town's children. They were invited to come by and play any time. I suppose it may have been his deafness that kept them away. He could not hear their questions or requests.

It must be obvious that Homer loved people. Like him, I take strength and sustenance from the company of good people. We aren't bored when we are alone, but there is never a time when we prefer solitude to good company. So there were many fine parties in the Richards home. For example, every year he and Eliza would invite the entire congregation of St. John's Episcopal Church to brunch. Nor was that all: Who but Homer Richards would invite every resident of Jackson Hole to a party? Homer invited all to his and Eliza's Golden Anniversary celebration. The paper reported, "Hundreds of friends stopped by to offer their congratulations." That was 1970.

For 48 years Homer had perfect attendance at Rotary. It was his ambition to make 50. Imagine! Fifty years of perfect attendance at anything! He didn't quite make it. Death was the only force that could have stopped him; and, unfortunately, it did. We miss him. When considering Homer's 48 years of perfect attendance, recall that there was only one Rotary Club in Jackson Hole in those days; and the nearest place to make up a missed meeting was Idaho Falls, 90 miles away. Amazing!

For quite a few years the Rotary Club of Jackson Hole met at the Wort Hotel. He worried because there was no meeting the day it burned. Would the fire destroy his perfect attendance as well as the Silver Dollar Bar?

For some reason he couldn't make it to one Rotary luncheon that was held at the Granary up on the butte. The following week he approached the president. "Jeff, I couldn't make it to the Granary last week; so I come over here to the Wort an' set fer an hour. Do I git credit?" He had sat alone for an hour in a dark room. What choice had President Jeff Woodruff?

The two Rotarians who sponsored my admission to Rotary so many years ago were Dr. Don MacLeod and Homer Richards. How could a person be better sponsored? Don, too, was hard of hearing; and he dropped out of Rotary because he missed all the banter and fun. Homer, typically, hung in there. So did Garl Riggan, another charter member who was extremely hard of hearing. Some of us felt we must not lose these fine men; so I set about finding a solution at least for Rotary meetings. The solution seemed to be an FM transmitter hooked up to the PA system, and an FM receiver for each member with a hearing problem. Those receivers with stereo earphones that could be individually adjusted, were worn at Rotary meetings in lieu of traditional hearing aids. The club purchased the transmitter and microphones; those members who desired them purchased the receivers and earphones.

I'll not forget the first meeting with the new equipment in place. Three men had FM receivers. I sat with Homer to see to it that his was on the right frequency. The high point of the proceedings for most of us was when Homer boomed out, "Jack, it's too loud!" That was in the middle of the invocation.

Some time later, I had to tape his receiver to our frequency because I caught him listening to a baseball game instead of our meeting.

At Rotary meetings, Homer commented on many local affairs, and he always made good sense.

On the Tuesday at Summer's end he always stood and reminded us Jackson Rotarians that the tourist season was running down, "Just remember: Pretty soon now we're gonna start livin' off each other agin."

A move was afoot, supported by Laurance Rockefeller and Grand Teton National Park, to move the airport out of Jackson Hole and down to Daniel Junction. Homer's comment said it all: "If you're gonna move the airport to Daniel, you'd better keep this one so you can fly back and forth."

When substituting concrete sidewalks for the town's boardwalks was being considered: "People come from all over the world to see Jackson's Hole. They travel over thousands of miles of blacktop. I want 'em to be able to see a few boards. I want people to see what it was like." I wish more residents of Jackson shared Homer's viewpoint.

He foresaw troubles for his beloved Jackson Hole. He said, "I always figgered this was goin' to turn out to be a rich man's country, that it was going to be hard for a poor man to live here." How unfortunate that, as usual, he was correct! What a misnomer is "common sense"! It is so uncommon. Homer had a great supply of it.

Homer was a loyal, generous, and reliable member of Saint John's Episcopal Church. When the bishops decided that the *Book of Common Prayer* should be replaced by a new translation (which is often a new interpretation rather than a new statement of the old), internal strife surfaced between those who wanted to go along with the change and those of us diehards who wanted to stay with the Jacobean English we loved. Typically, Homer put everything into proper focus when he arose at the congregational meeting and addressed the priest: "Well, Phil, it seems to me if we jest use it long enough, the *new* Prayer Book will be the *old* Prayer Book." End of discussion; we voted it in.

One time in the 1960s, when the young people of his church and a young priest wanted to try some pretty unorthodox things, Homer commented, "It seems to me that people in the older generation are supposed to *encourage* the younger generation. Let 'em try, I say." In the log sanctuary they performed *The American Dream* by Edward Albee. Reaction was divided, but never passive.

The Episcopal Church involves a great deal of congregational participation throughout its services. In his late years Homer could participate only in the Lord's Prayer. He could *see* when to kneel and when to stand; but he could *feel* the rhythms of the Lord's Prayer so could, and did, join in. Otherwise for him the weekly service at which his attendance was typically regular was a service of meditation, a sort of Quaker Meeting in an Anglican setting.

Homer was untroubled by theological debate. To his close friend, the well-known theologian Charles Carroll, he declared his thoughts about the various translations of the Bible: "Charles, them scholars kin say what they want, but I believe every word of the Bible just the way Jesus writ it."

Homer had a positive outlook upon everything and an unquenchable exuberance, an outlook and effervescence that even the loss of their sons, an infant in 1923 and Jim in World War II; the eventual loss of his lifetime partner, Eliza, in 1976; and his deafness could not extinguish. For a short time it would be dimmed as he mourned his loss, but gradually the ebullience resurfaced and took over once more.

At the annual storytelling potluck that Margaret and I hosted on our Rocking H Ranch for thirty-some years, we sat around a campfire after supper and told, and listened to, stories about "Them What's Gone." In his later years, Homer heard little of what was said; but he sat there mulling over old times until he, too, was ready to share something. His eyesight wasn't too good either, and he sometimes couldn't see that someone else was standing telling a story. Homer would just stand up wherever he was and begin: "Jack, there was this feller . . ." The person who had been talking would know that Homer was not interrupting intentionally and would sit down until Homer was finished. Then the first storyteller's problem was whether to try to pick up again the thread of the abandoned story or to begin another.

A favorite of Homer's stories is my favorite because it was about deafness, yet he told it with such delight. I wish you could hear that hard, flat voice and see his eagerness to share.

"Jack, there was this deef waitress at the Wort, you see; and there was this one feller who come in fer breakfast pretty much every mornin' an' she'd take care of him.

"Got to be so she'd watch fer him and allus see that he was seated at one of her tables. Not that they could talk much, 'cause she was deef, don't yu see? But anyhow, they enjoyed each other's company.

"Well, Jess or John hired a new hostess for the breakfast room, and she didn't know about that waitress and this feller. See? So when he come in next mornin' while that waitress happened to be in the kitchen, he was seated at another girl's table.

"By the time his gal got time to look around and seen him, he was pretty well finished. She slipped over to him and asked, 'Is there anything I can get you?' 'No, thank you,' he said quietly so as not to attract attention from the whole dining room. 'I've had a sufficiency.'

"She didn't quite catch that. 'You've been fishin'?' 'No, thank you. I've had plenty.' 'You caught twenty?' 'Oh, go to hell.' 'I'll say you did do well.'

"You see: Us deef fellers sometimes hear excitin' things the rest of you miss." And Homer sat down amidst laughter and applause which he could not hear, but could see.

Some years ago, Dick Peck, Dick Riddle, and the Lower Valley Power & Light Company joined homeowners in underwriting improved winterization of Valley homes to save energy. I happened to be there with Ed Roberts, a friend from Fort Worth, when two men came with an estimate for improving the winterization of Homer's house. Ed has never forgotten Homer's reaction. Evidently, Homer did not grasp the concept that the job was being underwritten by LVP&L in order to avoid the necessity of expanding their facilities. Homer said to me, "Jack, that's too cheap. You tell them young fellers to come back to me with a reasonable bid, and I'll sign it."

Did Homer really do this? Anyway, he loved to tell it.

One day Homer, driving around the Square in his Lincoln Continental Mark IV, spotted an empty parking space. As he pulled up alongside the car ahead and prepared to back into the slot, a young fellow in a VW bug zipped into Homer's spot from behind, jumped out, slammed his door, and called to Homer, "You gotta be young and quick to do that, Pops!"

Undaunted, Homer shifted the Mark IV into reverse and backed slowly but steadily into the spot, accordioning the little VW as he went.

To the young man standing there agog he remarked with glee, "Young feller, you gotta be old and rich to do that."

One sure thing about Homer, if he did do that to teach the young man a lesson, he subsequently bought another—and better—secondhand car for him. Homer was capable of doing both.

After he had a cancer cut from his lip and stopped smoking, Homer asked Olie Riniker to remove from around town a famous photo of him of which he had been justifiably proud. He wanted it removed because in it he was smoking a cigar. "It's a bad example fer the kids, Olie!"

"Olie, you and I are gonna live to be a hundred because of one word: *determination.*"

When Homer was about 85, his doctor told him he must take a daily walk for his health. For awhile he walked Broadway; then he moved one block south to Pearl: "Too much pollution on Broadway."

Until the day he died, in April 1989 at 93, of complications of diverticulitis, Homer was the eternal optimist. His attitude toward life and his increasing infirmities is illustrated by one of his last statements. His legs had weakened. As he and I approached the long staircase leading to the theater in the Pink Garter Plaza, I shouted in his ear, "Homer, do you think you can make it?"

"I alluz have; so I guess I can make it one more time." He did. What a wonderful way to look at life! If only more of us did!

For years, at the first Rotary meeting of each month, Homer stood and recited the following birthday poem for those of his

Collection of the Jackson Hole Historical Society and Museum.

48 Years of Perfect Attendance at Rotary, 1958.

fellow Rotarians at the Birthday Table. These lines had been written for him by Barbara Wood Gray's mother:

It isn't the years that count today
As we think of our love for you,
But how you have lived them,
Your cheery ways, and the kindly things you do.

That is the way it was with Homer, himself: the way he had lived his years, his cheery ways, and the innumerable kindly deeds he did. Jackson Hole without Homer can never again be quite such a good place to live.

What would Homer Richards have thought had he seen the mural honoring him that was completed in 1999 on the wall of the Round Up facing the Sundance Inn, formerly his Flame Motel? That mural, sponsored by the Morton family and painted by Greta Gretzinger, is 150 feet long and 10 feet high. It required three months to complete over three years, and features a fine likeness of the honoree extending a Tootsie Roll to young Hailey Morton, while her sister, Sally, and brother, Cooper, smile in anticipation. Homer would, I am certain, have been both bemused and delighted. His childlike innocence and joy would probably have led him to throw a party in front of it for his legion of friends.

Collection of the Jackson Hole Historical Society and Museum.

The Homer Richards mural, 1999.

CHAPTER EIGHT

Dance Halls

I write of dance halls, not of saloons nor casinos nor bars, but dance halls built especially and exclusively for dancing. I remember six in Jackson's Hole, and there was at least one before my time. Perhaps there were more. Before the dance halls was The Club, still standing on the northeast side of Jackson's Square. It contained a movie theater that doubled as a dance hall; so it was not, strictly speaking, a dance hall; however, for dances Ray McNabb's band furnished the music. It had quality. Glenn Exum was saxophonist/clarinetist/crooner for Ray, who was a trumpeter.

The farthest north of the Valley's dance halls was Beaver Tooth Neal's, which stood in Elk, Wyoming, about where the Heart 6 Guest Ranch now stands. It, also, was more than a dance hall, although that is what it was every Wednesday and Saturday night. Beaver Tooth's had an unusual aspect, in that it was a roughly circular dance floor with the bandstand in the center. It survived until after the removal of the town of Moran. My brother, Coulter, and I went there a few times with Julie and Nat Burt after they moved from the Bar BC to Three Rivers Ranch. McNabb's band played there, too, before moving to the Jenny Lake Dance Hall.

Photo by Harrison R. Crandall. Collection of the Jackson Hole Historical Society and Museum.

Invitation to Crandall's Dance Pavilion (Ester Leusch), 1925.

Crandall's Dance Hall

near String Lake, north of the road, flourished on Saturday nights; and it was a natural, since Harrison Crandall played the trombone and his wife, Hildegard the piano, giving them a strong nucleus of a band in residence. Crandall's Open Air Dance Pavilion, built in 1924, became history in two summers when the plank floor and four-foot-high side logs were used in his new studio building. Subsequently, Cliff Ward, who sometimes played his drums at Crandalls, had a dance hall closer to a better road in the growing Jenny Lake community where it became the center of much exciting activity.

Harrison Crandall, by the way, was the Valley's first resident commercial photographer. His beautiful photographs, some hand-painted in the days before color prints, are to be seen framed in the older homes and hotels of Jackson Hole and beyond. He built his log studio with its distinctive sky-lighting cupola on his homestead. The building stood near the forest edge on the north side of the road, northeast of today's Cathedral Group Turnout on the Jenny Lake Loop Road about a mile east of String Lake. The studio was later moved to the lakeside at Jenny Lake Campground after the National Park was established. The building was moved again to its present location and is now the Jenny Lake Visitor Center.

Later the usual band there consisted of Ruth Bremenstall at the piano; Jimmy Stevens and Glenn Exum, sax and clarinet. The May brothers (Clifton, Leland, Lester, and Murland) played saxophone, trombone, and drums. The hall belonged to Cliff Ward, who, when Grand Teton National Park acquired Jenny Lake, moved his dance hall lock, stock, and barrel 20 miles to a site just north of Jackson, alongside the highway about a mile north of Flat Creek Bridge and across the road from the Elk Refuge. A gas station occupies the site today. In its new location, this was Jackson Hole's last dance hall. After it, dancing moved to the bars, the "Joints."

Cliff Ward, who had run his hall when it had stood near Jenny Lake, ran it near Jackson. Most of his band moved with him. Harrison Crandall played the trombone; his wife, Hildegard, the piano; Glenn Exum played the saxophone and clarinet and was the crooner. And what a crooner he was! Glenn was definitely the most handsome man I have ever seen, an Errol Flynn with character. He sported the wavy hair, the pencil mustache, the dreamy blue eyes, the muscle; and when he crooned it was through a small megaphone à la Rudy Vallee, who at the time was the Crosby or Sinatra of the nation.

Glenn, a 17-year-old member of the musicians' union, had come to the Hole from Pocatello in the Summer of 1930 because he heard that the Jenny Lake Dance Hall needed a saxophone player. The band played on Saturday nights only, but since he couldn't live on what Ward could pay him, Glenn worked on a road gang that first Summer until Paul Petzoldt met him and transformed him into a mountain guide.

Paul, a few years Glenn's senior, had come over from Idaho with a friend and climbed the Grand Teton in 1924. He was 16 at the time and without climbing experience. Immediately famous and with Jackson's Hole yearly becoming more of a destination resort for dudes, Paul foresaw a future that was economically sound and fun as well, and immediately became the first commercial guide in the Tetons. By the time Glenn arrived, Paul was doing well enough to want an assistant. One ascent of the Grand together, and Paul declared Glenn a full fledged guide; however, Glenn reminded him that he needed to be off the mountain every Saturday afternoon in time to play at the dance hall.

Although I was too young to attend the Rainbow or the Jenny Lake Dance Hall, Mother, Dad, Coulter, and Gwyn did quite regularly in the Summertime; and in the years to come, I spent a lot of Saturday nights in each of the others.

Structurally, they were similar: barns without lofts or stalls—big rooms surrounded by a plank bench, continuous except for one corner, where there was a refreshment counter. I have been told by those who were there that during Prohibition, in addition to soft drinks and coffee, "Moose Milk" was served in tin cups. "Moose Milk" was moonshine disguised with milk.

The Saturday night routine was this: As a family, or other group that included girls, arrived, they found a place somewhere along the bench. That became their home base, so to speak. It was there that we boys went to ask a girl for a dance. It was to that spot that we returned her after the dance, unless she was willing to step outside "for a breath of air." There was no cutting in. The couples formed and moved out onto the floor; the band struck up and played a number entirely through four times. At the conclusion of the fourth run-through, the saxophone wailed, "That's all!" and each man escorted his gal back to her spot on the bench, where he thanked her and usually drifted away to some other desirable partner, where the cycle repeated itself.

Popularity is fickle. The Jungle, constructed about a mile north of Wilson on the Birchers' property, became the "in" place to spend Saturday evenings. Wesley Bircher had built it, and he retained ownership. The Jungle band featured Ray Reed on the drums; Cabot Cummins (tailor, hatter, and Town Clerk) on sax; Stippy Wolff on the fiddle; Ted Lozier, bass; on guitar, Karly Johnson, who in response to urging, still (in 1999) plays beautifully; Ruth Bremenstall at the keyboard; her husband on the banjo. Marion Nethercott and Louie Fleming played the "bones." It was quite a band! Karly reports,

"He paid us according to what he made: sometimes a dollar; other times ten."

Perhaps in these days and times the "bones" require explanation. My dictionary informs me: "Bones: flat clappers made of bone or wood originally used by the end man in a minstrel show." So far so good, but it doesn't tell you enough. Most "bones" were made of hard wood and took their name from the fact that they were shaped like beef ribs, which were, indeed, used as rhythm instruments on the frontier. A pair was held between the fingers of each hand, the middle fingers separating them, the arcs against each other, instead of nesting. They were shaken rhythmically with the music and were often the rhythm section of country orchestras. I suppose the sound most similar today is that of an outstanding tap dancer dancing with metal taps on his shoes. When the "bones" were clapping, any listener would have needed to be "deef" not to tap a toe at the very least.

In addition to the dancing, many and glorious were the fights that took place occasionally inside, but mostly outside, the dance halls. There were lots of fights, especially during the lifetime of the CCC, the Civilian Conservation Corps. In the 1930s the CCC took unemployed young men, usually from metropolitan areas, and sent them to the national parks and forests to build trails and otherwise improve the nation's lands under the supervision and command of regular Army officers. It was a great and successful program. The men were young and the experience of working for the CCC often gave real direction to their lives. They built roads and trails and monuments; they improved their health and muscle; they learned discipline. Each enlisted for a minimum of six months and was paid $30 per month, with the stipulation that $25 of it must be sent home. Although none of us suspected it then, because of the CCC they made better soldiers a very few years later, at which time, as privates in the United States Army, they received the same pay: $1 a day. While in the CCC, they generally stayed out of big trouble, but were frequently involved in small troubles such as fistfights at the dances.

It never occurred to me until many years later to feel sorry for the CCC boys. So far as I recall, no one did at the time; however, here were young fellows away from home and loaded with testosterone. They, quite naturally, wanted to dance with our sisters and sweethearts; we, quite naturally, did not wish to entrust our sisters and sweethearts to the arms of those strangers from Brooklyn, the Bronx, or Chicago's South Side.

Altercations occurred weekly, but those fights were small stuff when compared to the brawl in 1930 between Paul Petzoldt and Big John Emery.

Glenn Exum's fancy had been caught by a young local beauty, one Dorothy Redmond. Knowing that he could "sit out" a few numbers, Glenn had invited Dorothy to Saturday night's dance at the Jenny Lake Dance Hall. Dorothy, probably a bit worried about the potentials of this smooth character, said she would not come unless her girlfriend could come too. Exum approached Petzoldt to take this blind date. Paul finally agreed upon the condition that he might wear Glenn's best suit. "Done!"

It turned out that the girl was a University of Southern California cheerleader. Had he known that, Paul would not have needed bribing.

Saturday night arrived with no hint of the drama that was to follow. Glenn and Paul, in Glenn's best suit, picked up the girls at the Redmonds' Red Rock Ranch up the Gros Ventre and drove them to Jenny Lake. It was a beautiful night illuminated and glorified by an almost-full moon. Glenn eagerly anticipated "sitting out" a few dances with Dorothy.

Finally asking Cliff Ward if he might "sit out" the next dance, he led Dorothy to the dance floor. They were just becoming cozy when trouble struck in the form of Big John Emery.

John was not only big, he was more than ornery; he was mean. To illustrate my point:

One evening Bill Giles, Guy Kyle, Homer Richards, and Big John were playing poker in Mike Meeks's bar. Kyle was winning; John accused him of cheating and, suddenly reaching across the table, grabbed Guy and almost bit his nose off, as a result of which Guy Kyle was disfigured for the rest of his life.

And, by the way, Guy Kyle was no softy himself. He lived up the Gros Ventre, where he and a neighbor, "Pap" Dew, had a severe falling out. John Ryan tells me that "Pap" had three strapping sons, Pat, Ted, and Dick. "Pap" and sons spent one

Collection of the Huyler Family.

Glenn Exum atop his mountain, 1933.

Winter boxing with the notion of whipping Guy Kyle come Spring.

One fine Spring day, the four men went down to Guy's cabin and demanded that he come outside. "We're going to whip you," the father announced.

"How are you going to go about it? One at a time, or all three at once?"

"One at a time."

"That suits me fine." Guy beat each of the them in turn.

Eventually, Guy left the Hole and moved to Arizona, where he took up with a woman from South Chicago. Tiring of her after awhile, he drove her out onto the desert and simply dumped her out to fend for herself. No, Guy Kyle was no pushover, yet Big John had bitten off the end of his nose, disfiguring him for life.

At any rate, on the particular Saturday night at the Jenny Lake Dance Hall, Big John spotted Glenn and Dorothy dancing, went up to them, shoved his arm in between them and declared, "I want to dance with Dorothy!"

"John, I don't want to dance with you."

Refusing to accept that rebuff, John hauled off and hit Dorothy on the forehead. Glenn did the only thing a man could do under the circumstances: He drew back and hit Big John on the chin just as hard as he could.

Collection of the Jackson Hole Historical Society and Museum.

Young Paul Petzoldt already a legend in Jackson's Hole, c. 1925.

You will recall that Glenn made his living by hauling himself and clients up the Grand Teton. He was very strong; he was in top condition; and he had the satisfaction of feeling every ounce of his strength go into that punch. "I pulled that one all the way from the floor," says Glenn, "But Big John just shook his head and turned on me."

Some men grabbed John; and says Glenn, "I made darn sure that the guys who grabbed me held me."

Dorothy ran toward "Roan Horse" Smith's concession and ducked through the little access hole under the end of the counter. Big John had broken loose and was after her.

"Roanie, help me! He's going to kill me!" panted Dorothy. Roan Horse pulled a big .44 from under the bar, stuck it into Big John's belly as he arrived, and pulled the trigger. Click! But that slowed even Big John Emery down, and he retreated.

Did Roan Horse know that was an empty chamber, or was it a misfire? Did he leave the first chamber in the cylinder empty for just such a purpose: so that he could "put the cougar sign" on someone without shooting him? Another question that must forever go unanswered.

While all this had been going on, of course, the dancing had stopped as everybody watched. "Grab your horn and get back up there and blow it," muttered Cliff to Glenn in an aside.

The music began again and so did the dancing.

About that time Paul Petzoldt, outside enjoying the moonlight with the USC cheerleader when all of this took place, heard of the excitement, came barging up to Glenn, and demanded, "Who hit Dorothy?" Glenn pointed out Big John, who was leaning against the doorway brooding. Petzoldt started for him.

"Hey! That's my best suit!" yelled Glenn.

Paul stopped, removed the jacket, folded it carefully, laid it on the bandstand. Then, "He ran all the way across the dance floor and hit Big John, knocking him through the doorway, off the porch onto the ground."

Petzoldt is big; he is built like a grizzly bear; he was in his prime; and he was angry. Every time Big John got up, Paul knocked him down again—five times in all. A crowd had gathered cheering him on. Few people liked Emery, and no one liked what he had just done inside. After that fifth knockdown, someone yelled, "Look out, Paul! He's got a knife!" Big John had pulled a knife from its sheath in his boot. Not quite all was fair in love or war even in the Jackson's Hole of those days. Three or four cowboys jumped on Emery, dragged him to a pickup, and drove him back to the Bar BC. End of the affair? Not at all.

Exum and Petzoldt lived at Jenny Lake. The next morning, J. D. Kimmel, who built and owned the Jenny Lake Store, looked up Paul to tell him, "I've just come back from town. Big John is roaming around looking for you. Says he's gonna kill you. You'd better lay low for awhile or carry this gun." He offered Petzoldt his gun.

Paul responded, "Well, I want to be sure he finds me." Turning to Glenn, he said, "Come on, Ex. Let's go to town." So they jumped into his Model A and headed south.

In town they were soon informed that Big John Emery was in Joe Ruby's Café and Beer Garden and that he had been swearing that he was going to kill "that damned Petzoldt."

Paul went directly there. Emery was at the crap table; In fact, he was the shooter. As the dice were being slid back to him by the croupier, Petzoldt pushed in next to him, shoved him aside and took the dice, declaring, "Gimme the dice; I want to play." That was, of course, quite an affront to Big John's manhood; but he backed down and said not a word. I suppose that Paul's physical presence reminded John of the previous night's beating; and he wanted no more.

Dorothy Redmond later married Fernie C. Hubbard from Ennis, Montana, and went there to live. On a visit to her family in Jackson, she and Fernie stayed in one of the Crabtree Cabins. Big John, still insanely jealous, shot Fernie in the back one morning while he was shaving. The wound was not fatal, but John became, of course, a wanted man. He left our valley in a hurry and went north not to be seen again in Jackson's Hole until some years later, when he returned and surrendered for trial. During the trial, Big John changed his mind and escaped. The Jackson jail at the time was hardly a modern prison, and John was not the first to break out of it. To the best of my knowledge, he was never seen in Jackson Hole again.

It is an odd circumstance that Big John's brother, Olin Emery, later became a respected Sheriff of Teton County. I was one of his Deputies.

As soon as Fernie was well enough, the Hubbards went home to Montana. Dorothy and Glenn did not see each other again until 1993 at our ranch, the Rocking H, over supper. I believe that was a delightful evening for all concerned. I know it was for Margaret and me. Dorothy was embarrassed to be reminded of the fateful evening 60 some years earlier, but finally began chuckling about it as Glenn, in his inimitable style, "needled" her—despite remonstrances from his wife, Beth. I took the details of the Petzoldt vs. Emery affair from an audio tape that I made of Glenn Exum and Dorothy at our dinner table that evening. I realize that it differs in sequence and a couple of small details from Glenn's account of the same incident as it appears in his 1998 publication: *Glenn Exum: Never a Bad Word or a Twisted Rope*; however, I'll stand by his earlier account which I taped and which is word for word as I have heard him recount it at my urging probably two dozen times in the past 70 years.

Al Lysher was a fine man; his wife, Winnie, was the cause of many troubles. One of them exploded at the Jenny Lake Dance Hall around the same time as the Exum-Redmond-Petzoldt-Emery affair.

At the Rocking H Jack Neal had employed a young Blackfoot Indian horse breaker, Frank Parker, to help break the colts that we were busy raising. Al's wife must have felt that it would be interesting to be "sparked" by an Indian. A complication was that she and Al had an infant daughter.

Be that as it was, one Saturday evening she told Al she was going to visit her mother. On some pretext she left the baby with her mother and sneaked off with Frank to the Jenny Lake Dance Hall. Al was no fool. Guessing what was going on, he soldered the cylinder of a .22 revolver so that he could take no more than one shot with it. Satisfied with his modification of Colonel Colt's invention, Al tucked it into his waistband behind his vest and set out for Jenny Lake.

Mother, Dad, Coulter, and Gwyn, already at the Jenny Lake Dance Hall that evening, had noted Winnie and Frank dancing together. They saw Al come in; he was weaving. It seemed to them he had reason to be drunk. A few minutes later the sound of a shot focused everyone's attention. On the dance floor stood Frank and Winnie, each clutching a wounded forearm.

Al had staggered around the dance floor, pretty much ignored in his seeming condition, until he saw a clear line of fire to Winnie's right and Frank's left forearms as they came together while slow dancing. There was a moment when no one was behind them. At that moment Al pulled his revolver and fired his single shot.

He straightened up and walked out, no longer "drunk." How the woman got home I do not know; probably with Jack and Bernice Neal, since she was Bernice's daughter. Frank fled. Jumping into his car, he drove directly to the Rocking H bunkhouse, rolled his bedroll, grabbed his saddle, and headed back to the reservation without even waiting to draw his pay. We never saw him again.

Al left his wife and baby and went to Alaska, where he became a guide for big game hunters. Before he departed, he gave me that .22 revolver. Someone took it while I was overseas in World War II. It was an odd-looking weapon, with its big glob of solder on the cylinder. Al had been too hurried to do a careful and sightly job.

His ex-wife died in Boise, Idaho, in 1996, tenderly cared for until the end by the woman who had been that baby daughter.

I don't recall anything so wild at The Jungle, despite its name. There were the usual fisticuffs with the CCC boys, but nothing as dramatic as the John Emery or Al Lysher affairs. My brother, Coulter, was frequently a featured attraction in the fistfights. He was good at it; and although he maintained that he did not, he loved to fight, else how could he have been involved in so many? As for me, I avoided them whenever possible; but being my brother's brother, I'd had good training: I could duck.

Despite the fact that Wilson was derided in Jackson and Jenny Lake as Cannibal Island and the dance hall as The Jungle, it was known in Wilson as "Bircher's," where it flourished from 1926 to 1938. The Bear Paw went there en masse every Saturday night: family, wranglers, and dudes.

Cabot Cummins (tailor, dry cleaner, hatter, and for years Town Clerk of Jackson) played the saxophone here; Murland May (electrician), drums; Don Kent (Postmaster at Kelly) was a great deadpan piano player; Louie Fleming (rancher and cowboy who lived in Wilson) usually brought two pairs of "bones" in his pocket; Glenn Exum came down from Jenny Lake to croon and play his horn.

The old place really rocked on Saturday nights, especially when the band struck up Scott Joplin's "Twelfth Street Rag." To that number, and to that number only, we did the Jackson Hole Stomp, sort of a schottische in which we all stamped as loudly as possible—and, since we all wore boots, that was plenty loud!

Possibly the most sensational dancer of those "good old days" was Wilma. Although she admitted to 200 pounds, her true weight must have been closer to 300. Wilma was the only person I ever saw, man or woman, who rode one of the old, horse-drawn mowers without hanging a rock or cinder block under the seat to make it ride easier. Wilma's weight needed no help.

But this large Wilma was a fine and popular dancer, light on her feet and swift of foot. At the dances she was in demand.

Today's readers may be unaware of the fact that whenever the construction of a barn was completed, a barn dance was held in the yet-empty hayloft.

Mel Annis (the man who took Nick McCoy home to Kentucky to die) built a good many barns in Jackson's Hole, among them ours in 1928. As completion neared, Mel approached Dad with a proposition:

"Mr. Huyler, that's a good barn. I think it deserves a staircase, rather than a ladder, up to the loft."

Dad was well aware of Mel's motive, but he played it straight.

"No, Mel. A ladder's good enough for us."

"Mr. Huyler, that really is a handsome barn, if I do say so. A nice staircase sure would look good in it."

"No, Mel. A ladder will be just fine."

"Mr. Huyler, if you'll furnish the materials, I'll furnish the labor to build a staircase."

"No. Thank you, Mel."

Then came the truth: "Mr. Huyler, the truth is that Wilma can't reach the rungs of a ladder."

Our barn, as do several other of Mel's barns built during the Wilma Period, sports a staircase. Dad maintained that it was a good investment, for if the new hayloft would hold Wilma dancing, it would certainly hold a few tons of hay.

As stated previously, the Valley's last dance hall was Ward's, moved from Jenny Lake with only name and location changed. After repeal of the 18th Amendment ("Prohibition") in 1933, there was very little drinking inside the dance halls. Out in the cars or the bushes, perhaps; but drunkenness was not tolerated inside. They were safe and wholesome places for young and old, from grandmothers to babies sleeping in baskets.

By now the Saturday night dancers were about equally divided: locals and dudes from the dude ranches, who attended pretty much en masse except for those who gambled.

We men never wore our hats while dancing; customarily, we put our hats on our partners' heads.

Almost everybody wore jeans. Women and girls, men and boys wore silk or satin shirts. Nothing ever felt better to a boy than a girl through a satin shirt!

Throughout the 1920s and 1930s Tom Mix shirts of silk were in vogue for men: The collars were somewhat like those on Cossack blouses, or the Nehru collars of a later period. They stood three or four buttons high, snug against the neck. Each sleeve sported a dozen buttons. The openings of the two slit breast pockets were outlined in black thread; and black piping ran up both sides of the front opening and of the lines of buttons on the sleeves. Bernice Neal made these beauties for her men: Jack, Coulter, Clyde, and me; and we wore them without embarrassment. It was a gaudy period: bright colored shirts, silk bandannas, ten-gallon Stetson hats, Indian beaded gloves, silver belt buckles, made-to-order boots. The men were every bit as flashy as the women. Peacocks we may have been on Saturday nights, but working men the rest of the time.

Perhaps those were the styles that Gene Autry and Roy Rogers later carried to such ridiculous extremes: white silver-mounted saddles, bridles, and breast collars—or even white-and-blue to match shirts and pants; and ivory or pearl-handled revolvers, always two of them. Those Roy and Gene wore every day in the course of their normal day's work. And did you ever try to carry a guitar a-horseback? I did just once.

One evening, Margaret and I had walked to the neighboring Piton Ranch for dinner. I had taken my guitar as requested by Art and Sally Peters, our host and hostess. By the end of the evening, it was raining hard. We walked home, but I left my Martin until another time. The following morning was crisp and bright as mornings in Jackson Hole are wont to be.

Jeep was the only horse I've ever owned that I could ride anywhere—and I do mean anywhere—without bridle, halter, or even a piece of string. Since I enjoy walking only as far as the end of my bridle reins, I hopped onto Jeep bareback to retrieve my guitar.

Reaching the Peterses' cabins, I called and asked that Art or Sally fetch me my guitar. I don't recall which one handed it to me before several things occurred in rapid succession. Jeep disliked the look of that big black case, but responded to my repeated *whoas* by standing trembling. When I got the guitar case across my lap so that it wouldn't bump him when he moved, I signaled with my legs and weight for him to start home. Start home he did—as fast as he could run. When that guitar and I hit the dirt, it sounded the lost chord, but thanks to the case, was undamaged.

It and I sounded not at all like Roy or Gene as they rode along singing "Tumbleweed" or "Happy Trails."

Collection of the Huyler Family.

My Brother, Coulter, ready to dance, c. 1930.

CHAPTER NINE

"The Joints"

"The Joints" were something else again: Tuttle's, Joe Ruby's, the Frontier Saloon, the Cowboy Bar, the Log Cabin, and the Wort! Until the late 1950s, these bars were "gambling joints" as well as "watering holes," and each had a band and small dance floor. The musicians were pretty much the same people who played at the dance halls on Saturday nights, except that a small band drove over from Driggs, Idaho, every night they could make it to play at Joe Ruby's Café and Beer Garden. Let it be noted that John Ryan, local Jackson Hole historian, sang with that band.

I suppose drinking was the primary drawing card for most patrons; however, roulette, twenty-one, craps, poker, faro, a few slot machines, and, in the back of the room, a table or two of old-timers playing poker earned more money for the proprietors than did even their bars. Some of those old-timers arrived daily shortly after lunch and played until late every night. Since

Collection of the Jackson Hole Historical Society and Museum.

Gambling in Jackson's Hole, 1941.

gambling was illegal in Wyoming anyway, there was no law to prevent us as teenagers from going in. Although the minimum bet on any of the tables was two bits, we hadn't sufficient funds to do more than drop an occasional nickel into a slot machine. Slot machines were prominently displayed in virtually every store and gasoline station throughout the state. But we watched, and we saw which direction most of the money took. After a few years of watching, none of us youngsters became serious gamblers. It was a good and useful education. We saw who won: nine times out of ten, the House. The excessive drinking we sometimes witnessed affected us the same way: We saw nothing glamorous about making asses of ourselves.

The West had voted against paper money. It seemed insubstantial to ranchers, cowboys, and cowgirls. Silver dollars were the general medium of exchange. One rarely saw paper bills in smaller denominations than $20. On the craps, twenty-one, or poker tables, chips were used only for large bets. Stacks of silver dollars stood in front of all but the losers. Unless we were broke, our pockets did jingle.

Around the late thirties it became a regular thing for the adult dudes from the ranches to go to town midweek to do a little—or in a few cases much—gambling. We dude wranglers and our girls usually went with them or drove them to town in a ranch car. We watched them occasionally win, but usually lose their money; and we danced.

I know of no bar in today's Jackson that has more than a postage-stamp-sized dance floor. 'Twas not always so. Ruby's featured Karly Johnson on the guitar and Jimmy Stevens on the banjo and a dance floor roomy enough to accommodate the patrons. "In the old days" the saloons all had real dance floors with good bands; today primarily there are performances. Although Bill Pruitt might sing in the Cowboy Bar in the afternoons, and the Sons of the Golden West might play in the Wort, the show was incidental to the dancing to the band of six-foot-six Johnny Walker.

In 1946, right after World War II, playing in the Wort was an aggregation of Jewish refugee classical musicians who comprised the best dance band to which Margaret and I have ever danced—and we have had the pleasure of dancing to Count Basie, Paul Whiteman, Eddy Duchin, and Benny Goodman. Their chanteuse, whose name I cannot recall, had been a singer with one of the well-known touring bands. She had become tired of one-night stands and being on the road and was taking a Summer off. Wow! Could she sing!

That Summer we went to the Wort at least twice a week to dance to their music and to listen to her sing. They were terrific!

Until the mid-1950s there was a certain innocence, a local flavor, to the "joints." Locals owned them and operated them. We knew them; they knew us. Whenever there was a civic project in need of funds, we'd go to the "joints" for help; and we'd get it. That changed when riff-raff from Vegas moved in. Jackson was listed in *Fortune* magazine as "the second toughest town in the United States." Few residents were pleased. Butte, Montana, had the distinction of being first.

The gamblers even tried to get their toes into the dude ranches. They offered to install slot machines in our offices: nickle, quarter, and dollar. "If you will just instruct your secretary to use silver whenever possible when making change, you can pay your entire crew with your take from these three machines." Incredible! Three machines played by a maximum of 36 guests and some of the crew would pay the wages of 18? I was tempted, but not much. Margaret wasn't tempted at all.

I believe it was Governor Millward Simpson, son of Jackson attorney Bill Simpson and father of today's Senator Alan Simpson, who declared that so long as gambling was illegal, there would be none in his state—and he meant it. At first, the games moved to the basement of the Wort, and you had to know Steve Bartek to get in. Then, on a small scale, gambling moved to motel cabins. Even way out to Flat Creek Ranch.

It is my opinion that the Governor believed that gambling would be legalized in the next election, which, of course, would bring large revenues to the coffers of the state. If that was what he wished for, he underestimated the power of the church vote, especially the commitment of the Church of Latter Day Saints, the Mormons. Gambling was defeated and has never reared its head in Jackson again, although from time to time there have been abortive attempts to get it on the ballot.

Each of the "joints" had its own character and its heyday.

In the twenties Joe Ruby's Café and Beer Garden, and the Frontier Saloon had everything pretty much to themselves. They were old-time saloons without trumpery.

In the thirties "Miss Kaye" and her partner, Lew DeWitt, took over the south side of the Square west of Simpson's Hardware with the Bluebird Café and the Log Cabin Saloon. That was not today's Log Cabin Saloon, but stood on the southwest corner of the town square. The Log Cabin instantly became *the* place to go; and we did. A huge bar ran the length of the big front room. The equally large back room was for gambling and dancing.

In his ring Lew wore a diamond which could have done duty as a traffic light. "Miss Kaye" was right out of a "Western" novel: stout, heavily corseted, dyed red hair, lots of makeup, high heels, tight dresses of black silk—and a soft heart at least toward teenaged kids. I was a teenager and she was good to me. It was my habit not to eat lunch on rodeo days. If I won, I had a standing invitation to the Bluebird for not one, but two T-bone steaks "on the house"—rare and juicy. Thanks, "Miss Kaye"—whichever place you are—for a good many fine dinners.

A favorite recollection of the Bluebird Café occurred the first Saturday night of one August as I was consuming a pair of my steaks. The rodeo was in town. The rodeo was always in town the first weekend in August. In those days our August rodeo was big-time; it drew the best of the rodeo circuit riders, ropers, and bulldoggers. At a nearby table that particular evening sat a bunch of rodeo cowboys with their wives. "Breezy" Cox, a Professional Rodeo Cowboys Association cowboy, entered feeling no pain and carrying his rope. Sighting his friends at the table before they noticed him, he built a large loop, threw it over the whole bunch, let it drop to the legs of the chairs, and sat back hard on his slack. One man was tipped back in his chair talking. Over he went, while the rest were pinned to the table. Temporary pandemonium!

That same weekend came the Log Cabin Brawl. Not that there was only one brawl in the Log Cabin, but this is the one all of us recall with grins. Both rooms of the Log Cabin were packed with revelers, locals, dudes, and P.R.C.A. cowboys and their women.

Let me introduce to you the evening's cast of characters: Steve Bartek, the fastest bartender I have ever seen; Charley Brown, blacksmith, a giant of a man and deputy sheriff; Bob and Harry Brown, Charley's grown and powerful sons; and Pete and Harry Knight, professional rodeo cowboys, one of whom was at that particular time World's Champion Saddle Bronc Rider. Why the Knights wanted to start a fight nobody I talked to ever knew. Just feeling good, I suppose. Fighting was an accepted way of blowing off steam in those days.

At any rate, one of the Knights engaged Charley in a conversation, in which he spoke too quietly to be heard above the background noise. Charley bent over to hear. Knight bent over, too. Charley bent over even farther until the other Knight, who had been waiting for the right moment, stepped up and brought an uppercut from the floor. Charley saw it coming, not in time to duck it, but in time to turn his head enough so that the blow landed on his cheek rather than his chin. Immediately, women were shoved into corners for protection and locals started punching P.R.C.A. cowboys, who returned the compliment enthusiastically. It was quite a free-for-all, but it did not last long. I don't know how many of us were swinging; probably a hundred until big Charley Brown fought his way to the bar, climbed up on it, and released tear gas.

"Gas!"

I believe that not another blow was struck by either side. Everybody crowded toward the two doors. Out in the street couples and groups reunited.

Steve Bartek dashed out, took a couple of deep breaths of Jackson's Hole, ducked back in, and began serving drinks to the first customers to return. The Log Cabin Brawl was finished as suddenly as it had begun.

The next time I was to smell tear gas was in the Army during gas mask drills.

Another year another general melée was triggered by two women. Again it was at the Log Cabin; again it was locals vs. P.R.C.A. This one started in the Ladies' Room when a local girl slapped the face of one of the rodeo trick riders who, she thought, was "making a play for" her man. The professional athlete's response was to rake a set of long, painted, and pointed fingernails the length of her antagonist's cheek, drawing blood. The local gal, no piker herself, grabbed her and tried to wrestle her to the floor. The Ladies' Room was not very large. In the scuffle they burst through the door into the gambling room, where within a minute everyone had joined in, locals vs. rodeo cowboys. I don't recall what stopped that one. Had it been anything so dramatic as tear gas, I would remember.

From the previous three tales, might you conclude that the P.R.C.A. was unwelcome in Jackson? Not at all. We looked forward to their arrival in late July. Each side had good friends on the other; but when it came to the Saturday night sport of brawling, the teams naturally sorted themselves out as locals vs. outsiders.

The biggest gamble I ever saw? It was made on a roulette table in the Log Cabin. A nurses' convention was in town. I suppose one nurse had a long-time yen to experience the sensations of big-time gambling, when a lot of money rode on the turn of a card or the spin of a wheel. I don't know who she was or where she came from, but I saw her walk up to the roulette table and place $1,000 on the red. All of us witnesses gasped. The wheel was spinning; the ball made its rapid circuits, then bumped a few times and settled on a red number. The nurse picked up her stake and her winnings and walked out of the Log Cabin Saloon never to be seen again. That was in the late 1930s. That bet was comparable to $10,000 today.

I hope somewhere she has grandchildren who know that story well.

"Imagine! Grandma!"

"I can't!"

In 1939 Ben Goe bought out Joe Ruby and had Jack Kranenberg thoroughly remodel the building to lure the crowd back from the Log Cabin. There was a Grand Opening of the Cowboy Bar in 1940. Although I suppose it never occurred to Ben to use real saddles as bar stools, as in today's Cowboy Bar, by using knotty pine for supports, bar, and decoration, Ben created a remarkable room: gambling on the south side, bar on the north side, dance floor in the rear. "The Cowboy" as it was soon called by locals, did draw the crowd and became and remained the "in" place until the completion of the Wort Hotel.

"Curly" Walker's band held forth with an honest-to-God electric PA system for the crooners. In the late mornings and afternoons, Bill Pruitt, a real cowboy singer and one of the two finest yodelers I have ever heard, sang. I learned many songs and a few chords from Bill, but I never could yodel, try as I might. "The Lavender Cowboy," the "Bad Brahma Bull," "Yavapai Pete," "Utah Trail," the "Cowboy and the Lady" have stood me in good stead for almost 60 years now, but I still cannot yodel.

Memories of The Cowboy? Trading songs there with Bill Pruitt, dancing there with Margaret and once with Lily Pons, the coloratura diva of the Metropolitan Opera and of the world.

Miss Pons and her husband, André Kostelanetz, the orchestra leader, had come west to see the national parks. In Jackson, they dropped into the Cowboy to inspect the nightlife. About 16 years old, I was leaning against the wall with my friend Jack Hand when they came in. They participated in nothing, merely observed. After five minutes or so, being a 16-year-old, I turned to Jack and asked, "What'll you give me if I can get her to dance with me?"

"I'll bet you five bucks you can't." My big "Black Champie" Stetson in hand, I walked over to her and asked for a dance. It wasn't until some years later that I realized that her thought was undoubtedly, "Well, this kid can't be dangerous." At 16, of course, I thought myself a man and was flattered when she accepted. Nodding to the bald Mr. Kostelanetz, I led her to the dance floor, explained local custom, put my hat on her head, and we danced. She was dark-haired and petite, perhaps four feet eleven. Her famous voice was soft, with that French accent to her English which we Americans find so charming. I regretted that "Curly" and his boys did not play each number four times as at the dance halls. At the end of the dance I returned Miss Pons to her husband, thanked both, and walked back to Jack Hand richer by five dollars and feeling seven feet tall.

In 1936 we had neither horse trailer nor stock rack. There were few of either in the Valley. We rode and led our horses from ranch to town for the rodeos; but, since they knew where they were going and wanted to go there, a rider or two herded them home. One year at the end of the final day of the August rodeo, Dad asked Ed Neal, Jack's brother, if he would ride Silver King back to the Lower Ranch, 13 miles. It wouldn't do to try to herd a stallion. Ed, a quiet man, was agreeable. It was afternoon. Dad had no reason to suspect that Ed had been drinking. Swinging onto Silver King with his usual fluid grace that I never saw another man equal, he set out. The way home from the rodeo ground led through town; it would be a long, lonely, and dusty ride from there. Ed felt that he needed "one more for the road." You don't tie a stallion in the street; so he rode Silver King across the board sidewalk, through the swinging doors and right into the Cowboy, up to the bar, and, without dismounting, demanded a drink.

The horse was not mean, but he was unsophisticated, unused to bars. He was uneasy. He snorted and wheeled, clearing quite a swath for himself before Ed finished his drink, reached over, set the glass back on the bar, and rode out the door for home. Somehow people don't seem to do such things today. In fact, well past World War II one saw plenty of horses in town. Nowadays, aside from parades, the Summer "shoot out," and annual Fall cattle drives, it is a rarity to see a mounted cowboy within the city limits. A pity! There is a stagecoach drawn by one team (whoever heard of such a thing in the old days?) that hauls children and a few adults a prescribed route around town. Every year Jackson becomes more like Everyplace, U.S.A., and Davy Jackson's Hole is no longer Jackson's Hole, but Jackson Hole.

In through the swinging doors of the Cowboy one Saturday night strode a gigantic man. He was a barnstorming wrestler looking for a few dollars and offering to bet $50 that no one could stay in the ring with him for five minutes. He bragged and he challenged and he belittled the manhood of a town that produced no challenger. As he scoffed, he drank; as he drank, he became louder. Finally, Ike Neal, brother of Jack and of the horseman just described, could stand it no more. "Mister," he said, "I'm no wrastler; and I don't have $50 to spend on foolishness; but I'll finger wrastle you just to see which one of us is the better man."

What we all knew, but the wrestler didn't, was that Ike spent his Winters with his wife's family in Meteetse, Wyoming. Honah's family had a small coal mine, and Ike took his shift in there every day lying on his back using a pick above his head. He developed powerful shoulders and thick fingers, each the size of a normal two. But he spoke quietly, and the wrestler took him on without noting those fingers. Around the end of the bar slid Ike. Middle finger extended in a derogatory gesture now centuries old, he put his right forearm on the bar between himself and the wrestler. The stranger did the same and they locked fingers. Someone counted, "One. Two. Three!" The braggart expected a straight pull, but Ike's first move was a yank with a twist. The bully yelled in pain as his finger left its socket. Ike kept yanking and twisting, back and forth. The stranger moved toward him to relieve his pain. Up onto the bar and across it, Ike dragged that 250-pound man, who was now hollering, "Enough! I quit! You win!" Ike kept jerking until the man tumbled head first onto the floor behind the bar, defeated in every way imaginable.

"Mister," advised Ike, "next time you come into a town lookin' to wrastle, don't knock the men who don't want to wrastle you. They may be better men

Collection of the Huyler Family.

Ike Neal, the "Finger Wrastler," c. 1940.

than you are." And he turned and walked away.

"Giving the finger," by the way, that gesture of contempt, traces back to the Battle of Agincourt, October 25, 1415. The French had declared that when they won the battle, they would cut off the bowstring fingers of every English archer. It was those same English archers who won that battle, after which, jeering, they paraded back and forth before the French survivors showing off the middle fingers of their right hands. The gesture survived; its original significance has been long lost.

Another big man who kicked open those doors of the Cowboy was Wallace Beery, the movie actor, who owned a Summer home on Jackson Lake. Beery looked just the same off-screen as on: invariably rumpled and appearing the worse for wear. He used his red bandanna as a handkerchief just as he did in the movies, mauling his prominent nose with it. In Jackson's Hole, Beery was a popular figure. The following anecdote is a example of why.

In the early forties and fifties the streets and sidewalks of Jackson were pretty quiet at mid-afternoon. In the bars there might be a half-dozen hard cases plus two or three bored dealers and a bartender—just in case.

On one such afternoon Wally Beery and his daughter, Carol Ann, aged about 11, came swaggering down the boardwalk toward the Cowboy Bar. As all who saw his films know, Beery really could swagger; and the little girl was producing a pretty good imitation. At those swinging doors, Beery knocked them open, and the two swaggered up to the bar; both put their boots on the brass rail; Wally thumped the bar and demanded in a loud voice, "Barkeep! Two milks!"

Without a blink, the bartender took two shot glasses from his counter and slid them expertly down the bar to his customers. From under the bar he produced probably the first and last bottle of milk ever to be seen in the Cowboy Bar. He filled both shot glasses. Father and daughter lifted them, clicked them, looked each other in the eye, then tossed down the "cow juice." The father crashed two silver dollars on the bar, and the two swaggered out.

If there was ever a happier little girl in Jackson's Hole, I don't know who she might have been.

That same doorway of the Cowboy Bar was key in Margaret's and my romance. It was August 1938. Riding in the back of Slats Helms's white

Chevy coupe, we had come to town on our first date. Slats parked off the Square; and he and Madeline, the ranch bookkeeper, headed for the Log Cabin, while Margaret and I, anxious to be away from their surveillance, walked across the street toward the Cowboy Bar. As we were about 30 feet from the door, out of it surged Ben Goe, Jr., the bouncer, with a hammer lock on a great big guy six inches taller than he. The streets of Jackson were dirt in 1938. Across the dirt street Ben pushed his man. At the park fence, he released him, spun him around, and hit him so hard that he went over the railing, and landed unconscious. Margaret grabbed my hand, and we've been holding hands ever since 61 years so far.

They turned a hose on the unconscious man to bring him around. With Margaret holding my hand tightly, it would have taken more than that hose to get my attention.

Are there still such exciting goings on at the Cowboy Bar? I don't know; at my age, I hardly go in there anymore; but in the Summer of 1974 . . .

Walt was a young bull rider with aspirations. Carol was a truly beautiful innocent who was a bar girl at the Cowboy. Does that sound like an oxymoron to you? An innocent bar girl? If you know Carol, you'll agree with me. Tall, slim, curvaceous, wearing tight jeans and a blouse that clearly suggested beauty beneath; with a lovely face set off by brown hair to the small of her back, and with the biggest blue eyes you ever saw, and a habit of batting them, it was inevitable that she would attract attention, both good and not so good.

On this particular Saturday night after the rodeo, Walt was sitting in the Cowboy having a beer with a couple of friends. As Carol passed lissomely between his table and the next, a young man sitting at the other table offered a rude remark. Walt turned his head and said, "Hey! Cut it out!"

"I don't see anybody here who can make me."

Turning around in his chair and looking the other man up and down, Walt responded, "Well, I know somebody who'll sure give it a try if you make another crack like that."

On Carol's next trip, the man directed another snide remark at her. Walt stood up. "Outside!" They and most of the bar moved into the street, where the two squared off.

Most barroom fights last only seconds. This one lasted ten minutes, for the other guy was tough and proud of his local reputation for toughness. Walt knocked him down repeatedly, finally breaking his own right hand on the other man's head, and knocking him down with his left. Eventually his opponent stayed down.

When it was over, Carol came up to Walt, batted those blue eyes, thanked him, and offered to pack ice on his hand. Today Walt and Carol are ranchers. On their cattle ranch in British Columbia, they have three strapping sons, yet Carol would still attract attention anywhere, both the good and not-so-good.

John and Jess Wort built their Wort Hotel during the early years of World War II. It featured the Silver Dollar Bar, into which 2,032 silver dollars had been set in resin. To the east of the barroom was the gambling room; to the west, the dance floor already alluded to. The Wort (the o pronounced as in work, not wart) was *the* place until the good old days had become today and the Worts had sold it. Not only the bar and gambling rooms, over which Steve Bartek of Log Cabin Brawl fame now presided; but the restaurant and café became the social center of town. "I'll meet you at the Wort" became a local byword—and still is with old-timers.

No one—or at least none of us around Jackson Hole—had seen anything like the Silver Dollar Bar; and to some those dollars seemed easy pickings. The bartenders would watch as some guy would try surreptitiously to pick one loose. Of course, no amount of finger picking would do it, no matter how strong the fingers. The next step was sneaky use of pocket knives. While this was going on, the bartenders would ply the guy with drinks, and he'd keep buying them because he wanted to continue his attempted theft. One of the maintenance men told me that it was very little problem for him to replace chipped resin; a lot of drinks were sold to the would-be thieves and to those who were aware of what was going on and hung around to watch. Even the Wort brothers were amused to watch from time to time. Of course, silver dollars were worth only their face value then; I don't suppose any bartender would tolerate picking at them today.

During the filming of *Shane*, the "in thing" to do in Jackson was to gather in the lobby of the Wort at about 7:00 A.M. to watch Jean Arthur exit for the day's shooting. She would appear on the balcony at the head of the big staircase in the lobby, throw her coat down to the floor below, then slide down the banister to the laughter and applause of those watching. Those who have seen that western classic, *Shane*, will recall that Miss Arthur usually wore jeans.

Since the post-fire remodeling, she could not have slid the banister anyway; it's angular with knobs.

The fire was probably the biggest event in the Wort's history so far. When it broke out, it moved fast, but not too fast to thwart Steve Bartek, who somehow assembled men with chain saws, who sawed the Silver Dollar Bar into manageable sections, which were carried directly to the Jackson State Bank.

"The Joints" still thrive; but they are today just bars with entertainment: no gambling, insufficient space for dancing, no horses, few fights. Oh, well, at least a few of us can remember when.

I am flattered that in the hallway of the Wort along with a series of historic photos hangs a plaque comemorating my singing of "Just Passin' Thru"—words by Old-Timer Howard Ballew, music by Old Jack Huyler. The poem appears at the end of this little book.

CHAPTER TEN

Rodeos

When I was a boy in the 1920s and 1930s, Jackson rodeos took place only three times each year: Fourth of July, Labor Day Weekend, and the first three days of August.

The Fourth of July rodeo was a rodeo for and by locals, the cowboys and dude wranglers putting on the competitions for their own fun and for the enjoyment of dudes and townsfolk. Brahma bulls had not yet been seen in Jackson's Hole; but there were saddle and bareback bronc riding, calf roping, bulldogging, wild cow milking, and horse races: quarter-mile, half-mile, novelty races, packing races, cowhide races, and one-man relay races. The latter were my specialty and the source of my steak dinners at the Bluebird.

Wild Cow Milking was a great event rarely if ever seen anymore. A horse, a roper, a mugger, a pop bottle, and a range cow were the ingredients. The roper caught his critter; the mugger grabbed her by the nose and a horn and tried to hold her still enough for the roper, by now dismounted with his pop bottle, to squeeze enough milk into it to be poured out at the finish line. With his milk he sprinted in his high-heeled boots to the judge at that finish line, where the clock was stopped and the judge held up the bottle for all to see as he tipped it over. Milk must be seen to come from that bottle—no specific amount of milk, but visible milk. Those were not milk cows, and they objected to being "violated." They bucked and bawled and kicked and struck, doing their best to break loose. I bear a permanent scar on my neck from one of those events, a scar left there by a tight rope between a good horse and a fighting cow.

For the Cowhide Race each team must supply a cowhide with a lariat attached to it, a willing cow pony and rider, and an idiot. I was frequently one of those idiots—idiots because most of us lay on our bellies on the cowhide hanging onto the rope while the horse dragging us threw dirt and gravel into our faces and our bellies were bruised by small and not-so-small rocks. I say "most of us" because there was one exception: I once saw Mike Taylor, currently foreman of the Fish Creek Ranch, ride a cowhide while kneeling perfectly balanced on one knee and holding the rope with one hand.

He deserved to, and did, win. I've seen lots of Cowhide Races, but only one memorable performance.

The Novelty Race I have already described in Chapter Three.

The One-Man Relay Race was my favorite. I have neither seen nor heard of one in 50 years. Each rider used three horses. Each horse ran a half-mile. Riders began mounted, but at the end of each lap each rider must leap off, saddle in hand, hurtle toward his second horse, saddle him, mount on the run, and repeat the entire process at the end of the next half-mile. Since the distance was half-a-mile per horse, Thoroughbreds rather than Quarter Horses were the horses of choice.

One of three kinds of saddles would be specified by the rodeo management: a "lightning rig," a stock saddle with tongueless tackaberry, or a stock saddle with standard cinch and latigo. We didn't use saddle blankets. I preferred the lightning rig. Such a saddle weighed only eight pounds, had a high horn like that on a trick riders's saddle, a set of overlapping six-inch harness rings sewed to the near fender, and a stiff-but-curved leather cinch on the near end of which were a wide band of elastic, a formed leather loop handle, and a metal hook. The horses were teams trained together, fed and corralled together. In the excitement of the rodeo and the race, they sought each other. At the end of the first lap as his horse ran to its mates, the rider reached down, grasped the handle with his left hand, and peeled off, unhooking the cinch as he hit the ground and carrying the light saddle with him in his right hand as he ran. Impelled by the still-running horse, he was running fast as he approached his next mount and slapped the saddle on its back. When he heard the slap of that saddle the holder released the horse and slapped him on the rump as it went by. The rider ran alongside for the first stride hooking the cinch, which because it was stiff, came under the horse's belly to his hand. At about the second stride, the cinch was hooked as tightly as the rider could stretch it. Then his left hand joined his right on that long horn; he picked up both his feet, hung for a moment, hit the ground hard with both feet and catapulted into the saddle in a "pony express mount." A bat lay ready to his hand under the headstall between the horse's ears.

Relay Racing was fun, a lot of exercise, and rewarding because the prize money was good. I had the best teacher imaginable. Owen Barkdall rode Relay professionally for years at rodeos and fairs all over the Rocky Mountain area. He was never beaten in a Relay Race to my knowledge. His training of me was excellent and paid off in "Miss Kaye's" tender steaks as well as in hard cash.

As we galloped our horses, morning and evening, Owen would suddenly yell, "Bail off!" And I was to step off whenever and wherever without slowing my horse. I never was a fast runner, but I could step off a racehorse running full speed, and that paid off in getting to my second and third horses. It paid off because I was off sooner than my opponents and, hurtled by the speed of my horse, I was running much faster than I could have on my own.

If "lightning rigs" were prohibited, we used latigos with tackaberries from which we had removed the tongues. The lightest stock saddles weighed in the neighborhood of 20 pounds; so our changes were slower, but we stiffened our cinches with leather backing so that they came under a horse's belly to us and all we had to do was to put the cinch ring into the lip of the tackaberry, give a pull, mounting in the usual way and wrapping the latigo around the saddle horn in the first couple of hundred feet.

If we were not permitted to use tackaberries, we made two wraps through the cinch ring, pulled as hard as we could and wrapped the latigo around the saddle horn, where we held it tightly with our right hands as we rode. This was the most dangerous of the Relay Race techniques, as without those harness rings and hook, or without the leverage of a tackaberry, we could not be certain that we had our cinches tight enough to hold the saddle in place for a half-mile on a running horse. Falls were common.

Photo by Harrison R. Crandall. Collection of the Huyler Family.

Dreamy and author after our racing days, 1936.

I detail all of the above because, as I mentioned at the beginning, One-Man Relay Races are now extinct.

I wish I had that little eight-pound "lightning rig" saddle still. It disappeared with my bridle, saddle, chaps, and spurs while I was overseas during World War II. I'd like to hang it in our barn and reminisce of Owen Barkdall, Dreamy, Willie, and June. There is a lightning rig saddle hanging in Flat Creek Saddlery. I wish Scott and John didn't want so much for it.

For three hundred and fifty-nine days of each year "Appendicitis" was a faithful work horse on a local ranch. Six days a year he was as wild and woolly a bucking horse as you've ever seen. As soon as he was put into a chute, he went wild: He pawed; he bellowed; he tried to get out even while being saddled. At some time he must have been terribly mistreated in a chute. A bucking strap was not needed on Appendicitis. He wanted out of there and he wanted to get rid of that spurring, fanning cowboy on his back.

For several years no one made a qualified ride on Appendicitis. Dad had a standing offer of $50, the monthly wage of a good cowboy, to anyone who could ride Appendicitis for the regulation eight seconds. Many tried. It was Clover Sturlin, later to become "Clover the Killer" in the town's nightly shoot-out, who first rode Appendicitis. And he not only rode him the requisite eight seconds, but rode him all the way around the half-mile racetrack; Dad took movies that prove it.

That was a memorable sight, but no more memorable than the tri-annual ride made on him by two towheaded kids when the rodeo was over. Appendicitis, now unsaddled, outside the chute, and tied behind the grandstand, returned to his alter ego, that of docile work horse. His owner, realizing that it was an important part of that day's entertainment, would boost his two little kids onto Appendicitis's bare back, slap him on the rump, and send them off home. What a sight after having watched him destroy cowboys! Would he have tolerated a saddle outside the arena? I don't know, but I doubt it.

As mentioned in my description of Jackson's war memorial, probably the most replicated picture of a cowboy riding a bronc is that of Guy Holt on Steamboat. It appears on every Wyoming license plate. The savvy viewer will immediately note that Guy is doing something they no longer do in rodeos: he is "fanning" Steamboat; that is, he has his hat in his hand and is waving it as the horse bucks. When I was a kid, all bronc riders fanned. It was picturesque, western, and it was fun. After years, some bucking judge realized that fanning could be more than that; it could be a help to the rider, for if he slapped his hat alongside the bronc's head, he could frequently turn him in a predictable, and therefore anticipated, direction. That judge must have pointed out his observation to other bucking judges; they must have put their heads together; and fanning was outlawed. Too bad, for it was "wild and woolly" and more than a little bit western. Why couldn't it be permitted again so long as the hat did not touch the bronc in front of the saddle?

Another major change in rodeo is in the design of chute gates. In the earliest days of rodeo, no chute was used. Each bronc was roped and choked down until he could be haltered. The halter rope of each bronc was snubbed up tight to the saddle horn of a cowboy on a good, stout saddle horse, while the contestant saddled and mounted. Usually the bronc was also blindfolded to make saddling easier. When the rider was seated deep in the saddle, he would pull off his hat—the hat with which he was prepared to fan his horse—and say, "Let 'er buck!" The snubber would loose his dallies, hand the rope to the rider, remove the blindfold—and the show was on.

By 1926, when we Huylers came along, chutes were in use at most rodeos; but those chutes, like the chutes for calf roping, pointed straight into the arena. When the cowboy "called for air" and the chute gate was thrown open, he frequently injured a knee on a gate post, sooner or later seriously. Most old cowboys limp. Many of those limps came from chute gates.

Eventually, someone thought of building the chutes parallel to the side of the arena so that the chute gate swung open away from the bronc's head and shoulder. That revision helped a great deal. Although a right knee occasionally hit a gate post, the left knee brushed the gate at worst, and a fast gate man usually had the opening wide enough to avoid rider contact as the bronc turned 90 degrees into the arena.

Then came a genius. He reversed the bronc in that same chute so that the gate swings open from the horse's tail. By the time he has room to turn his head and bolt into the arena, the gate is wide open. Nowadays, some bronc riders don't limp and those who do were injured by something other than the chute gate.

Yet another change in rodeo is in the style of riding. The wilder the ride, the higher the score. Casey Tibbs was the first rider I saw who deliberately lay back on a bareback bronc's rump every time that rump came up. It made the ride look harder all right. Now all bareback riders come out of the chute leaning back as far as possible. Were I a bronc rider, I might like that style; as a horseman spectator, I deplore it. Horsemen sit erect and tall in the saddle. As a matter of fact, that style has pretty much destroyed my pleasure in watching Bareback Bronc Riding. It looks so contrived.

Saddle Bronc Riding is something else. All riders today must use approved "Association Saddles," on which the saddle horn has been omitted, thereby eliminating many injuries caused by that saddle horn's violent blows to the rider's belly. Top riders today ride a balanced ride saddle and as a result can do something the old-timers could not: spur from the shoulders back until you can hear their spurs click together behind the cantle. Amazing!

Changes in calf roping that helped reduce times were lowered saddle cantles, and lowered boot heels. Lowered cantles made fast dismounts easier; and college athletes used to football and track shoes realized that roping heels would lower their times. Since time was money, literally, away went the two-inch and two-and-a-half-inch heels of the old-time cowpoke. Today it is virtually impossible to find boots with the kind of heel I like—the high, undershot heel that dug in when you roped a horse in the corral and that helped keep your stirrup where it belongs. I ordered one last pair of those old-style boots for my 79th birthday. They were made to order by Paul Bond of Nogales, Arizona, bootmaker to the Cowboy Hall of Fame and once a hand on the Rocking H. I love them! They are no good for walking, but who wants to walk farther than to his horse?

The greatest change in calf roping, however, came when some smart waddy figured out that the shortest way to tying position on a calf was to dismount from that side of the horse. For a right-handed roper that meant dismounting from the "off," or right, side. Ropings are won by fractions of seconds. That shorter run won lots of money. Now every good right-handed roper dismounts on the run from the off side, and every left-handed roper, from the near.

Photo by R. R. Doubleday. Collection of the Jackson Hole Historical Society and Museum.

Bob Crisp riding high at Jackson's Hole Frontier Days, c. 1920s.

As mentioned earlier in this chapter, in the "good old days" Jackson's rodeo the first weekend of August (Frontier Days) was a big one. The best P.R.C.A. (Professional Rodeo Cowboys Association) riders, ropers, and 'doggers, came. Our rodeo took place between two other big ones—as I recall, Cheyenne Frontier Days and the Pendleton Roundup. At any rate, the big-name professionals came to Jackson; and a good many of them camped out on the Bear Paw: Joe "Tuffy" Welch ("World's Champion All-Around Cowboy"); Elmer Hepler ("World's Champion Bull Rider"); "Heavy" Wheeler; "Big Bill" Bennett; Chester "Chet" Byers ("World's Champion Trick Roper"); Homer Hokum ("World's Champion Clown"); and John Jordan ("World's Champion Saddle Bronc Rider") were regulars.

Since I have matured, I have often been puzzled by our American need to be "World's Champions." Who from the rest of the globe competes with our "World's Champion" for the title? "World Champion Dodgers." "World Champion Lakers." Even "The World Series"! In a long lifetime, I have never heard of a Japanese, Puerto Rican, or Cuban team playing in "The World Series." Wouldn't it be great if they did? Meanwhile, what's the matter with "National Champion"?

Back at the Bear Paw before the then-big Jackson Rodeo, everyone was always practicing his skills one way or another. Homer would teach Orphan Annie new tricks. Chet would get out his magueys and work on new catches for which I would sometimes ride Dreamy. I thought it big stuff to be roped by "The World's Champion Trick Roper."

These men were physical and, therefore, were practical jokers. The old Bear Paw was a circus for the week they were there. They were always "jobbing" each other.

One of their jokes struck me the wrong way. Heavy Wheeler was mounted on my little palomino racing mare Dreamy when all of us rode down to the Lower Ranch and the Snake River. Jack Neal, a practical joker himself, lured Heavy into riding Dreamy off a bank into what Jack knew to be a deep hole. Rider and my mare disappeared for a moment, a dreadful moment for me. I thought that big man might drown my mare. After seconds, which seemed to me eternity, the little mare surfaced with Heavy hanging onto her tail. She was still blowing water as she dragged him ashore. I didn't think it was very funny, but I was only 11 or 12. What could I do? In those days kids didn't yell at or even protest loudly to adults, or they would have been banished. I hero worshipped that crowd so kept my mouth shut.

Like Trigger in later years, Orphan Annie, Homer Hokum's little mule, was housebroken. One time when the boys were in Chicago for the rodeo,

Homer, wearing his clown's makeup, rode her into the Gladstone Hotel, into the elevator and up to the floor where Dad happened to be staying alone. Everybody was so startled by this apparition of donkey and clown that nobody prevented them. Tuffy had helped to set things up by obtaining from the front desk the key to "my uncle's room." Arriving at Dad's room, the conspirators eased the door open, and Homer rode in. Joy! They could hear splashing from the bathroom. Dad was taking a bath. He was more than a little startled when Annie stuck her head around the bathroom door.

The very worst practical joke I knew those boys to play was at the New York World's Fair of 1939–40. The arena fence was constructed of wooden planks. Homer, seeing a good opportunity, removed three contiguous planks, constructed from them a little trapdoor, and swung it from a pair of small hinges. It was not noticeable. Then in his bull baiting at the rodeos, he would let a big Brahma get close behind him as he ran to the fence too high for him to climb. As all seemed lost and the crowd gasped, Homer would dive through his swinging panel. The crowds loved it. So did Homer until one day it occurred to some of his pals—Tuffy, Elmer, Heavy, and Big Bill among them—that it would be pretty funny to nail up Homer's door. They would see to it that several of them were mounted and casually nearby to deflect the bull. The moment came: Homer was only a couple of strides ahead of a big, vicious brahma. The crowd came to its feet and gasped. Homer dived and hit solid wood. His "friends" rushed in on their horses and drove the bull off before he could do any harm to Homer. Very funny? They thought so, and, more surprising, so did Homer, despite a fractured collar bone.

Perhaps that wasn't the very worst "joke." Tuffy and Elmer decided it would be fun to make their wives jealous. While the "boys" were on the road, of course, their wives read all the mail, paid the bills, and decided what needed forwarding. In Chicago, the men hired two women whom they met hanging around the rodeo to write passionate love letters to them at their home addresses in Carlsbad, New Mexico.

Naturally, as the wives read these letters, they became more and more jealous and angry until by the time the "boys" reached home a month after the letters began, the women were talking divorce. Tuffy and Elmer thought it a great joke, but the wives smouldered and brooded over sweet revenge.

Rodeo cowboys are wont to arrive home unexpectedly. They suddenly become homesick and detour 500 miles between shows for a night at home with their wives.

The next time the men left home for the rodeo circuit, the two wives swore another P.R.C.A. cowboy, a close friend of their husbands, to silence and had him promise to telephone them the very next time their "boys" got the yen and headed home.

A month or so later they received a call: Tuffy and Elmer were on the way and should arrive in time for supper. Aha!

All gussied up, the women got together at the Heplers' house as the afternoon drew to a close. The men stopped first at the Welch house, surmised that the women were together at the other house, and headed for it. An alerted neighbor phoned the girls so that their timing could be perfect.

As the men jumped out of their car, the two women came out of the house gloved, hatted, and pursed. Feigning surprise, they asked, "Why didn't you boys let us know you were coming? We have dates. You'll find leftovers in the icebox. We'll be home early." (Ah! Sweet revenge!)

The boys looked at each other. This was not what they had in mind.

"Who are your G— d— dates?"

The girls hadn't counted on that. They grabbed the names of the first two eligible bachelors who came to mind.

The husbands headed for their car and took off. It dawned on the women that trouble was brewing for the two innocents. They tried unsuccessfully to reach them by telephone in time to avert trouble. Surely there would be no violence! Surely there was. The more the two innocents proclaimed that innocence, the angrier became the two husbands. Not only were these guys double-crossing them, they were too cowardly to admit it. Wham!

The girls arrived at the feed store where the first worked. Too late! He was nursing a black eye and serious bruises. Calling that they would be right back, the two women drove off in search of the other at the drugstore where he worked. Too late again!

In tears they explained that this was their attempt to "get even," that there were no dates, that the two who had been beaten did not even know about their plan and had in no way been involved. Rueful apologies, pats on the back, and brushings off took place.

I wonder if that was when the expression, "With friends like those, who needs enemies?" was coined.

To me, the only funny aspect of the entire debacle was that the six remained friends and, after a little time, laughed together about it.

By the way, the last time I saw Tuffy, in Carlsbad, California, he told me to keep my eye on a rising film star, Racquel Welch, who came by her last name by being his daughter-in-law.

Plano, Tuffy Welch's roping and bulldogging horse on which he won the title of "World's Champion Bulldogger" and "World's Champion All-Around Cowboy," was the first Quarter Horse I ever saw. He was a cross between Kentucky Thoroughbred and Steel Dust. The Thoroughbred gave him speed and stamina; the Steel Dust gave him heavily muscled hind quarters and forearms for quick starts. He was a beautiful liver sorrel with white markings.

The horse acquired his name the very first time he was ridden. As has been mentioned, Tuffy hailed from New Mexico. He first saddled the colt in a ranch corral. When they opened the corral gate for him, the horse just ran instead of bucking. He ran like the wind; and as he tired, Tuffy could guide him a bit in a large circle until back at the corral the horse stopped breathless. A vaquero who had observed the entire procedure commented, "Señor, he run like ze aeroplano." Hence his name, Plano.

In those days, the Madison Square Garden Rodeo was the last of the rodeo season. I was in boarding school when Dad, Wintering in Greenwich, Connecticut, received a telegram from Tuffy saying, "Been called home unexpectedly. Please take care of Plano. Will pick him up sometime in the Spring."

Dad drove into New York to Madison Square Garden: no horses. The Garden was being prepared for ice hockey. Where was Plano? It was typical of Dad that he thought to inquire of the mounted police on duty in the area. "A liver sorrel with a star and snip? Yeah. He was left here. Too good a horse to let go to the pound. We've got him down at the Mounted Police Stable." Plano spent the Winter in a paddock in Greenwich, Connecticut.

Not only did Jackson's three-day August rodeo draw cowboys; it drew spectators from afar. The Diamond G Ranch of Dubois each Summer sent out a one-month pack trip into the Absarokas, Yellowstone Park, and the Tetons. Before riding the 100 miles back to the ranch, they would take in our three days of rodeo. They pitched their tents in the open space on the far side of the track. It was quite a sight to watch them, already packed up, mount up and ride away at the close of the show. They could have spent that extra night right where they were, but they, too, had an eye for showmanship. As I recall, they comprised roughly 50 riders and 80 horses.

Somehow I cannot quite imagine such a trip today. Few of my acquaintance would relish a month-long pack trip.

Our Labor Day Rodeo was like the Fourth of July Rodeo, in that it was primarily by locals for locals and dudes. I refer to rodeos as "shows" because that's what we who live around them usually call them; but they are not shows in the sense that Buffalo Bill's Wild West Show or John Dodge's were exhibitions. They are competitions. In rodeo, professional athletes, instead of being paid as in all other sports I can name, pay entry fees; and 90 percent of them go home having lost those and being out their traveling and training expenses as well. Only the winners of each event take home any money. Among other reasons, I suppose that is one why rodeo events are never "fixed."

For several years, prize money for Jackson's Labor Day "show" was donated by Henry Stewart, whose JY Ranch was the largest dude ranch in the Valley and who used the rodeo to entice dudes to extend their stays beyond August 31.

Those three rodeos disappeared during World War II. In the immediate postwar years a Dude Ranchers' Rodeo commenced first at the old rodeo grounds (on the same site as today's rodeo grounds), and later transferred to the Teton Valley Ranch in Kelly. The Dude Ranchers' Rodeo was different from other rodeos in that the primary contestants were the dudes and dudines from the ranches. The events were tailored accordingly. Mule Riding was substituted for bronc and bull riding. Bulldogging and calf roping were eliminated. There were many races, including such special events as the 100-Yard Slow Race, in which each contestant moved forward as slowly as he could possibly make his mount go without stopping. Anyone who lost forward motion entirely was immediately disqualified by the judge who had been walking behind him or her from the starting line.

This event is not to be confused with the Slow Horse Race, a quarter-mile event into which were entered the slowest horses from each ranch. The dude or dudine contestant rode his or her ranch horse out to the quarter-mile post. There each rider changed to a mount from another ranch. At "Go!" each rider applied all possible pressure to get that mount going as fast as possible, since the last horse to cross the finish line was the winner and the person who had ridden that horse to the starting line got the prize.

There were also a Packing Race, dude quarter-mile and half-mile races, dudine races at both distances, a form of Team Roping in which a wrangler roped a calf while a dude tried to tie it; Ribbon Roping, in which a calf with a ribbon on its tail was let out of a chute with a rope around its neck held by a dude. His dudine partner's job was to catch up with the bucking, kicking calf, remove the ribbon and race it back to the judge.

The final event of the Dude Ranchers' Rodeo was always the Dude Ranch Owners' Race. We dude ranchers loved it and so did our dudes, who felt great loyalty to their ranch—so much loyalty that it sometimes led to serious arguments.

On December 20, 1948, Dad sold the Bear Paw to John D. Rockefeller, Jr. From then on I was the rodeo announcer—announcer, not judge. In the early 1950s at the end of a close Packing Race, "Dad" Mapes, the packing judge, decided in favor of a debatable hitch thrown by the Triangle X team. The problem was that the Triangle X was owned and operated by Mapes's daughter and son-in-law. "Dad" Mapes was an experienced packer; he knew his hitches, diamond, three-quarter diamond, double diamond, squaw hitch, box hitch, possibly even the basco. In one of the rodeos before the war with cowboy packers, such a decision would have been shrugged off by the losers. Not so in the Dude Ranchers' Rodeo. The losing team wanted to fight; their ranch mates wanted to fight. "Dad" Mapes was an old man. They couldn't fight him. How about that young guy, the announcer. He had announced the decision, after all.

"On with the show! Let joy be unconfined."

I have a voice like a PA system. It is both a blessing and a curse. I rarely have laryngitis. By the end of that particular afternoon I had to practically swallow my microphone to be heard. I could barely whisper.

That night Margaret and I were in the Wort dancing and visiting with a tableful of friends. A doctor from the ranch that had lost the race came to our table and began to abuse me verbally. He wanted to do so physically. I couldn't make myself heard, but I got up and gestured him into the hall. There I whispered, "I'll only listen to you if you will listen to me."

"Okay!"

He lit into me. His team had really won the packing race. The other hitch should have been disqualified. I was a crook or in the pay of the winning ranch.

Finally, he paused for breath, and I whispered, "Hey, you s.o.b.! I was the announcer, not the judge. Remember? I just announced the results I was given. I never even saw that hitch except from the crow's nest."

He let out his breath, puzzled a couple of moments, then offered his hand. We shook, and I put my hand on his shoulder as we started back to our respective parties.

"Okay," he said, "but why did you call me a sonofabitch?"

"Why did you act like one?"

Walt Callahan had a nephew, Arlo Curtis, who became one of the nation's top bronc riders. In order to give Arlo the practice and experience that might take him to top, Walt built a rodeo arena beside his Stagecoach Bar in Wilson and there put on a rodeo every Saturday night. The only P.R.C.A. hands competing there were men such as Arlo who lived or worked in Jackson's Hole, which by that time had become Jackson Hole. Those were good little rodeos. Locals and dudes loved them. No longer, however, were horse races a part of our rodeos.

Next, Bob McConaughy and Hal Johnson bought out Callahan, leased the rodeo grounds in Jackson, updated its facilities, and put on rodeos every night for awhile and then every Saturday and Sunday evening. These rodeos drew competitors from the Valley and from as far as Idaho Falls to the west, Montana to the north, Lander to the east, and Pinedale and Afton to the south and were popular with locals and tourists. They came because rodeo is a great sport in which good sportsmanship is usually obvious, because the setting is gorgeous, and because the bucking stock (horses and bulls) is remarkably good for a small-town rodeo. There are, however, still no horse races except for Girls' Barrel Racing.

The Jackson Hole Rodeo Corporation has changed hands a few times. When Hal Johnson went to a job at the Thacher School in California, Russ Moses bought his half-interest. Later Bob McConaughy sold out his interest to Russ. The rodeo still flourishes. The bucking stock remains top-notch and the contestants good. A rodeo announcer's, "Let's go! Let's go! Let's rodeo!" still draws me as a magnet does steel.

CHAPTER ELEVEN

Dude Ranches

In 1926, the year the Huyler family came to Jackson's Hole, the population of Jackson was 500, but there were several flourishing dude ranches: the JY, Bar BC, White Grass, Circle H, Crescent Lazy H, Double Diamond, and STS spring to mind. There may have been others.

Dude ranches were an important influence in the opening of the West. The very first dude ranch, Eatons', had been opened in North Dakota Territory in 1879, just three years after the Custer Massacre (the Battle of the Little Bighorn), a year before Wounded Knee, ten years before Nick Wilson brought the first group of settlers into Davey Jackson's Hole. Eatons' became a dude ranch by accident rather than by design. The three Eaton brothers came west to become cattle ranchers, but eastern friends would not let them alone. "The Wild West" was already the glamorized subject of dime novels and the tabloids. Their friends wanted to have a look, and they came west to visit the three, to see "The Wild West" firsthand.

When the brothers moved their ranch in 1903 to Wolf, Wyoming, near Sheridan, they wrote their eastern friends not to come until they were settled. Did those friends heed their advice? No. They came in droves "to help you build and get settled." Of course, few were carpenters or had any other construction skills; but they had enthusiasm and will. As soon as a cabin was finished, they moved in. What to do? These friends weren't really worth their keep. The Eatons discovered to their dismay that they had served 2,000 free meals in one year. That could not continue; so they decided to charge each of their guests $1 per day for room, board, and horse; and the first dude ranch was born. It is greatly to the Eatons' credit that their ranch is still an operating dude ranch managed by the same family. It is a treat for anyone to visit Eatons' Ranch in Wolf, Wyoming.

"*Dude*—A man who is very fancy or sharp in dress and demeanor," declares the *American Heritage Dictionary*. Was it their dressy eastern tweeds or, as I suspect, was it that they espoused so heartily all the accouterments of the wild and woolly west: ten gallon hats, high-heeled boots, chaps, spurs, neckerchiefs, vests, revolvers? Look at a photo of Teddy Roosevelt in the west in those days.

Why was it that Philadelphians especially seemed drawn to dude ranches?

The first dude ranch in Jackson's Hole was started by Louis Joy, who named it JY for reasons that are obvious. That was in 1908. Soon Struthers Burt, a Philadelphian, a young graduate of Princeton's Class of 1907, my father's college and class, bought in as partner.

It is part of the nature of the place that every rancher in Jackson Hole thinks his is the best view in the Valley. The JY's is! It is not a view of the Grand Teton, but across beautiful Phelps Lake to Death Canyon and the Three Sisters: Static Peak, Mount Hunt, and Buck Mountain. The cabins are nestled among the pine trees that border the southeast end of the lake, the mouth of Lake Creek. The soughing of the wind through the pines harmonizes with the constant lapping of the waves. What a lullaby!

The corrals, saddle house, barn, and necessary sheds were built along Lake Creek. The builders did not have to search for cabin or corral logs; they had to remove lodgepole pines to make room for their construction. The JY was an instant and inevitable success.

My suspicion is that Joy and Burt each had strong ideas as to how a dude ranch should be run, and that those ideas did not coincide. I did not know Lou Joy, but Struthers Burt I remember well; he was authoritative.

At any rate, in 1912 with Dr. Horace Carncross, another Philadelphian and a pupil of Sigmund Freud, Struthers homesteaded the Bar BC on the west bank of the Snake River directly opposite the Grand Teton. Another fabulous view and fabulous location except that each of their logs and most of their stove wood had to be hauled by wagon a couple of miles from Timbered Island or Beaver Creek.

Stove wood was as essential as were building logs and corral rails. We cooked with wood. With wood we heated shaving and bath water, each little cabin, and the main cabin, where everybody ate and socialized. I must say that Joy chose better than did Burt when it came to life support. All ranches in the Hole had plenty of good water. Even the Snake River was potable until "civilized man" polluted it.

"Dudes winter better than cows" wrote Burt after a year or so; and he and Carncross solicited the patronage of their Philadelphian friends and of their friends' friends. Dudes and dudines came in a steady flow although it was no mean expedition in those days. Each eastern dude bound for Jackson's Hole came west by Chicago Northwestern and Union Pacific trains to Pocatello, Idaho, changed to the Oregon Short Line for Ashton, Idaho, where a car—or two if required—was shunted off the Yellowstone-bound trains onto the spur line for Victor, still in Idaho. That's the way we Huylers arrived in 1926.

Considering the time it took to get to the Jackson's Hole ranches, is it any wonder that the average stay was a month?

A teamster from the JY or Bar BC would meet the man, woman, or family in Victor. Trunks (people traveled with trunks in those days), duffel bags, and valises were loaded into the bed of the wagon; the customers climbed to the seats; and a very long day began. It is only 11 miles from Victor to the Snake River; but Teton Pass, steep now, was far steeper before a road was graded on its back. Both ranches were west of the Snake, so a ferry crossing was not needed. Once in Jackson's Hole, however, it was 11 miles north to Joy's ranch and another 11 to Burt's; and a team, tired from pulling Teton Pass, could not be expected to trot briskly up the wagon track which led home. The views, however, would have been awe-inspiring from the beginning. The guests would arrive at the ranches about the time the golden glow of sunset illuminated the Tetons; so I imagine that, weary as they must have been, they were thrilled and content when they were shown their tiny cabins and served a hot supper before they crawled wearily into bed.

Collection of the Jackson Hole Historical Society and Museum.

Cissy Patterson, "The Countess," c. 1920s.

The celebrated Cissy Patterson arrived at the Bar BC by wagon from Victor with her daughter, Felicia; a French maid; and six trunks. The story as Cissy told it was that when they arrived at the Bar BC and met their hostess, Katherine Burt, Mrs. Patterson informed her that she would like a bath drawn immediately and supper served in her cabin. When she recovered from shock, Mrs. Burt told her new guest firmly that she could find a zinc washtub hanging on an outside wall of her cabin; inside the cabin, a bucket of water and a Yellowstone stove with which to heat it. Furthermore, supper was served only in the dining room and that was soon. The bath would have to wait.

On the early ranches—be they dude or cattle—all hot water was heated on a stove, be it kitchen range or trash burner. Bathtubs were round, galvanized laundry tubs. It is not difficult for a child to bathe in such a tub, but I recall feeling sorry for Dad as he crouched in one and Mother poured water on him. To Cissy Patterson, reared as she was in the lap of luxury, the washtub on the wall of her Bar BC cabin must have seemed outrageous.

Mrs. Patterson turned and called to her maid, Abigail, to unpack nothing as they were leaving in the morning. Mrs. Burt countered with the information that after a pull such as today's, the team needed, and would have, a day of rest. They could leave day after tomorrow.

But, oh, the next morning! The transfiguration they must have experienced as they stepped out of their cabins for the first time. There is nothing like a clear morning in the Tetons! Air so thin and clear that you instinctively draw it to the bottom of your lungs. The scent of pine or sage, of wildflowers. The sounds of lake, of river, of horses, the whistles and calls of wranglers as they bring in the remuda. I can smell those odors and hear those sounds as I write these words on a freighter off the coast of Chile.

Photo by Bob Willcox. Courtesy of the Jackson Hole News.

Luxury bath in the wild country. Bob Disney at a cow camp in the Gros Ventre Mountains, 1989.

God, I love them, treasure memory of them, and am grateful for them. If ever I take them for granted, let me die, for I shall be already dead in all significant senses of the word.

Those sounds, sights, and scents transformed Mrs. Patterson her first morning; she and Mrs. Burt became great friends; and she even bought a ranch of her own, taking colorful cowboy Cal Carrington of the Bar BC with her to run it. As a matter of record, she bought her ranch—still known by old-timers as "The Countess's Place," from Cal.

Cissy and pretty much everyone else in Jackson's Hole knew that Cal Carrington was not his real name. Like others of the earliest residents, he was hiding from his past. I sometimes wondered whether the Old Man had once ridden under a name we would all recognize, a name that he had left behind when he came to the Hole. (As a matter of record, Cal was born Enoch Julin, as I was told by the Countess's great nephew, Joe Albright.)

The Homestead Act was still open and remained so in Jackson Hole until 1927. Harold Hammond was a wrangler on the JY, where he met Tucker Bispham, and the two dreamed of a ranch of their own. They began prospecting for land to homestead. They found and filed on a beautiful spot at the head of Wister Draw, just below Static Peak and over the ridge from Phelps Lake. In 1911 Harold and Marie Hammond and their partner, Bispham, concurred with Burt's conclusion, "Dudes winter better than cows," and their H Quarter Circle B became the White Grass Ranch, where

Collection of the Huyler Family.

Guest cabins at the Bear Paw, c. 1930s.

they not only entertained paying guests, but raised silver fox for their pelts so in demand by furriers for the collars, muffs, and even full-length coats of fashionable ladies. They also harbored what became the only antelope herd in Jackson Hole. Marie and Tucker were Philadelphians, as were most of their paying customers.

So were Frances Estes (wife of Buster, and with him owner of the STS Ranch), the Roeslers, and the Spears. Mr. and Mrs. Brown of the Crescent Lazy H were not, neither were Harry and Ethel Harrison, nor were John and Louise Turner of the Triangle X, Frank Williams of the Double Diamond, the Gabbeys of the Square G, Jimmy Manges of the X Quarter Circle X, "Turp" Turner of the Turpin Meadows Ranch, Miss Ida Tarbell of the Half Moon Ranch, or Weenie and Mary Ellen Wilson of Teton Valley Ranch. Nor was Coulter Huyler; however, the guest books of all those ranches were replete with Philadelphia addresses.

Why did people flock to the dude ranches from most of the non-ranching, non-farming states? How was it that throughout the Great Depression our dude ranches bulged with guests? The scenery, the air, the joy and fun of "playing cowboy" did it.

The Eugene Wilhoits came from Stockton, California, for three months every Summer. At the end of their stay one year, Ike Neal remarked, "You know, I feel sorry for Old Wilhoit. He keeps his nose to the grindstone for nine months every year to make enough money to do what I do all the time." Good point succinctly made.

Collection of the Huyler Family.

"Jingling" the Bear Paw horses, 1946.

Since few who read this will have spent time on a dude ranch, they may well wonder what daily life was like on a dude ranch? What did people do?

For a few moments, just imagine with me that you are a guest on the Bear Paw. How would your day begin? How did the ranch's day begin?

At 5:00 A.M., two wranglers mounted and left the corrals to gather the horses. Frequently a couple of dudes or dudines went with them. They were off for the horse pasture four miles south on the Rocking H. At the Bear Paw, 6,300 feet above sea level, there was usually frost on the ground at that hour.

Shortly after the horse wranglers departed, the Cook's Helper entered the kitchen with an armload of wood to start the woodstove. By 6:00, the Cook showed up and began preparations for huge breakfasts for the crew and a variety of offerings for the guests. The cowboys ate meat three times a day.

At 7:00, breakfast was served in the kitchen for the crew.

All this time you would have been snuggled under a down comforter in your warm bed. The only sound you would have heard had you awakened, would have been the babbling of the irrigation ditch at your cabin door and, in the background, the muted roar of Granite Creek.

Between 7:00 and 7:30, the Chore Boy and Cabin Girl, making their rounds of the guest cabins, would have knocked on your door. He would have lit a fire in your Yellowstone stove, while she poured hot coffee at your bedside.

Their departure was a sign that you should consider arising. Between 7:30 and 8:00 you would hear the sound of galloping horses and the whistles and calls of the horse wranglers returning with the remuda, which was herded into

Collection of the Huyler Family.

Saddling up at the Bear Paw corrals, c. 1930.

a large pen down the center of which ran a long grain trough. Those sounds—so Western—would have reminded you that you were no longer in your home town.

While that morning's wranglers went to the kitchen to eat, the other two, who had not wrangled that morning, walked the length of the trough dispensing oats from two hundred-pound grain sacks. Just a few mouthfuls daily made quite a difference in the condition, energy, and stamina of our cavvy.

Once their oats were cleaned up, the horses were herded into the round corral, where it was easier to catch or rope them. Mostly we roped them—I suppose 40 out of 45.

Breakfast for the dudes was served from 8:00 to 9:00. Anyone could have virtually anything that tickled his or her fancy: Eggs Benedict; shirred eggs; scrambled, boiled, poached, or fried eggs; French toast, waffles, pancakes, biscuits, or toast from the sourdough bread baked daily. During your breakfast, I would appear with options for the day: "What would you like to do today? How many would like to go fishing with Wayne Connor? How many would enjoy a picnic ride up Death Canyon or to Taggart and Bradley Lakes or a swim at Phelps Lake? I have to go down to the Lower Ranch to move some yearlings. Anyone want to join me? We'll be back for lunch. Name your choice."

From 9:30 to 10:00, rides departed the corrals bound for the selected locations. Virtually everyone, no matter what age or which gender, rode every morning for two to three hours. I recall only one guest, a lady with a bad back, who did not ride. After all, "playing cowboy" was what it was all about;

Collection of the Huyler Family.

Brownie keeps five people occupied, 1936.

and how can you do that without riding?

For safety's sake, a wrangler led each ride. In all our years we made only one exception, the Wilhoits. Although they were, I suppose, in their seventies, they had spent two or even three months of each Summer in Jackson's Hole at the JY for 15 years. They knew the trails, didn't take risks, and we had bought for them two single-footing horses that could cover the ground faster and more comfortably than non-gaited horses. To keep up with them any companions needed to trot all the time; not many wanted to.

I suppose other ranches also made a few exceptions to the ride-only-with-wrangler rule. I know that the White Grass did with the Laidlaw family, who owned their own cabin and horses. There were probably a few others; however, we chose our wranglers carefully: always good and reliable horsemen of demonstrated sound judgment who knew the terrain and the wildlife. Unlike a few of the other dude ranches, we hired only genuine cowboys as wranglers. What we were selling was ranch atmosphere, and our dude wranglers must be what they seemed to be. Most of our dudes enjoyed their company and what they learned from them of terrain and nature (human, animal, and vegetable) in the course of their rides. Our wranglers led the rides in both senses of the word. We wanted them up front in case of an unforeseen obstacle or danger in the trail; and we wanted them there because, more often than not, if a rider gets in trouble, the horse bolts ahead, rather than turning back. So the head of the line was the spot from which to cope with most problems that occurred on the trail.

Suppose you had chosen to go on a picnic ride. What should you expect

Collection of the Huyler Family.

A morning ride comes home, c. 1935.

other than beautiful terrain, wildflowers, and a variety of game and bird life?

Our kitchen sent out two types of lunches: hot and cold; and each trip chose whether they wanted sandwiches or preferred to stop long enough for a fire, a grilled hamburger, steak, or chop, a salad, hot coffee, and tea. The cold lunches would be bacon-tomato-and-lettuce on toast, broiled or fried chicken, and peanut butter and jelly—no deli stuff; always Mother or Margaret sent along peeled and sliced cantaloupe, grapes, cherries, plums, or other fresh fruit. We drank the fresh, clear, cold water wherever we happened to stop. Those were the days before young people who professed to love Nature so much and who condemned us for "unnatural" practices—such as burying our feces and trash—infected our streams forever with giardia through their sloppy personal hygiene.

The hospitality between ranches was spontaneous and generous. You might have chosen to visit another dude ranch for lunch in order to observe its facilities and operation or to lunch with a friend. Whenever a group of Bear Paw riders wanted to lunch at the White Grass, they could count upon being invited in if they arrived at the right time. What would have been a problem at dinner was no problem at lunchtime, since from each ranch some guests were always away at lunchtime picnicking, fishing, visiting Yellowstone or another ranch. Those invitations to dismount and come in for lunch, although sincere, may have been a bit less spontaneous than they seemed, since from the mid-1930s on, each ranch office had a party-line telephone.

After lunch, most adults on the home ranch or on a picnic took siestas. The young, of course, didn't; so on picnic rides they would swim, swim the

Collection of the Huyler Family.

Bear Paw roping arena, 1946.

horses, or be pointed toward a patch of snow which appeared in the thin air of high altitude to be a 15-minute climb, but proved to be an hour's. Which would you have done: hiked, snoozed, or read? Meanwhile back on the ranch, someone took the young for a fast afternoon ride while their parents napped. The kids liked to gallop and to jump logs. We obliged them.

The balance of the afternoon for those who were not riding was usually devoted to reading in the shade or to bridge. That might have looked like a good option to you on most afternoons.

Before dinner, guests at the Bear Paw might have a highball in their cabins, even with another couple, but no cocktail parties, and no drinking at all in the Main Cabin—ever. I wonder if we could get away with that policy today. It was clearly stated in our literature. We had seen drinking get out of hand at two Jackson Hole dude ranches. You would have joined the other guests at 7:00 dinner, all sitting down at once at three tables with the Huyler family at the ends, and grace asked.

On Sunday nights cold buffets replaced the usual dinners, as most of the crew had time off from after Sunday dinner until Monday morning.

You could not have failed to observe the flickering of the electricity in the Main Cabin, the only one of our cabins that boasted electricity. That electricity was produced by a homemade generator powered by a homemade paddlewheel at the foot of a homemade millpond. The Bear Paw was sold before rural electricity reached Jackson's Hole. The paddlewheel was saved and relocated on their property by the Fred Inglis family.

Knowing that your cabin had no electricity, on your way to dinner you would probably have left your gasoline lantern on the kitchen stoop to be filled and pumped up while you ate.

I'd wager that at least once after dinner you would have gone to our roping arena, where we wranglers sharpened our skills; and the dudes were welcome to have a go at roping, just tying a calf one of us had roped, or managing the holding pens and chute.

Until it was superimposed year-round upon all states during World War II, Wyoming did not observe Daylight Saving Time—even in the Summer. That far north we didn't need it. It stayed light until 9:00 P.M. in midsummer. Personally, I wish we did not have Daylight Saving Time now. No matter what the hour, it's mighty difficult to get children into bed before it gets dark.

As darkness fell, some of the guests drifted to their cabins to read before turning in; many stayed around the Main Cabin to chat and to listen to cowboy songs—no Country Western or Bluegrass. We had never heard of Country Western; to us, all western songs were country. We knew of the songs of Appalachia, and I sang some; however, this was a dude ranch, and what we were selling was cowboy atmosphere.

Cowboy:
"Red River Valley"
"Yavapai Pete"
"Tumbleweed"
"The Bad Brahma Bull"

Country:
"How Can I Miss You If You Won't Go Away"
"You Done Tore Out My Heart and Stomped That Sucker Flat"
"I Was Hangin' in There When You Hung Me Out to Dry"

And the Number One Country Song in 1999:
"I Haven't Gone to Bed with Any Ugly Women,
But I've Sure Woke Up with a Few"

Bluegrass:
"Foggy Mountain Breakdown"
"Stony Mountain"
"Salty Dog"
"Rocky Top"

On Wednesday evenings, would you have accompanied some of the other adults going in to Jackson to gamble? If you needed transportation, one of our wranglers and a ranch vehicle would have been at your disposal. Mr. Wilhoit loved to play twenty-one.

We called him "The Boss" because he had announced that he was. The first Summer he and Mrs. Wilhoit came to the Bear Paw, Dad arrived after they did, for he usually worked as a realtor in the New York area until around July 1. Dad's first evening at the dinner table, Eugene Wilhoit of Stockton, California, arose, tapped his glass for attention and announced without a trace of a smile, "I'm glad to welcome Dad Huyler to his ranch, but I just want him to know that I'm the Boss around here." He sat down to laughter and cheers. From that moment on no one on the Bear Paw, young or old, cowboy or paying customer, ever called the old man anything but "Boss" or referred to him by any name other than "The Boss." We loved him. He always wore a sour expression, but behind it was a sense of humor biding its time.

Yes, "The Boss" loved to play blackjack. Why? Why wouldn't a banker of all people figure the odds? Anyway, he loved it. Mrs. Wilhoit didn't approve of gambling. He was delighted when she discovered roulette and enjoyed it. That meant that he could go into town more often.

Once, "The Boss" made what seemed like a mistake at the time, the mistake of telling Lew DeWitt at the Log Cabin that he would be good for Mrs. Wilhoit's losses if she ran out of cash. Was it a mistake, or was the old gent as foxy as he looked? You be the judge.

The next time they went to the Log Cabin, Mrs. Wilhoit won. Not much, but she won. Oh! This was fun!

The time after that, she won big, $800 or so! Oh! This was great fun!

The following day they departed for California, "The Boss" asking me to inform Lew that he had received a call to come home. There was a problem at his bank. Hmm! I won't say that roulette wheel was rigged, but I do declare that Lew lost his composure and swore under his breath. Had they been setting Mrs. W. up for a big loss? No wonder! Eugene Wilhoit was a bank president. The Wilhoits never returned to the Bear Paw. Her health failed that Winter, and she died. He never came back to the ranch that loved him—to the place where he was "The Boss." He had no heart for it without his beloved.

On Saturday nights, as has been said, everybody but the families with little

Collection of the Huyler Family.

Riders and stagecoach at the Chapel of the Transfiguration, 1930.

kids "duded up" in clean jeans and silk or satin shirts, brushed their big hats and boots, and "headed for town." Some went to the joints; most to the dance halls while they lasted.

Sundays were different. From the Bear Paw, everyone except the Wilhoits went to the Chapel of the Transfiguration in Moose. "The Boss" sent $50 conscience money by me. John D. Rockefeller, Jr., and I were the only members of the congregation who regularly dropped a fifty into the plate. I know; I took up the collection on the left side of the church, where Mr. Rockefeller always sat.

The riders left the ranch for church in small groups beginning around 9:15. The stagecoach left at 10:00, because the teams trotted up hill and down.

The aim of the dude ranch riders was to converge upon the Chapel from all directions at the same time: the Bear Paw from the South; the White Grass over the ridge from the west; the Half Moon, the Elbo and the Bar BC from the north.

As our stagecoach came down the dugway half a mile from the Chapel, the driver lifted his teams into a gallop. That was the signal for all the riders in sight to gallop, too. In those days the road cut straight from the dugway to the Chapel. Inevitably, a few boys would war whoop—girls rarely did that in those days. The Bar BC stagecoach and riders would see the dust, hear the whoops, and follow suit. Ours was an undignified descent upon a church, but it resulted in attendance by many people who might otherwise have skipped church while on their vacations.

Stagecoaches and drivers, perforce, waited outside; but riders ducked their

Collection of the Huyler Family.

Horses tied at Chapel during service, c. 1930s.

heads and rode under the belfry, each making thereby an inadvertent bow toward the altar. Was that part of the builder's plan as it was the plan of the architect of the Taj Mahal, where every visitor, however unwittingly, must bow to the tomb of the Empress Mumtaz Mahal?

Throughout the service a hundred horses might be tied to hitch rails inside the buck-and-rail fence. They made quite a sight and were the subjects of many photographs! That buck-and-rail enclosure was considerably larger than it is today.

Riders departed for their ranches without the hoopla, with lunch on their minds. The ride home was usually uneventful except a couple of times each Summer, when White Grass riders would decide to hold up the Bear Paw stage.

As had professional bandits before them, they would select a place where the teams must be moving slowly: the top of the steep little hill between Wister Draw and the northern gate to the JY. As the teams labored around the final curve at the top of the hill, there would be a dozen masked riders demanding, "Your money or your lives!" We had lots of inter-ranch fun in those days.

Dinner was midday on Sundays, rather than in the evening, and featured homemade ice cream. The wranglers and some competitive dudes took turns cranking the two old-fashioned churns. Each churn contained a gallon of real cream, eggs, and the other goodies required for the flavor desired. It was not difficult for "Cookie" to get volunteers, since the person who gave the handle

Collection of the Huyler Family.

Bear Paw riders leaving Chapel (Glenn and Beth Exum standing to the left; Margaret and Jack Huyler leading riders), 1946.

of each churn its last full turn got to lick its dasher. Turning that handle became a contest of strength because as the ice cream became firmer and firmer, turning became more and more difficult. It was the last full turn that counted.

At the Bear Paw, there was no riding on Sunday afternoons; the horses and the crew got well-deserved rests.

Whenever there was a full moon during the Summer months, dude ranches held moonlight picnics and moonlight rides. For us young wranglers those rides were particular fun. I suppose other young fellows on other ranches did as I did.

Invariably, there were some older persons who opted to go to the picnic by car rather than by horse. I would ride the horse and saddle assigned to one of them. As the moon rose over the campfire and we sang, that person would begin to regret being afoot. To her—usually a her—I would say, "Miss So and So, don't you wish you had ridden?"

"Yes, Jack," was the usual response, "Why didn't you urge me to?"

"Well, it so happens I rode your horse this evening; and if you would like to ride him home, I have another horse to ride."

"Really? That would be wonderful!"

I would adjust the lady's stirrups, hop on Margaret's horse behind her, and get to hug her legally all the way home. I thought I was pretty clever; hind-

Collection of the Huyler Family.

A pan of high country cutthroat, c. 1940s.

sight makes me suspect that I was probably about as subtle as the proverbial crutch. In fact, some of those dear old ladies may well have gone to the picnics by car just to give Margaret and me our opportunity. They were dear old ladies, and much smarter than I. Oddly enough, the spinsters seemed most eager to put us together. Had they regrets?

Pack trips were popular at all dude ranches, and we sent out several each season for two to five days apiece.

A veteran of more than 150 pack trips, I have always wished that just once I could take one as a paying customer. I am, however, too penurious to spend the necessary money. It's not that dude ranches overcharge for their pack trips, but Margaret and I could take one by ourselves any time we wished; and it was free.

So I have never been a "guest" on the kind of pack trips we dude ranchers put out regularly. We took a pack horse for every two guests, tents to erect for them, and air mattresses to inflate for them. Foam pads for sleeping bags were a later development introduced by backpackers. Blowing up a half-dozen air mattresses with lung power is "heady stuff" at 10,000 feet and above, and rendered the blower quite dizzy.

On the trail, one wrangler led the riders, while another one or two, depending upon the size of the group, led the pack string. When the riders stopped for sandwich lunches, the pack string kept plugging up the trail so as to reach camp and have a fire going with water on when the dudes and dudines arrived.

Canned soup (those were the days before dehydrated soups) and Dutch oven chicken were usual the first night, accompanied by canned vegetables, "mashed spuds," fresh salad, and fresh fruit. (Frozen vegetables were not yet available.) Onion soup, steaks, and Dutch oven biscuits, the second (in Jackson Hole, we had never heard of reflector ovens). Mulligan stew was frequently the last dinner.

Breakfasts were hearty: canned tomato juice, eggs, flapjacks, bacon or ham, and frequently trout, as those high country lakes provided excellent fishing.

But before breakfast came a favorite spectator sport of dudes and dudines.

Have you ever watched an old-time cowboy dress? The order is not what one would expect. Consider Slats as a typical example. He always smoked; so the first sounds from his sougan were of deep coughing and lung clearing. Next, long-john-clad legs appeared, and the cowboy sat up, put on his hat, and rolled and lit a cigarette. More coughing. Next came socks and boots; the Levis after them. Then he stood, put on his shirt, buttoned it, tucked in its tail, and put on his jacket. He was ready. Have you ever tried boots before jeans? I told you old-time cowboys prided themselves on having small feet.

Each Summer the White Grass, Bar BC, and Bear Paw put on a benefit barbecue for some worthwhile civic project: the library, the ski shelter, the hospital. A whole steer was pit barbecued; the entire Valley, invited. Tickets were first offered to the other dude ranches, then to the populace.

Frank Bessette, First Deputy Sheriff already mentioned in connection with the last shooting up of Jackson, was everybody's barbecue cook. Frank had once been chef at the Colonial Club at Princeton University.

The ranch prepared the pit, large enough to hold an entire steer; lined it with rocks to hold the heat; and built the fire. The pit was filled with logs and torched. After several hours, when the logs had become coals and the rocks were white hot, Frank arrived.

The steer was already wrapped in chicken wire. Employing a large paint brush, Frank applied his seasonings from a gallon bucket; a pipe was run through the carcass, and willing hands lowered it into the pit. A cover of corrugated metal was dragged across the entire thing and covered with dirt for insulation. Everybody but Frank licked their lips in anticipation and went home to bed. Frank stayed with his project all night, at just the right times removing the cover and basting the beef.

By morning the odors permeating the ranch were tantalizing and mouth watering.

About five in the afternoon the paying customers arrived, and the party began. It's difficult to believe today that at those gigantic barbecues in those days no alcohol—not even beer—was served, yet a fine time was had by all.

Having eaten their fill, people gathered around the campfire for music before leaving for home shortly after dark—some on horseback.

The Bear Paw barbecue of 1940 was particularly memorable. Reg and Gladys Laubin had just brought their authentic Indian dances to the Valley. None of the assembled crowd had seen them dance; this was their Jackson's Hole debut.

As people arrived, they noted on the eastern edge of the Bear Paw pond a closed tipi set up next to a small campfire. As the sun dropped behind the Tetons, which were reflected in the mirror of that pond, an Indian stepped quietly from the tipi, lit his peace pipe with a coal from his campfire, and addressed the four points of the compass, calling upon the Great Spirit to bless him and this assembled tribe. As he finished his eerie cry, a lone coyote in the woods behind him lifted its head and howled. Although there are few of us left, no one who was there will forget that moment. Then, from within the tipi came the sound of a drum, and the Indian brave began to dance. Singing in a high-pitched falsetto, his squaw emerged still beating her tom-tom.

Mrs. Henning Prentis of Lancaster, Pennsylvania, was the Bear Paw guest who did not ride. She was elderly. She walked. She had seriously injured her back in some unspecified way and informed us that she would happily walk alone, enjoying Nature. She rode only once on the Bear Paw and that was double with me.

A group of us was riding up the Granite Canyon Trail one day. Mr. Prentis was not in this group. I was riding drag because, at trail's end, we must turn each horse where it stood for the ride home, and horses were more likely to become "antsy" on the way home.

As we reached a spot perhaps 15 vertical feet above the roaring, rushing stream, we spotted Mrs. Prentis, who stepped up the bank above the trail to let us pass. Last one to pass her, I made some flippant remark about foot versus horse travel and, surprised that she hadn't her usual quick quip of a reply, turned in my saddle and watched her. I had ridden perhaps 30 feet when she collapsed in a heap and began rolling toward that precipitous dropoff. I was young; it was easy to leap from my horse and block her roll before she went over the edge and onto large granite boulders in white water. Had we not come by at that precise moment, she would have fallen into that stream, probably suffered a concussion and drowned. Quickly the others joined us, some climbing down to the creek for hatsful of water. Mrs. Prentis soon regained consciousness and was embarrassed by all the attention. Nonetheless, she was still faint; and I insisted that she ride back to the ranch. The bank made it easy for her to mount my horse, and I vaulted on behind her.

The ride home was unremarkable, and I suppose that my reaction to the whole situation was shameful; so I have never shared those thoughts with anyone until now. The Prentises were elderly; they had no children; and I wondered whether they might not remember in their wills the young man who once saved her life. Not a fortune, but perhaps a new hat, silver-mounted spurs, or even a saddle. I had clearly saved her life. I'll bet I wasn't the first dude wrangler to entertain such thoughts in similar circumstances.

Mother and Dad felt that to be the best, a dude ranch needed good food, good beds, and good horses. If we had those, the good people would come. As a matter of record, in all the years the Bear Paw operated as a dude ranch, we had only two families and one individual whom we would not have welcomed back. Do you wonder about them?

One was just uncooperative: He would hike into the mountains with his daughter telling us he was going one place and sometimes going another. One night when they had not returned by 10:00 P.M., we became concerned, notified Park Headquarters, and prepared to send out search parties at dawn. Meanwhile, by automobile, all night I patrolled the Moose-Wilson road in case they should come out of the mountains somewhere along it. A guest, John Outwater of New York, volunteered to keep me company. The road was totally empty; I knew it well; I was worried; I drove fast. The road was dirt and washboarded; the car bounced about a little and rattled a lot. At one point I looked over at Mr. Outwater. He was clutching the door handle with both hands; his head was down protectively. Realizing that he was traumatized, I attempted to jolly him up, "You know, John, these washboard roads are like waves on water: If you cross them slowly, your boat climbs up one side and flops down the other; but if you have a speedboat and go fast, the waves slap the boat noisily as it passes, but it stays pretty level." I did not expect him to believe me; but he did, and I caught the devil from his wife after their next drive to town in their own car.

As for the object of our search, at the first gray of dawn, we sent out search parties on foot and horseback. Someone in each group was armed and instructed to fire two shots if the lost were found and three shots if found seriously injured. Shots can be heard a long way in the mountains, especially early in the morning before the bustle of day.

In those days the Granite Canyon trail ended no more than a half-mile from the Fleming homestead cabin. I, who dislike hiking, climbed Granite Canyon with a Park Ranger. We came across man and daughter strolling in the opposite direction all unconcerned that they were reversing the course they had identified before leaving and unapologetic for the discombobulation they had caused. "You shouldn't have worried about us." We who had been out all night looking for them did not need that kind of noncooperation. We would have appreciated a simple "Thank you."

Mr. S., on the other hand, meant well. We accepted his application without having met him because we had a mutual friend. Mr. S. lived on Long Island, was a manufacturer, and had in his employ a young cowboy who would drive his car to Wyoming while his employer flew. Commercial air travel had reached Jackson Hole in 1946. Employer and employee would share a cabin—the cabin that today is Margaret's and my bedroom.

True to plan, Curt, the young "cowboy," arrived in a Chrysler convertible the day before his employer. I directed him to his cabin and helped him unload the car. In the trunk there must have been six or eight pairs of dress boots, and three hatboxes. Handsome cowboy shirts were there in garment bags. When we finished unloading, I noticed Curt's belt buckle. A veritable billboard, it proclaimed to anyone within 50 feet his name as recent winner of the calf roping at Pendleton. Welcome, indeed! I quickly spread the word while Curt settled in. Slats, Ed, Cliff, Tuffy, and I looked forward to improving our roping and tying. Thereby hangs the tale.

The next day, Curt fetched his boss from the airport. The latter, considerably overweight, was dressed in a sports shirt unbuttoned down to the navel at a place and time when people did not wear shirts open to the navel. Silently I hoped that he would button up before dinner. He did not. Curt, on the other hand came to the table beautifully dressed. All of us cowboys admired his buckle and welcomed him most heartily. We looked forward to roping with him the following evening. Something prevented Curt's joining us that next evening or the next or the next.

We began to wonder, and our wondering divided us into two camps: 1) He's a fake! 2) He couldn't be a fake. If he were a fake, his belt buckle would not show date and rodeo. It would show his name and Champion Calf Roper; and when asked where he had won it, he would inquire whether the questioner had ever been to such and such a rodeo. Yes? Well, he had won it at such and such (a different place). But there emblazoned on his buckle were his name, the rodeo, and the year! We bickered and continued to press Curt to join us. He just could not find time.

Mr. S. announced his plan to buy a couple of good horses to take back to Long Island. He directed Curt to drive down to the N. Porter Saddlery in Phoenix and buy the needed equipment. Curt left in the Chrysler and performed the impossible. He was back within a week with a brand-new tandem, two-horse trailer painted to match the Chrysler and with a pair of matched Porter saddles with handsome coronas. I think those saddles could not have been made to order in that amount of time no matter how much money was offered. The fenders of each saddle had been custom made, however, for each sported Mr. S.'s brand worked into the full flower stamping. With the saddles came matching bridles and breast collars, not just matching each other, but matching the saddle, each with the S. Now for the horses!

They purchased a Tennessee Walker from Duke Durkee, our local saddle and boot maker. The gelding needed shoeing. He wasn't our horse; under the circumstances, we weren't about to shoe him. We watched. Somewhere, Curt had learned the rudiments of shoeing; however, the horse was fidgety. Curt, with a mouthful of horseshoe nails and a front hoof on his knees, requested, "Will someone please pick up another foot so that this damned horse will stand still?" Did you ever see a horse stand on two legs? Neither had we.

Finally, Curt could postpone the roping no longer. This would be the test, the proof. And to double his chances to show us, we devised a new kind of competition: Cliff would rope and I would tie; I would rope and Cliff would tie. Then Curt would rope and Slats would tie; finally, Slats would rope and Curt would tie. Even a good roper might conceivably miss; however, no one who knows how to tie a calf can forget.

Virtually the entire ranch was there to watch a champion roper do his thing.

I cannot recall Cliff's and my luck, but I recall Curt's as vividly as if it were yesterday instead of 50 years ago. When he rode one of our good rope horses into the chute, he was carrying a loop as small as only the very best ropers carry. Ah ha! Perhaps he is good. He settled the horse and nodded for the calf. As he made his run, he was sitting on the horse's kidneys instead of standing in the stirrups. He swung and cast his little loop. It hit the calf on the rump. No apology, no explanation as he rode back up the arena.

Had Slats missed, we might have killed him; but he didn't. We did not see Curt's dismount, for we couldn't help watching Slats throw. But we did see something we had never seen before: We saw a man gather a calf's legs together and wrap them over and under with his piggin' string rather than around and around.

Although we grinned at each other, we managed not to laugh while we waited for an explanation. Had Curt come to us and said something to the effect of, "Well, you caught me. Mr. S. had bet me $100 I couldn't fool you," we would have clapped him on the shoulder and had a good laugh together. He never offered any excuse or explanation. Had he been intelligent about his deception, he could have said that first day, when I welcomed him, "I tore my shoulder at Madison Square Garden that year and haven't been able to throw a rope since." We, being trusting souls, would have accepted that. To this day, however, I have heard neither excuse nor explanation. As you can tell, it still puzzles me. How could he have been so blatant a liar?

Throughout all this, Mr. S. changed from one unbuttoned shirt to another. He didn't catch on to that, either. Had he been young, slim, and hairless, it wouldn't have been so bad; but none of those attributes was his. Yet, as I stated at the beginning, he meant well.

It's difficult to remember that nylon stockings were once a rarity. Mr. S. manufactured nylons, and he had brought more than a handful with him. He gave them to the female employees without seeking any payoff.

He and Curt began their search for just the right second horse to take east in that great new trailer. Cliff Proctor, one of our dude wranglers, had been trying to buy a "typey"—or classy mare from Walt Callahan, who at the last minute had sold it to a pal at the JY—or had he? Was he just trying to jack the price up? At any rate, the price had risen beyond Cliff's means; so we spoke of her and took Curt and his boss to see her. They looked the mare over and liked her. Mr. S. stepped aside with the owner. We saw them shake hands. Mr. S. opened his fat wallet and produced several bills. They shook hands again; the new owner took her lead rope, led her over to Cliff, and handed him the halter rope. We were all flabbergasted. There had been no indication of what he had in mind. That mare's ride back to the Bear Paw was her last ride in that fancy new trailer.

Yes, he had a kind heart, but he and Curt did not fit in and would not have been welcomed back. They didn't try.

The demise of Jackson Hole dude ranching began a long time ago. It was a lingering death given impetus by the growth of Grand Teton National Park. Lou Joy sold his JY Ranch to Henry Stewart, who sold to John D. Rockefeller, Jr. in 1932. It is now a Rockefeller Summer home. For all they have done for Jackson Hole, that family deserves the best spot in Jackson Hole, and they have it.

Struthers Burt sold the Bar BC to Irv Corse and, with Katherine and two of their former guests, moved to Three Rivers Ranch north of Moran. In 1930 Irv Corse, in turn, sold to the Snake River Land Company, later to become Grand Teton National Park, retaining tenure until his death or that of his wife, Maggie, whichever occurred last. Maggie died on August 3, 1988; and the Park took over its property.

Tragically and nonsensically, the then Park Superintendent made no attempt to obtain funding to preserve that historic property, but chose to let the ranch return to nature. Tragically, because it had been the wish of John D. Rockefeller, Jr., as expressed in a letter to Horace Albright, to maintain for the edification of Park visitors one of the early dude ranches, one of the early homesteads, and one of the cattle ranch headquarters. I know that Superintendent knew of that letter, for I accompanied Albright's daughter, Marion Albright Schenck, when she presented a copy of it to him; yet he chose to ignore the wishes of the two men without whom he would not have had his job, for without them, Grand Teton National Park would never have existed as it does today. Nonsenically, because it would really have cost the Park very little to have restored some of the Bar BC buildings to 1920 condition for tourists to see, and other buildings to modern standards for use as housing for the Park's Summer employees. Public subscription would have poured in to assist. With the JY an impossibility, the Bar BC was the historic dude ranch to preserve.

The final opportunity to preserve an historic dude ranch was addressed in the same way by the same Superintendent. Harold Hammond had married Marion Galey after the death of Marie. Mrs. Galey's son, Frank, with his German war bride, Inga, took over management of the ranch upon his return from World War II. Some years later he and his second wife, Nona, sold to the Park, retaining tenure until the death of the last of them. Frank died; a house fire destroyed Nona's home; the Park took possession and instituted the same policy: deterioration until back to nature.

Margaret and I attended both the Bar BC and White Grass dispersal auctions, as did virtually every Jackson Holer who had known those ranches in their heyday. Antique dealers were there "from outside," buying most of the furniture for transport elsewhere; but the primary motive of local buyers was to preserve some souvenirs of the old ranches we had loved. I must admit that those two auctions were sad affairs. They reminded me of that horrible scene from *Zorba the Greek*: The old woman is dying, and all the other old women in town are sitting around her room like Harpies waiting for her to die so that they can grab some of her possessions. I think all of us locals felt a bit like Harpies.

Harry and Ethel Harrison had sold the Circle H long ago. It became a private home; now most of its former land belongs to the Park.

The Browns sold the Crescent Lazy H when I was still a boy. It is now a subdivision, but a subdivision I respect, for every dwelling must be log construction.

Frank Williams and his Double Diamond, Jimmy Manges and his X Quarter Circle X, the Gabbeys and their Square G, all are gone; the Danny

Ranch, Slash G, the Elbo, the STS, the Half Moon, and the Bear Paw, too. All are parts of the Park. Of the old prewar dude ranches, only the Triangle X, the Teton Valley Ranch, and the R Lazy S continue today. Our hats are tipped to them. Of these, the Triangle X already belongs to Grand Teton National Park and is operated via a lease.

Several younger ranches have opened their doors to guests: Betty Woolsey's Trail Creek Ranch near Wilson, the Moose Head Ranch above Moose, the Heart Six farther north in the Buffalo Valley, the Gros Ventre River Ranch, and the Red Rock Ranch. Long may they thrive! God and the dude ranches made the Jackson's Hole we loved.

Many dudes and dudines fell so in love with the area that they bought their own ranches in Jackson's Hole. Owen Wister, then Roesler and Spear, then Bob and Florelle McConaughy, and finally Howard and Cara Stirn owned the R Lazy S Ranch; the Frews, the Four Lazy F; Elena Hunt, the HS Ranch; the Resors, the Snake River Ranch; the Wesleys, the Trail Ranch; the Balderstones, the Sky Ranch. The list goes on and on.

But no matter how wealthy they were, the places they built fitted in, and the owners tried to. They were never ostentatious—and I do mean never. I cannot recall an exception. Their homes were of log and hidden in trees insofar as possible. That's a big difference today. Just note the difference between the cabins on the Snake River Ranch, the JY, Sky Ranch, and the "trophy homes" now scattered around the Valley. Margaret and I have good friends who live in some of those homes—even a couple of chateaux. They are good people, but they are changing not only the face but the character of the valley we and they love, the valley whose "atmosphere" brought them here.

I suppose that while I am offending people, I might as well take on the architects, so many of whom seem dedicated to building monuments to themselves. Trophy homes, rather than homes that fit into their surroundings! Wesley Bircher and Paul Colbron did not do that.

Yes, the homes of those dudes turned ranchers fitted in; but no matter whether they tried to or not, they, themselves, could not. Again, I cannot call to mind an exception.

Have you had experience with Americans who have lived abroad for a lifetime or with foreigners who live here? Ninety percent of them can't "pass." Indeed, my father and mother and most of their "immigrant" friends never tried to pass, which is just as well, because there was no way that they could have.

That inability to "pass" embarrasses their kids, who want to pass, and can.

The dudes' and dudines' dress betrayed them, no matter how they tried—especially their hats, the way they wore them, and still do. It wasn't the size of the hat, but the way it was blocked, handled, and placed on the head. Mike Sullivan, recent Governor of Wyoming, and Cliff Hansen, former Governor, United States Senator, and owner of Teton County license plate Number One, wear small-brimmed Stetsons; yet anyone can recognize either man as "the genuine article" just by a glance at his hat as his pickup goes by. A dude wore his hat lower in back than in front; a cowboy pulled his hat down in front to shade his eyes. It was as simple as that.

It is not quite so simple today. I believe it was the great Jim Shoulders who changed the style. Other bull riders began to wear their large hats down in back. They set the style that virtually all young cowboys seem to be following still. If he is young, I can no longer distinguish the Real McCoy from the Summer cowboy by a quick glance through the window of an automobile or truck. In fact, sometimes it's hard to guess their gender with a quick look. I hate that.

Undeniably, the heyday of dude ranching has passed, not only in Jackson Hole but throughout the

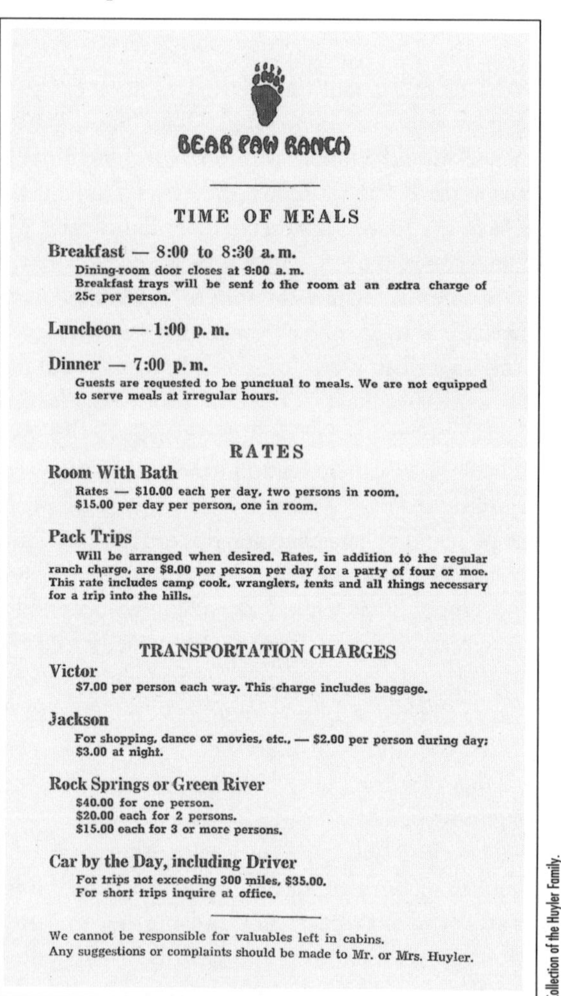

BEAR PAW RANCH

TIME OF MEALS

Breakfast — 8:00 to 8:30 a. m.
Dining-room door closes at 9:00 a. m.
Breakfast trays will be sent to the room at an extra charge of 25c per person.

Luncheon — 1:00 p. m.

Dinner — 7:00 p. m.
Guests are requested to be punctual to meals. We are not equipped to serve meals at irregular hours.

RATES

Room With Bath
Rates — $10.00 each per day, two persons in room.
$15.00 per day per person, one in room.

Pack Trips
Will be arranged when desired. Rates, in addition to the regular ranch charge, are $8.00 per person per day for a party of four or moe. This rate includes camp cook, wranglers, tents and all things necessary for a trip into the hills.

TRANSPORTATION CHARGES

Victor
$7.00 per person each way. This charge includes baggage.

Jackson
For shopping, dance or movies, etc., — $2.00 per person during day; $3.00 at night.

Rock Springs or Green River
$40.00 for one person.
$20.00 each for 2 persons.
$15.00 each for 3 or more persons.

Car by the Day, including Driver
For trips not exceeding 300 miles, $35.00.
For short trips inquire at office.

We cannot be responsible for valuables left in cabins.
Any suggestions or complaints should be made to Mr. or Mrs. Huyler.

Collection of the Huyler Family.

Bear Paw rate sheet, c. 1940.

West; however, Jackson Hole dude ranches are filled every Summer, the best of them filled many months in advance. The legacy of dude ranching is strong. It commenced the flow of Easterners west and of West Coasters eastward. When will that flow stop? Our valley is full to overflowing. Every additional home, no matter its style, in some way destroys what drew its owner here in the first place. It cannot be denied that the Huyler family and all the other dude ranchers contributed to the Valley's growth—and did so early on. We liked our guests, and we urged the best of them to buy and build, even though in doing so we lost our best customers.

There are, no doubt, good people yet to come—people who will love this Valley as I do and who will cherish it; however, they cannot avoid bringing with them growth, which inevitably dooms the way of life we love—the way of life which attracted them here in the first place.

Why is it that people find a place they like—or even claim to love—and immediately begin converting that place into the place they left? It is totally incomprehensible to me.

Collection of the Huyler Family.

Margaret Huyler (authors wife), M.N.A. Winning Dudine Race

CHAPTER TWELVE

The Park

My father once asked John D. Rockefeller, Jr., "Mr. Rockefeller, how much money is enough?"

Mr. Rockefeller smiled and replied, "Just a little more than you have, Coulter—just a little bit more than you have."

This seems a good place and time to write of the origins of Grand Teton National Park, which saved so much of the beauty of Jackson's Hole while it "gobbled up" so many dude ranches.

The concept of National Parks may well be the greatest contribution of the United States of America to the world.

The State of Wyoming contains the world's first National Park (Yellowstone—1872), the first National Forest (Teton Forest Reserve—1879), and the First National Monument (Devil's Tower—1906). In addition, Wyoming gave the nation its first woman governor (Nellie Tayloe Ross from 1925-27), its first all-female town council (Jackson's in 1920-23), its

Collection of the Jackson Hole Historical Society and Museum.

The nation's first all-women town council, c. 1920.

first woman mayor (Grace Miller of Jackson), and, perhaps, its first woman marshal (Pearl Williams).

Yellowstone remains America's premier park; however, it is Grand Teton National Park which, probably, most directly affected Jackson's Hole. I say probably because Yellowstone Park continues to affect Jackson Hole's primary industry, tourism, every day of the short Wyoming Summers and appreciably during ski and snowmobile seasons. Teton Park, however, in 1999 draws approximately 3,000,000 visitors per year; and all of those are, of course, in Jackson Hole.

In 1915, my father's good friend Horace Albright, whom many refer to as the "Father of the National Park System," first visited Jackson's Hole and determined that this glorious Valley must be preserved for and against future generations.

An historic meeting was held in Moose at the cabin home of Maud Noble on July 26, 1923. In attendance were Horace Albright, Burt and his partner, Dr. Horace Carncross, representing the dude ranchers; Jack Eynon, representing the cattle ranchers; Joe Jones, representing the Valley's businessmen; Dick Winger, owner of the local newspaper; and Miss Noble. They were interested in obtaining for Jackson's Hole the designation of Recreational Preserve, which was accomplished in 1925, the year Dad bought his first land here. They envisioned that Recreational Preserve's eventually becoming part of Yellowstone National Park. At that time, they did not foresee a Grand Teton National Park.

In 1926, Albright persuaded the John D. Rockefeller, Jr., family to leave Yellowstone, which they were visiting, and to drive with him to see Jackson's Hole. Mr. Rockefeller was greatly moved by the peaks and the lakes at their feet. Mrs. Rockefeller was disturbed by the beginnings of exploitation that they saw, and she urged her husband to do something about it. He agreed to purchase on a willing-seller-willing-buyer basis such lands as he could to protect the peaks: those lands to include a significant area of the range, specific mountain lakes (Leigh, String, Jenny, Bradley, Taggart, and Phelps) and streams, and enough of the floor of the Valley to preserve and showcase the rest. Horace Albright pointed out that there was an urgency, as the Forest Service proposed to dam Jenny Lake for agricultural use. Mr. Rockefeller subsequently formalized his offer to purchase lands and to set them aside for future absorption as the Department of the Interior generated funds to manage those lands. Specifically, he authorized the purchase of 14,170 acres on the west side of Snake River and 100,000 acres on the east side. Current landowners will find it almost unbelievable that on the west side the authorized price per acre was $28; on the east side, $10.

As Albright, at that time Superintendent of Yellowstone Park, pointed out, it would not do for Jackson Holers to find out that "the richest man in America" was buying land. Prices would have soared. Behind a screen based in Salt Lake City and called the Snake River Land Company, John D. Rockefeller, Jr., through agents, began buying land in earnest. At one point he contemplated buying all private lands in Jackson's Hole. An attorney from Salt Lake City, one Beverly Clendenin (father of Claire McConaughy, today manager of Jackson Hole's R Lazy S dude ranch) was in charge of purchases. The attorney on site was Harold Fabian, who moved with his wife, Josephine, to Jackson's Hole from Salt Lake City the better to perform his duties. Locally, Dick Winger was the preeminent agent. Hindsight suggests that Robert Miller, owner of the proprietary Jackson State Bank, and the first purchasing agent for the Snake River Land Company, learned who the real source of funds was. He is said to have foreclosed more than a few mortgages and to have sold those properties to the Snake River Land Company at a nice profit. Although Miller sold those lands willingly, such transactions were hardly what Mr. Rockefeller meant when he referred to willing buyer, willing seller. "Old 12% Miller," indeed!

When he was a high school kid, Valarz "John" Hagen was hired by Robert Miller to mow the Miller lawn weekly during the growing season. It took Valarz a day and a half each week. The president of the Jackson State Bank paid young Hagen 50¢ a week for the job

By 1929 the Tetons themselves, with a handful of lakes at their bases,

Photo by Olie Riniker. Collection of the Jackson Hole Historical Society and Museum.

Robert Miller homestead, 1990.

comprised a small but spectacular Grand Teton National Park. In his scholarly and interesting book, *Crucible for Conservation*, Robert Righter writes:

> In truth, Miller was never trusted by the Rockefeller associates, and it was felt that the less he knew the better . . . While Rockefeller, Fabian, Miller and others were intent on offering a fair price for the land, their agreement spoke the language of hardfisted business dealings . . . Rockefeller was motivated by both a desire to do good works and a commitment to accomplish those good works fairly and without injury. (p. 51)

By the end of 1930, the company had purchased 35,310 acres for $1,400,300, and its true purpose and ownership became known. My family's 20-acre ranch would today bring appreciably more than that total acreage brought then. The purchases averaged out to $39.66 per acre, a fair price at the time. (Dad bought 160 acres of good land for $10 per acre as late as 1940.)

It must be re-emphasized that every purchase made by the Snake River Land Company, with the exception of those mortgaged lands foreclosed by banker/buyer Miller, was freely sold. Agriculture had suffered when the United States stopped feeding Europe via the Hoover Plan some years after World War I. Farmers were going bankrupt all over the nation. For all its charms, Jackson's Hole was not—and is not—prime agricultural land. The growing season is too short. Many rancher/farmers were anxious to sell. As the world knows, the Great Depression had hit in November 1929, and already low property values declined further.

Nonetheless, when the name of the real purchaser became known in Jackson's Hole, there was a great hue and cry. *The richest man in America should have paid more for the land he purchased.*

In 1944 President Franklin Delano Roosevelt vetoed a bill to destroy Teton Park. Just imagine that: a bill not only to preclude any further acquisition of lands for the Park, but requiring the dissolution of those lands already designated as Grand Teton National Park! It seems impossible that such a bill could have passed both houses of Congress and reached the President's desk. I believe that even the most ardent Republican would today applaud Roosevelt's veto.

On March 15, 1943, at the urging of Mr. Rockefeller, who threatened to sell the lands if something was not done to relieve him of the property taxes and to move his plan along, the President established and set up the Jackson Hole National Monument to hold those lands that Mr. Rockefeller had purchased until the Park Service should have sufficient funds to support them. It was 1950 before the Jackson Hole National Monument merged with Grand Teton National Park.

The press jumped into the fray. The front page of the *Jackson's Hole Courier* on Thursday, June 24, 1943, carried several significant headlines:

I shall utilize all police authority at my disposal to evict from the proposed Jackson Hole National Monument any federal official who attempts to assume authority. — GOV. LESTER C. HUNT

Noted Columnist Likens Jackson Hole Monument to Nazi Trick!

Westbrook Pegler Brands Action
By Ickes and Roosevelt
As Typical Hitler Act

> President Roosevelt and Harold Ickes [Secretary of the Interior] have recently perpetrated in which [sic] follows the general lines of Adolph Hitler's seizure of Austria. They have anchlussed [sic] a tract of 221,610 acres for Ickes' domain by a subterfuge after congress had twice rejected proposals for the same annexation. (p. 1)

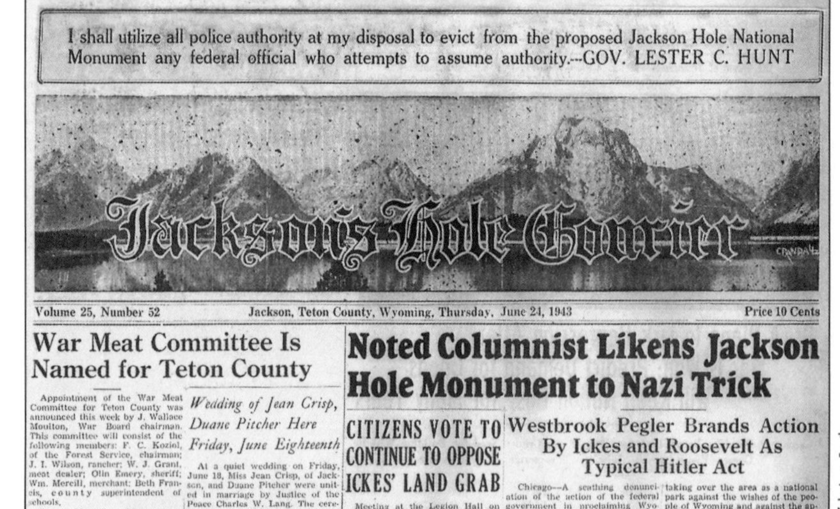

I shall utilize all police authority at my disposal to evict from the proposed Jackson Hole National Monument any federal official who attempts to assume authority.--GOV. LESTER C. HUNT

Jackson's Hole Courier

Volume 25, Number 52 — Jackson, Teton County, Wyoming, Thursday, June 24, 1943 — Price 10 Cents

War Meat Committee Is Named for Teton County

Appointment of the War Meat Committee for Teton County was announced this week by J. Wallace Moulton, War Board chairman. This committee will consist of the following members: F. C. Koziol, of the Forest Service, chairman; J. I. Wilson, rancher; W. J. Grant, meat dealer; Olin Emery, sheriff; Wm. Mercill, merchant; Beth Francis, county superintendent of schools.

County Meat Committees organized under instructions of the War Food administration, U. S. Department of Agriculture, will function under the Wyoming Meat Marketing Supervisor, J. Marius Christen-

Wedding of Jean Crisp, Duane Pitcher Here Friday, June Eighteenth

At a quiet wedding on Friday, June 18, Miss Jean Crisp, of Jackson, and Duane Pitcher were united in marriage by Justice of the Peace Charles W. Lang. The ceremony was performed at seven o'clock at the Lang home in the presence of a few close relatives and friends. Room decorations were white tapers and bouquets of columbine.

Noted Columnist Likens Jackson Hole Monument to Nazi Trick

CITIZENS VOTE TO CONTINUE TO OPPOSE ICKES' LAND GRAB

Meeting at the Legion Hall on Monday, June 14, for the purpose of listening to a report from the committee which went to Washington, D. C. to testify in opposition to the recently established Jackson

Westbrook Pegler Brands Action By Ickes and Roosevelt As Typical Hitler Act

Chicago—A seathing denunciation of the action of the federal government in proclaiming Wyoming's Jackson Hole country a national monument has been made in his nationally-read column by Westbrook Pegler, writer for Scripps-Howard newspapers and the United

taking over the area as a national park against the wishes of the people of Wyoming and against the approval of congress is an action which is very similar to Germany's annexation of small countries in Europe which it desired to take into the reich.

Collection of the Lucas Family.

Jackson's Hole Courier, June 24, 1943.

Pretty strong stuff, I am sure you will agree. And it was trumpeted throughout the Scripps-Howard newspapers and the United Feature Syndicate during World War II, when all citizens tended to rally around the nation's leadership.

In that same issue of the *Courier* appeared an editorial from the *Augusta* (Georgia) *Herald:*

> The other day I mentioned in one of my columns the matter of Jackson's Hole, where the government was trying to take over all of the worthwhile land in a county in Wyoming, and the citizens were protesting because there would not be enough left to pay expenses, since the federal government pays no state or county taxes . . .
>
> Then a day or two ago I saw where President Roosevelt, without any say-so by the people involved or by their congressmen or senators, had issued a directive and signed it, taking over the whole tract for the federal government to be held as a national "monument.". . . Just what it is to be a monument to I do not know, but the inscription might well read, "In Memory of Democratic Rights, Buried Here." (p. 1)

Cattlemen protested the loss of some of their ranges and the closing of some of the routes to ranges on the National Forest. Their protests had little if anything to do with the identity of the purchaser, but much to do with what they perceived as losses to the cattle industry and with some of the high-handed tactics employed by the government forces.

Local notables, including Cliff Hansen and movie star Wallace Beery, a Summer resident, notified the press that on a certain day they would mount their horses and drive cattle across the Valley on traditional cattle trails and to Hell with the consequences. The photos hit front pages of newspapers everywhere and appeared in such magazines as *Time*, *Newsweek*, *Life*, and *Look*. Nationally, the populace protested vehemently to their congressmen and senators the government's abuse of the little man, in this case the rancher.

I quote former Wyoming Governor and United States Senator Clifford P. Hansen writing to me on the subject in 1999. Senator Hansen is, without doubt, the most respected man in Teton County, if not the state. He was there; he participated; he knows whereof he speaks (my comments are in italics here):

> For a number of years, repeated efforts were made to write a bill acceptable to the majority of the divergent groups interested in Jackson Hole. There were two hearings by Senatorial

subcommittees in Jackson. In 1933, John C. Pickett, U.S. Attorney, handled one. Later, in 1938, Milward Simpson *[also governor and senator]* played a leading role.

I've read Robert Righter's *Crucible for Conservation.* I suggested he get the transcript of those hearings in the early 1930's. Among other things, word was given to some post office patrons at Elk, Moose, Kelly—and there may have been others—that continued opposition to park expansion would result in the closure of their post offices.

An invitation for bids to perform work improving Togwotee Pass was summarily withdrawn, recognizing greater travel from that entrance to Jackson Hole would result in appreciation of land values.

If memory serves, I think it was Sam Woodring *[Superintendent of Grand Teton National Park]* who had a survey crew working from Wilson north to Moose ostensibly planning a widened and improved road if Jackson continued opposing plans to expand boundaries of Grand Teton. (Insofar as I know, the Rockefellers had no hand in these activities.)

There was a great interest throughout the valley and Wyoming when Mr. Rockefeller's role became known. I have the recollection that most of the ranch sales to S.R.L.C. were willing buyer-willing seller. As you point out, times were tough. The Great Depression was felt in Jackson Hole as elsewhere.

The motivation for the Wallace Beery armed intrusion into Monument Lands was not connected in any way to your statement that *[people felt]* the richest man in America should have paid more for the land he purchased. Rather our motivation was to attract national attention to: 1) the county's losing much taxable property as title passed from private ownership to the federal government; 2) loss of cattle range—at the time there were many cattle ranches in Jackson Hole; 3) loss of hunting—no one believed hunting would be continued in a National Monument.

In retrospect let me note that we were: 1) successful in getting written into the Act of Congress abolishing the Monument and expanding the Park a provision to reimburse Teton County for a period of 20 years—taxes levied on the real estate as ownership passed from individuals to the federal government; 2) recognition of the State of Wyoming to continue big game hunting and further providing for the Wyoming Game and

> Fish to meet with Park officials setting areas to be hunted and dates of hunting seasons; 3) recognition of right to graze in Grand Teton National Park as well as permits to cross the park grazing to forest ranges; 4) the right to continue dude ranching a) if base property owned and b) right of concessionaires.
>
> Having said all this, as you know, I've said many times how grateful I am to the Rockefeller family for their prescience in protecting this valley. (Letter from former U.S. Senator Clifford P. Hansen to Jack Huyler, Fall 1999.)

It seems incredible today that anti-Park feelings were as strong as they were and lasted as long as they did. Nowadays I am aware of no one who is not grateful for Grand Teton National Park; but at one time, those who supported the Park—I am proud to say my parents were among them—could have met in the telephone office if not in one of its four telephone booths.

As I declared in the second paragraph of this chapter, national parks are defensibly the greatest contribution of the United States of America to the world. We Americans are proud of our Parks; we visit them in hordes; we trample them until Park officials wring their hands. We are loving them to death.

I feel sure that every resident of Jackson Hole feels a proprietary interest in Grand Teton National Park. It is ours, and for a significant portion of each year it is ours alone. We like and appreciate the Park personnel.

I, and no doubt others, even solicited the President of the United States on behalf of our national parks: Grand Teton and Yellowstone. While vacationing in Jackson Hole in 1996, President Clinton was sufficiently gracious to ask me if I had any questions that I would like to ask him as President.

"Yes, sir," I replied, "two of them: Why should the New World Mine be permitted on the borders of Yellowstone Park, where it would surely contaminate the Greater Yellowstone ecosystem; and why can't each national park retain the fees it generates?"

"Jack," he has an uncanny ability to recall names, "as long as I am President, that mine will not be located there, on the edge of Yellowstone. You can count on that.

"As for the fees generated by each Park, I'll look into that."

"Thank you, Mr. President."

Those of us who can recall Burma Shave signs along the Jackson-Moran Highway admire and approve the removal of highway billboards, the absence of trash and graffiti, the maintenance of trails, the control of visitors, and the assistance given to the Teton Science School and to Mardy Murie.

We who have been here long enough recall the memorandum of March 17, 1945, from Newton B. Drury, Director of the National Park Service, addressed to Secretary of the Interior, Harold L. Ickes, and approved by the latter four days later. It states (italics mine):

> *One of the purposes of the Jackson Hole plan since the beginning has been the perpetuation of those aspects of the region that represent the "Old West."*
>
> Administration and interpretation of the Monument will take this into account. Not only the earlier and nationally significant places of its history, but also the recent and local phases will be revealed to the public. *Pioneer structures like Menor's Ferry and the Cunningham Cabin will be restored, protected, and displayed. The "dude ranches" represent a colorful native institution . . . They should be continued and fitted into the over-all program of accommodations.*

Thirteen years later a memorandum from George B. Hartzog, Jr., Director, National Park Service, dated October 10, 1968, conveys a similar message (italics mine):

> *It has recently come to my attention that the Service is still demolishing historic structures within some of the older National Parks for the reason that the structure has deteriorated. From my personal observation this deterioration results, in most instances, from a lack of any creative effort on the part of the Service to maintain the structure in the first place.*
>
> The Service stands as perhaps the single most vital force in promoting historic preservation throughout the country. It, thus, is incongruous for us to be dismantling structures in National Parks which, were they outside of National Parks, we would be in the forefront of those opposing demolition.
>
> Accordingly, hereafter no structure 50 years or older shall be razed or modified without my personal approval. Moreover, any structure less than 50 years old that is significant in interpreting the cultural heritage of a location or region shall not be razed or modified without review and concurrence of the Chief, Office of Archeology and Historic Preservation.

In addition to the above, there was that letter, mentioned in the previous chapter, from John D. Rockefeller, Jr., to Horace Albright urging the preservation of at least one dude ranch, one old cattle ranch, and one early homestead.

Why did Park Superintendents choose to fly in the face of those directives and to stand by as historic sites in Jackson Hole fell apart—even razing some? Why is it that socially delightful men, though remaining accessible and approachable, when they sit behind that Superintendent's desk frequently seem to develop severe cases of hubris, and become unreachable? They no longer respond to the wishes of their patrons, the people. One even bragged that he did not read letters sent to him on specific issues. Is there truly a bureaucratic schizophrenia, or does it merely seem to exist? What is it that permits a Superintendent, after being shown an historical inaccuracy on a Park map, to remark, "Well, this is the way it is going to be now!"?

Yes, we love and admire our National Parks and the beauty they guarantee to future generations. We support the G.T.N.P.'s administrations in most things, though a great many of us have deplored, and do deplore, specific actions, especially:

- the style of housing selected when Park Headquarters moved from the lovely log cabins at Beaver Creek to Moose;
- the extravagance of moving the road that ran to and past Jenny Lake;
- the closure of certain major trails to horseback riding (after all, those trails were built for horseback riders);
- the elimination of the Jenny Lake horse concession operated for

Photo by Latham Jenkins. Collection of JHStock.com.

Saddle shed at the Bar BC, 1992.

so many years by Cornell Rudd and his family;

- the extravagance of the proposed construction of a new Visitors' Center at a time when our Parks are moaning about lack of funds;
- the proposal of a toll booth and ranger cabin or house in the Poker Flats area;
- and above all else, the minimization of the importance of human history; and the resultant neglect of the Bar BC and White Grass dude ranches and of the Antelope Flats/Mormon Row homesteads.

The good news is that at long last a Superintendent is responding to the clamor of local citizens for restoration and maintenance of a few areas. Superintendent Jack Neckels recently submitted for public examination and comment five options for preservation of the Chambers and Moulton homesteads on Mormon Row. He has, moreover, accepted "a sizeable donation to stabilize at least three of the buildings at the historic Bar BC dude ranch." Perhaps the tide has turned and some of what is left will be restored and preserved; much, however, is beyond redemption: gone forever.

To many of us in Jackson Hole, human history is as significant as geologic history. Human history is in the long haul part of natural history. We are the Anasazi of the future.

CHAPTER THIRTEEN

Reigo

Reigo Nethercott had been born on the ranch where he lived his life. His father, Al, had homesteaded the place early on in the settling of Jackson's Hole. Al had at one time been one of Brigham Young's Avenging Angels. He must have been hot-tempered. It was he who put the bullet through Linn's hat, sicked his dog on the Linn brothers' calves, and shot and killed his own team, thinking it was the Linns'.

Reigo was a Mormon bishop, our mailman and good friend, a cracker barrel philosopher of intelligence and intuition, a hunting guide with one stiff leg, an outfitter, and the owner of Shorty.

I have never seen another horse like Shorty. He was a good-sized horse except for the short legs that led to his name. Nothing to look at, Shorty could and would do anything. He was a reliable saddle horse and a good ride; he was a good hunting horse, for he would stay around camp rather than trying to go home; and he could be packed with a load of game and frequently was. One thing he did, no other horse ever did, to the best of my knowledge.

Reigo delivered the mail by pickup truck. The roads were snow in the Winter, dirt in the Summer, and mud in the Spring and Fall. Those were days before four-wheel drives, which came on the Jackson Hole scene after World War II and were, at first, all of them GI surplus vehicles. Whenever Reigo was worried about getting stuck, he would harness Shorty, lead him to the back of the pickup, drop the tailgate, and command Shorty to get in. The horse would hop from the ground to the truck bed without benefit of a ramp. Reigo would close the tailgate, fire up the truck, and away they would go on his mail route. Whenever they got stuck, and that was not an unusual experience on those roads, Reigo would get out and drop the tailgate. Alone in the truck bed, Shorty had barely enough room to turn around. He would turn around, hop down with great dignity, and wait for his master and friend. I saw it several times.

Reigo would lead him to the front of the truck and fasten the traces to the bumper braces, Shorty standing idle all the while. Bumper braces were strong in those days; would they were still. Shorty wore neither bridle nor reins, just a halter. Getting back in his cab, Reigo would start the engine, throw the clutch, put the truck in gear, lean out the window, speak crisply to Shorty, "Shorty!" Shorty would take up the slack, and lean his weight and muscle into the pull. Depressing the accelerator a bit and easing the clutch out, Reigo would help Shorty, and together they would pull the truck out. On solid ground, "Whoa, Shorty." Reigo would get out, unhook Shorty, lead him to the tailgate. "Shorty, get in!" Shorty would hop in; the tailgate would be slammed shut; and they would be on their way to the next ranch mailbox. I never heard of Reigo's needing more help than Shorty's, although I suppose sometime he may have. Those mud holes were pretty bad.

When Reigo arrived with the mail, he also brought the news and, along with that news, his commentary on it. His evaluations of happenings, local, national, and international made sense, were delivered in a style that made one listen, and were always worthy of consideration. We looked forward to Reigo's daily arrival. I miss him.

Annually at the full moon in August, Dad, Mother, Margaret, our kids, and I invited friends for a potluck supper at our Rocking H Ranch. After eating, we sang around a bonfire until it was time to go home. Reigo changed all that.

One year, after Dad and Mother's deaths, a heavy thunderstorm drove half the crowd home and the other half into our livingroom. In light of what he was about to say, it was appropriate that Reigo sat in Dad's chair. It was appropriate

Photo by J. Thralls. Collection of the Jackson Hole Historical Society and Museum.

Spring driving in the old days, 1936.

because Dad loved stories and storytelling.

"Well," began Reigo to everyone and to no one in particular, "we all wonder about "Them What's Gone." We're a-goin' to see them again, we know that; but we wonder what they're gonna look like. Will they look the way they did when last we seen 'em? Will they look the way they did when we was kids? Or will they look the way they did when they was in their prime?"

How do we remember "Them What's Gone:" as kids, as we last saw them, or in their prime? How do we remember Reigo's handsome son, Byron Nethercott, who was killed by a combine?

Byron and his wife had moved to Montana. The day he died they were haying their fields. She was driving the mower; he, the combine. She noticed the combine unmoving on a windrow. Byron was not to be seen. On her next pass, she still could not see her husband, and the combine was still in the same spot. Surmising him to be working on it, she shut down her mower and walked over to see if she could help. As she drew closer, she could hear that the combine was still running. That was strange. The horrible truth was that Byron had stopped to clear a jam in the big machine. One always shuts down to do that. Evidently Byron felt he could clear it better while it was running. As he cleared the jam, the boom swung around and struck him, breaking his neck and crushing his skull. Instant death, but what a traumatic discovery for the young widow!

"Reigo," I said, "you've just given me a great idea: From now on this party will not be devoted to visiting and singing, but to telling stories about "Them What's Gone"."

For the next 20 years we did just that; but we became old, and Margaret said, "Enough." We had more than 200 participants at our last storytelling potluck in August 1992, probably because the word had spread that it would be the last. Usually the number was 150 to 170.

After we dropped it, the Snake River Institute, God bless 'em, took over the project. It amused me that when I gave them our guest list they said it was more people than they could handle. They an institute with employees; we a small ranch without employees. We were, however, delighted that the storytelling would continue indefinitely, giving a form of immortality to "Them What's Gone" and indirectly to Reigo Nethercott. Now, most unfortunately, the Institute, itself, is one of "Them What's Gone". Margaret and I wonder if anyone will pick the storytelling up. The Jackson Hole Historical Society and Museum would be the logical successor.

Although professional storytellers throughout the nation have banded together into a union that meets annually and that advertises its members, amateur storytelling is declining. Skilled storytellers are becoming scarce because of radio, movies, and television. Before those inventions, when two or three people met they swapped tales of local happenings or news they had heard from "outside." When people got together for "socials," they told stories: stories of local happenings mostly, but also stories of the past, true and tall. Favorite storytellers were called upon to retell favorite tales time after time. Good storytellers were much in demand for social functions. It was worth a person's time to try to hone and polish narrative skills, a sure way to the attention of the opposite sex.

Mrs. George Lamb, Mardy Murie, "Doc" MacLeod, Rex Ross, Earl Hardeman, Evelyn Elmore, Lou Wilson, and Coulter Huyler were superb storytellers. Bill Ashley, Bob Kranenberg, Bob Rudd, Cliff Hansen, Dick Barker, Fern Nelson, Gene Hoffman, Gene Linn, Glenn Exum, Irene Brown, Lester May, Lou Demorest, Nels Dahlquist, and I continue the tradition today. Charlie Peterson is as good as the best ever. But if you know the folks listed above, you will have realized that most of us are "pretty long in the tooth." From that long list only two are not well past our prime. The tradition is dying. Would it were not so.

"Come along, boys, and listen to my tale; and I'll tell you of my troubles on the old Chisholm Trail . . ."

CHAPTER FOURTEEN

Mose Giltner
1857-1941

I remember Mose Giltner. According to his own account, he had been the 22nd man to make Jackson's Hole home. That was in 1886, three years prior to the arrival of Nick Wilson and the wagon train of settlers. In those days Jackson's Hole was halfway between hither and yon. The 21 he found in the valley consisted of 20 bachelors and one squaw man (the term for a white man married to, or living with, an Indian woman).

Mose had been born into a solid, respectable, churchgoing family near Kansas City, Missouri.

When he was a young buck, he and his brother, Bob, decided to build a house together. Over the weeks that they worked on it, they agreed that the first of them to marry would get the house. The day after it was completed, Bob married.

Minnie Single, Mose's girl friend, was furious. She was counting on that house. She was so angry that Mose left town—not for a short while, but for 30 years, 30 years during which he made no effort to maintain contact with family or Minnie. First, he went northwest to Washington prospecting, but after a few years of that he immigrated to Jackson's Hole and homesteaded on Poverty Flat. He prospered, bought more land, and became one of the leading cattlemen of the Valley. A great admirer of ladies after some arrived in Jackson's Hole, he, nonetheless, formed no lasting attachment. Was he pining for Minnie Single?

Thirty years after his departure a member of the family in Kansas City read in the *Kansas City Star* that one Mose Giltner of Jackson's Hole, Wyoming, had recently sold a shipment of 750 yearlings. A "Mose Giltner" was hardly a "John Smith," so they wrote him, urging him to come home. When he came for a short visit, he found Minnie Single had lived up to her name; and they "went around together" until once again he departed with no strings attached.

Fifteen years after that, the family planned a large reunion and again invited Mose. Again he came, and again he "went around" with Minnie throughout his visit. This time, when he left still without proposing, she became angry and shortly thereafter married a more reliable suitor. After 45 years! She must have been in her sixties by then.

It was 1936 when he returned to Jackson's Hole this time; and he was accompanied by a grandnephew, Jerry Bonar, who told me this story in September 1996. Jerry had decided that here was a rich relative with no children and that if he spent a couple of years helping the old man, he might well become his heir. A cattle baron! Little did he know. Mose was 82; Jerry, 18. Jerry stayed two years; they tested his fortitude.

Mose, by this time, was downright odd. For example, he wore one-buckle rubber overshoes no matter what the weather. On the train from Pocatello to Victor, the odor emanating from the old man's feet nauseated young Jerry. Mose told him to "stick my head out the window and watch for Victor. I had no idea where Victor was," Jerry added, "nor how far; but I took his advice."

Crossing the Pass, they stopped in Wilson long enough for Mose to purchase three dozen loaves of bread. Bread, beans, and coconut were the staple diet. Three times a day!

At the ranch after supper, Jerry started to pick up the dishes to wash them. "No. No!" said Mose. "Just turn them over on the table and they'll be there ready for the next meal."

In the morning, Jerry found a broom and started sweeping. "Get the Hell out of here with that broom!" yelled the old man "You just move the dust around."

When a fresh supply of bread, beans, and coconut was needed, they snow-shoed over Teton Pass and webbed all the way to Driggs and back because, "Things are too high in Jackson's Hole."

Mose had by that time sold his first ranch to the Elk Refuge and moved to his spread on Lake Creek, now part of the Snake River Ranch. His old house and barn can still be seen a quarter of a mile east of Bill and Story Resor's house.

The Elk Refuge today is comprised of 24,300 acres. Ideally it carries 7,500 elk through the Winter, with another 3,500 on the Gros Ventre and Fall Creek feed grounds. Actually, the numbers are more like 10,000 on the main Refuge alone. Roughly 3,000 elk are killed each year by hunters. It would require 5,000 to keep the herds stable.

Jerry Bonar was in Mose Giltner's cabin the day Stanley Resor, Sr., walked in and handed the old man a check for $25,000 for the property. The next day they couldn't find it; nor the following. It had temporarily disappeared in the litter.

On their rare expeditions to town, the old man and the boy appeared so down and out that tourists frequently took them for panhandlers and gave them money. That infuriated Mose, who, although he didn't look it, was one of the Valley's most successful ranchers. Jerry, however, accepted all gratuities. It was about the only money the boy saw.

Not that Mose was always dirty. Once a year, according to his nephew, he went all the way to Lava Hot Springs, 50 miles south of Pocatello, Idaho, for an annual bath and change of clothing. It was a prolonged stay, and there Jerry got a job that paid cash. Using that as a lever, he managed to squeeze a token wage from the old man when they returned to the ranch.

Unable to locate a will; concerned about the state of Mose's estate; and, no doubt, hoping to be mentioned prominently in any new instrument, Jerry urged his great-uncle to draw up a new will. It was done; however—again according to Jerry—Dr. Huff and Bill Simpson (grandfather of Senator Al), had the old man declared mentally incompetent about that time; so the revised will was unacceptable.

After Mose's death in a Salt Lake hospital, the earlier will surfaced, and each of the relatives received a check for a $100 with advice to wait for more to come. They waited and waited—and waited. Eventually 13 heirs employed 13 attorneys to sue the estate for settlement. "The lawyers got all but that $100 apiece," reports Jerry Bonar.

So what's new? The only people I know who *never* lose money are the attorneys. They win, win or lose. No wonder there are so many of them!

CHAPTER FIFTEEN

Mule Man

So far as I know, Jack Davis was the last of the old-time mule men. He rode horses, but he loved and packed mules.

Tall, craggy, stooped from broken bones, he wore always a big black hat. Although I knew him for years, I never knew him young. He was so weathered that he always seemed older than his years. Born in 1898, he must have been in his forties when we met, but he was already Old Jack Davis.

He said that he had left his Arizona home when he was 14 or 15 because "They was lotsa kids, and the jackrabbits had got pretty hard to find." He never encountered any member of his family again.

Jack first saw Jackson's Hole when in 1919 he rode more than 75 miles from Mosquito Lake on Green River—75 miles to a Jackson rodeo. He stated that he and a buddy rode those 75 miles in one day but took two to go back.

He returned in 1938, trailing ten head of green mules from the Indian reservation south of Casa Grande, Arizona, to Jackson. The trip took him five months. At the end of it, he sold his mules, most of them to Slim Bassett, and signed on for the rest of the season with Slim on Lower Granite Creek Ranch.

In 1942 he went to work for Weenie Wilson and his Teton Valley Ranch. He stayed there for 28 years, the rest of his working life.

In his mid-seventies he could no longer handle the packing at Teton Valley Ranch, and Wilson was shutting down his operation and renting the camp to Rawhide Camps. The Triangle X bought the string of mules. To the surprise of Weenie and Mary Ellen Wilson, when the mules left, so did Old Jack. He went with his mules.

The Turner family welcomed Jack warmly and gave him a home for the rest of his life. He could no longer do the packing, but he repaired pack and riding equipment, and when they weren't in the mountains, he could talk to his mules.

Jack slept outdoors most of his life. He preferred sleeping under the stars. Weenie Wilson assigned him a cabin of his own on the Teton Valley Ranch; however, unless it was storming, Jack carried his cowboy bedroll outdoors at bedtime. A sleeping bag? Not by a long shot.

How to describe a cowboy bedroll—a sougan?

The essential is a canvas tarpaulin, about 7 by 14 feet. Three or four buckles have been sewed equally spaced along the outside of one seven-foot edge. Three or four rings—also on the outside—have been sewed, equally spaced top to bottom, about a third of the way in from the other edge.

To make his bedroll, the cowboy laid his cover on the ground (with the 14 feet as width, not length), the rings and snaps on the outside, with the snaps to his left. About a third of the way in from the right edge and about a foot from the bottom of his tarp, he laid down a kapok mattress or a quilt—or both. Around this he made his bed, sometimes with sheets as well as blankets. Next, he folded the entire bottom of his tarp to tuck in the foot of the bed. Finally, he folded the right-hand flap across his bed, followed by the left-hand flap, which resulted in the three or four snaps meeting the three or four rings. Snap into the rings, and he had a cozy bedroll—a sougan.

One of these bedrolls weighs at least ten times as much as a modern sleeping bag and is bulky to pack; however, once laid out on the ground, it is far more comfortable than is any sleeping bag. On cattle ranches with bunkhouses and roundup wagons, the old cowboy bedrolls are still seen. The cowboy spends a lot of time sleeping on the ground, so comfort is more important to him than weight; moreover, the bedrolls customarily travel by wagon. His bedroll is also the cowboy's bed in the bunkhouse. He merely removes a blanket or two. No matter where he sleeps, he is sure to wear his "long-handled" underwear—a custom that protects his bedroll from body dirt. As has been said, when on the home ranch, Jack Davis dragged his bedroll outdoors at night.

Old Jack chewed and smoked cigars. It seemed to me that he chewed them more often than he smoked them. Of course, he was often in areas where smoking would have been dangerous, but chewing was not. I suspect that in his later years he may have preferred cigars to chewing tobacco as a sign of affluence.

In Jack's vicinity, the first sounds of dawn were not a crowing rooster, but a deep and terrible clearing of lungs and spitting. He stammered a bit: "W-well, I kin s-see my h-hat, J-J-Johnny. G-guess it's t-t-ime to g-git up."

In 1940 Dad bought three little mules from Jack because he now had a year-round job that would no longer allow him time to pack up his mules and ride to Arizona. That's right: ride from Jackson to Tucson and Phoenix, where he replenished his cash by shoeing horses at the racetracks until it was time to start north again. Nor did Jack ride south by the shortest route. He visited along the way down and the way back. It took him a couple of months each way. He didn't need to lead his little mules; they followed his mare.

As you know, every mule had a mare for a mother, and every mule I ever saw would bond with a mare if given opportunity. That is why Jack always rode a mare. That is why his mule strings at Teton Valley Ranch were each pastured with one mare—and one mare only—away from other horses.

It was a great sight to see Jack's Teton Valley Ranch pack string set out. He packed them out in the open and without tying any up. Each mule wore its halter always. Attached to each halter was a leather blindfold. Jack or the other packer would walk up to a mule talking to it until he could take hold of its halter. Then he would slip the blindfold over the mule's eyes. After that, there was no worry about spooking the mule with some strange object brought by some kid.

The campers were not limited as to how much duffel they could carry. They could take anything and everything they wanted. There were enough mules to accommodate a small army.

When a mule was fully packed, the hitch snapped to be sure it was taut, and the end of the lash rope tucked in, the blindfold was slipped off his eyes, and he wandered about nibbling grass until all packing was finished. At that point, Jack would mount his mare, reach over, shake her bell, and call, "Ho-o-o-o-o-wah!" All the mules would raise their heads, point their long ears in the direction of the call, and crowd in behind the bell mare as Jack led her off. In fact, until a narrow trail caused them to fall into line, several mules would try actually to touch the mare as they moved along. The mare, incidentally, wore a pack, but carried nothing but bells and hobbles. To see a couple of dozen mules coming down a trail without a single lead rope was a memorable sight.

One of Jack's tales illustrated why he preferred mules. In 1922, he was living in Arizona just north of the Mexican Border. Prohibition was the law of the land. Jack made a good living for a while by riding south across the Border with a pack mule and filling its panniers with bottles of tequila.

On the return trip he would, from time to time, meet a member of the Border Patrol or an Arizona Ranger. They dearly wished to know what Jack was packing on his mule. They would, of course, stop and chat. Most mules are skittish. They may trust one man or two, but that doesn't mean that they trust all men. Jack's trusted nobody but Jack and not even him too much. When a stranger showed up, the little mule would drift off 50 to 100 yards and "just stand and snort" while Jack and the stranger palavered.

The patrolman would invariably eye the mule and wonder what was in that pack. Veiled questions elicited veiled answers. If the man, hoping to get a closer look, showed interest in the hitch or some other particular of pack or mule and moved closer to it, the snorty animal just moved away that much farther.

"T-them f-f-fellers s-s-sure w-wanted to s-see wh-what that m-mule was a-carryin'; b-but t-they'd a d-d-damn w-well h-had to shoot him to a d-done that; a-and they'd b-better be damn sure t-they was r-right!

"T-t-that m-mule an' me, w-we made a pretty good l-l-livin' out there f-fer several y-y-years. Th-th-that was in '22 and '23." And Jack would grin and spit his tobacco juice.

"Th-then they finally g-got after me there, and I-I had to go down to Mexico for awhile. Went to work for th-the Green Cattle Company, O-Old Bill Green's RO Outfit. At the-the t-time I was down there, t-they was a-runnin' f-f-forty thousand head of cattle in four divisions; t-ten th-th-th-thousand in each division. F-four ch-chuckwagons and f-fourteen riders with each. Th-th-that was a damn fine outfit. T-t-that was in '23."

Jack switched to catching wild horses, rough breaking them, and bringing them up to Teton Valley Ranch Camp, where he and the other wranglers would wrangle on them in the mornings and then turn them over, still winded, to the camp counselors. If one of the mustangs bucked a counselor off three times, the wrangler took him back for more hard riding. If not, the counselors rode them until they could turn them over to the kids.

On May 9, 1945, Jack and his woman (his term) were caught in a blizzard on the Utah desert. They set up their tent in the lee of a snow fence. "It-it s-stormed so hard, horses and mules were scared to death by the blizzard. W-w-we could hardly catch 'em to unpack 'em. One little h-half-coyote mule we never d-did catch. He w-wore that pack clear th-through the storm. Every l-last one of them, except for a few old ex-ex-experienced horses, just t-turned their backs to t-that storm and ran. Them o-others j-just snuggled up to that tent and that snow fence. H-Helen an' I, w-we burnt th-that f-fence in our stove to-to-to stay alive. In the m-mornin' I found two o-old mares fr-froze to death. Had to s-shoot one; the other was-was already dead. That was as r-rough an ex-experience as I-I-I ever did have.

"Had for-forty h-head when the s-storm hit. Afterwards, spent t-two weeks r-riding l-l-looking for them. F-finally, I just took my b-best s-saddle horse, a n-nosebag h-half f-full a grain; s-s-stuffed my pockets full a c-c-c-candy bars and rode out on that d-desert till I had 'em all b-but one. I n-never did f-f-f-find h-him.

"Wh-what I did f-find I h-herded back f-f-45 miles beween o-one o'clock and d-dark of one afternoon. That's pretty good time with a herd of horses. Every time I caught up with a broke one, I-I-I'd rope him and ch-change horses."

Jack's method of catching wild horses, as he described it, seems inappropriate for a man who loved horses and mules. Locating a herd on the desert, he would first build his trap, then take his rifle and kill the stallion. "I-I'd w-wait u-u-u-ntil th-the s-stud stood c-clear; then I-I-I'd dismount, l-lay d-down, g-g-git a g-good b-b-bead on h-him, and d-drop h-him." Confused, the mares, foals and yearlings could more easily be herded into his trap. Sometimes it was necessary to kill the lead mare, too.

One Spring when Jack camped outside Moab, Utah, he awoke in the morning to find that someone had taken the hobbles off his animals and had stolen his bell. "And I-I-I've never gone th-through Moab s-since then without s-s-stealing somethin'. Th-th-they'll never g-get that debt paid off. I'll probably never g-get the r-right one, but I'm gonna steal s-somethin' every time I go thru M-Moab."

Does Jack Davis sound like an immoral or amoral man? If so, consider this:

Until he became too old, Jack was in charge of Wendell "Weenie" Wilson's Currant Creek Ranch during the Winters, a property that included four townships outside Rock Springs, Wyoming. In the Fall, Jack and a few cowboys would drive the Teton Valley Ranch herd of around 150 horses and mules from the Hole to the ranch, roughly 200 miles. Other Jackson Hole ranchers who wished to could throw in their remudas for a fee. Jack would head out with 250 to 300 head. The only regret I have ever had about being a schoolteacher was that I could not make that drive just once. It would have felt like the Old West.

Snow does not remain long on the ground in the Rock Springs region; the horses and mules did not need to be fed; they could fend for themselves all Winter. All Jack needed to do was to keep his eye on the lot, doctoring any who might need it from time to time.

Early one February, Weenie, wintering in Southern California, was surprised to see in his mailbox an envelope with penciled address in Jack's scrawl. Inside the envelope was Wilson's check for Davis's January wages and this scribbled note: "Ain't done nothin'; ain't earned nothin'."

Jacks repeated advice was, "D-d-don't t-take n-n-no gift what eats."

Jack was 76 years old when he died; his memorial service took place on the bank of Snake River opposite the Triangle X Ranch, where Jack had spent his last years. The service was just right and is unforgettable. Some wildflowers and one candle on a big cottonwood log, with the sound of the river for organ music. A sizable group assembled there to pay their respects not only to Jack Davis, Mule Man, but to a vanishing American, a way of life, a man of great independence, a man of absolute integrity when judged by his own criteria of "An eye for an eye, a tooth for a tooth." A Mule Man.

His former employers spoke of his skills and his reliability. Friends illustrated his ingenuity and independence. The sun set behind the Grand Teton, and we mourners departed remembering a man of mountain and desert whose sun had just set.

Lucky those generations of Teton Valley Ranch Camp boys and girls who had the great fortune of going pack tripping with Old Jack Davis. One of those fortunate boys was our elder son, John, who as a boy of 12 spent a Summer as close as he could get to Jack.

"W-w-well, J-John, I-I kin s-see mah h-hat. T-time t-to get up."

Would that he could.

CHAPTER SIXTEEN

Dick Winger, Agent

Anyone who did not know better might have sized him up as a dude. He usually wore a tweed sports jacket, a tie, and rimless spectacles, rarely wore jeans, and was never dirty. Dick haled from Iowa; and he and Marta Winger arrived in Jackson's Hole in 1913 the hard way, as you will hear. In his years in Jackson's Hole he wore several hats: editor, publisher, reporter, rancher, agent for the Snake River Land Company, and the man who incorporated the Town of Jackson.

The story of Winger's arrival in the Hole, when I heard it from him, radically altered my view of him.

A bridegroom, he reached Jackson without a bride

On February 17, 1913, Dick and Marta Winger were wed. Precisely a week later, the groom and his brother-in-law, George Kelly, left their brides in order to locate and see their homestead in Jackson's Hole.

Neither had ever seen the Valley.

Dick had heard of the beauty of Jackson's Hole and that there was land to be homesteaded there. One day in 1912 had found him in Kemmerer, Wyoming, the County Seat of Lincoln County, examining maps and descriptions of parcels available. He filed on one "simply from the description." Teton County, which nowadays reaches north to Madison Junction, did not exist in 1912. Jackson's Hole was part of Lincoln County until 1921.

It is not clear from his account as taped by Josephine Fabian in 1957 whether or not George Kelly was part of that initial action. The homestead is always referred to as "our homestead" or "the homestead" without clarification. Did the Kellys share ownership in it? Unlikely. Had they a contiguous parcel? It does not seem so when one hears that there was only one set of improvements. Did the Wingers own the land and the Kellys merely help them establish it? That seems to have been the situation.

Be that as it may, one week to the day after marrying Marta, the bridegroom and his brother-in-law hauled goods and chattels to the railroad and loaded them into an "immigrant car" bound for Driggs, Idaho, the end of the line. An immigrant car was a boxcar assigned to an immigrant family for transportation of family and goods, including livestock. Strictly speaking George and Dick were not immigrants, although they were, indeed, immigrating to Jackson's Hole.

Into one end of their car Dick and George loaded farm machinery, furniture, feed, and "five or six head of cattle." In the other end they set their kitchen range and constructed bunks of sorts. To keep from freezing, they kept a fire going in their range with coal cadged from the tender of the steam engine. That way they managed to survive a Rocky Mountain Winter. February is midwinter in those parts, and boxcars are neither insulated nor draft-proof.

After ten days in their immigrant car, they unloaded in Driggs on March 7, 1913. What a relief it must have been to humans and livestock to get out of that car!

In Driggs, Dick and George beheld a sight they had never before seen: men from Jackson's Hole shipping elk to zoos throughout the nation. Those men had constructed boxes on their sleighs, each sufficiently large to contain one elk. Trapping or roping elk which were feeding from their haystacks was no problem; however, the sleigh rides over Teton Pass must have presented several. Quite a difference from today's helicopter rides!

Always one to recognize an opportunity in whatever guise, Winger arranged with the freighters to freight his household and farm goods over Teton Pass as they went home with their empty elk stalls.

That done, Winger and Kelly began a ten-mile walk to Victor, herding

Collection of the Jackson Hole Historical Society and Museum.

Freighting the Pass, c. 1920s.

their cattle in front of them. Progress must have been slow, since after ten days in that immigrant car, those cattle would have tried to stop every time they saw a blade of grass, no matter how dead it might be. Nonetheless, before dark, men and beasts made it to Victor, where they passed the night. The following morning, March 10, they "walked over the Pass to Wilson, where we spent the night in the old Wilson Hotel. The snow was quite deep; there was nothing but a sleigh road in those days."

What was a sleigh road? It was a packed track, "sometimes as high as 25 feet above the earth—just packed snow and ice." No snowplows in those days—only that packed track.

It must have been some hike for men and cattle, yet it is so simply understated by Winger: "Walked over the Pass to Wilson, where we spent the night in the old Wilson Hotel."

The following morning, men and beasts walked on to Jackson and four miles farther east to the cabin of Bishop James I. May, whom they had met in Driggs and who had offered the use of his cabin, "You can't even find those homesteads of yours because the snow's so deep." Encouraging news, indeed! He had added that he had a small root cellar in which was a good supply of potatoes. "Help yourselves to them if they aren't frozen." They were, but they did.

"It was nearly two months there before we could get up to the homestead, where we started a barn outa rough boards and set up a couple of tents. I think that's when I wrote to Mart and told her that the homestead was all ready for her. I was anxious for her to come out. They didn't know

Collection of the Jackson Hole Historical Society and Museum.

The Summit Roadhouse, c. 1920s.

any better, and they came.

"We were to meet them in Driggs on the 9th of May. We went from here to the foot of the mountain in a wagon. Had to ford Snake River because we couldn't track the ferryman. We wired the wagon box down. and got across somehow. Then we changed to a sleigh. Got over the Hill and met the train in Driggs the next afternoon. [No mention of the joys of reunion.] After the train came in, we drove back to Victor and spent the night there in sort of a cottage. The only room available was occupied by a traveling veterinarian, who moved out and let the wives sleep in his room, while we men slept in the wagon.

"The next morning we left at 5:00 and started for the Pass. After about a mile, we met a man named Nate Stevens, who had a very fine snow team. He hooked on in front of our team and agreed to take us to the top. This was the 10th of May, and the snow was beginning to break up and was quite soft. We were breaking through all day. No dugway then; you just came straight up the canyon and down the other one. We had one young horse who was inexperienced and kept falling through. The road was only wide enough for one sleigh or wagon; so we couldn't go around him when he'd fall. We'd just tie the doubletree up and go right on over him. It didn't hurt him any. We'd drive on up 300 or 400 yards to a wide spot, and then go back and get him. He'd be lying right where we left him. We'd get him up, bring him up, and hook him up again. It took us 12 hours to get to the top of the mountain. That was as far as Nate Stevens was going; so he unhooked his team and started back down home; and we started down this side.

"We'd only gone a few rods till we fell in a hole somebody else had made. It was just impossible for our horses in the condition they were in to get out and to pull the sleigh out; so we just unhooked them and turned them loose.

"We took a suitcase and walked down to a cabin about where Betty Woolsey's place is now, where Frank Crandall had a roadhouse. We spent the night there."

"By the next morning the team had come on down. There was no place else for them to go. It had frozen a little during the night; so we [presumably Dick and George, without the women] went back up and using the team dragged the sleigh out of the hole by stages with a logging chain, then hooked up and come on down and went as far as Ma Reed's [hotel in Jackson] that night.

"'Dick, how will we ever get out of here?' demanded Marta. 'I just don't know,' I replied.

"It was some years before we left [for a visit]. It was four years before we ever heard a train whistle.

"After three or four days at Ma Reed's we took 'em on up and showed them those two tents and the one end of the barn finished: Home Sweet Home.

"We'd set up the stove in that one end of the barn, where we had the boards up, but hadn't had time to bat them yet. The boards were green, and they shrank until there were two-inch gaps between them. The next morning when the girls got up to get breakfast, it snowed a regular blizzard and it blew right through those cracks. They were just about fed up."

"Stayed at the homestead three months until we decided we were city people. One day Bill Kelly, for whom the town of Kelly was named, rode up and wanted to know if I could run the *Jackson's Hole Courier*. The editor had got into a jackpot and had to leave the country, and the homesteaders didn't want it to die, not only for the news but, more important, for the legal notices. I said I guessed I could run a paper as well as I could ranch. I'd been raised around a newspaper office.

"We just had $24 to our names when we went to town, and Marta needed a new pair of shoes. The bottoms of her shoes were wearin' out, an' the soles of her feet were rubbin' the ground. I bought her a pair at Deloney's store."

Pap Deloney wanted to give him the shoes on credit against future advertising in the *Courier*, but Dick wouldn't do it. "No, sir. I'll pay cash, and I'll expect you to pay cash for advertising.

"Got out our first issue on August 28, 1913. I assumed the mortgage from Bill Crawford for $400 at 12 percent interest and took the place over and ran the paper for six years. A man named Rodebeck had started it in 1909. There were four editors before me."

The Valley's first "newspaper" of record was John Kelly, brother of that same Bill Kelly who asked Dick to take over the *Courier*. John was in actual fact a real courier, riding from ranch to ranch from Jackson Lake to the Hoback spreading the news, both local and "outside." Perhaps that was where Rodebeck obtained inspiration to name his newspaper the *Jackson's Hole Courier*.

John Kelly was a cattle buyer, who rode over from Idaho Falls in the Fall to buy. That was no mean ride, probably more than 300 miles by the time he reached home again. Little and plump, and with a nose for pies, Kelly rode from ranch to ranch on Goldie, a fat little mare, usually managing to arrive at lunchtime or just as the housewife took a fresh pie or loaf of bread from her oven. The homesteader and wife felt the trade to be a good one: lunch or a sizeable hunk of pie or bread in exchange for the news. Those early homesteaders were pretty isolated and were as hungry for news as Kelly was for pie.

Kelly ate so much pie over the years that climbing up on Goldie became a problem. From then on, he rode with a mounting block tied to his saddle horn. The mounting block served a double purpose, for its thumping against the mare's shoulder kept her from dawdling, and John Kelly didn't have to kick her along.

The Valley's newspapers in order to date have been:

John Kelly	
The *Jackson's Hole Courier*	1909-1961
The *Grand Teton*	1931-1934
The *Jackson Hole Guide*	1952 to present
The *Jackson Hole News*	1970 to present
The *Jackson Hole Daily*	1978 to present
The *Jackson Hole Guide Daily*	c. 1980s to present

So with the acquisition of the *Courier,* the Wingers became townsfolk. Marta recounts, "We stayed at Ma Reed's for a couple of weeks. The Episcopalian minister [Rev. Seth Caulfield Hawley] boarded there, too; but his rectory had just been built; and he offered us room and board if we would take care of him. 'If you will come and live with me, you may have the Rectory to live in.' 'If you don't mind someone cooking for you who never cooked a meal in her life, we'd be glad to take you up on that proposition.' He said, 'That's all right by me. I'd much rather have companionship than food.'"

On that priceless tape recorded by Josephine Fabian and preserved by the Historical Society, is also the account of incorporating the town:

"In 1914 the citizens wanted to incorporate the town so that they could levy a licensing fee on the saloon. Until incorporation, any fees exacted went to the County Seat in Kemmerer.

State law required a population of 150 souls before a town could incorporate. Stretch lines as they might and did, they could find only 149; so Dick Winger, as a smooth talker, was sent to call on a local lady who was pregnant. He asked her to name her unborn baby, selecting a name that could be either masculine or feminine. Dick added the name to the list and went ahead with incorporation. Unfortunately, in 1957 Dick declared, "I'm sorry. I just can't remember that baby's name."

Dick and Marta Winger had a very tall son, older than I, and a very lovely daughter, Louise, my age. As a teenager, I was in and out of the Winger house some. I thought of Louise's parents then as just a successful Jackson businessman and his wife. I wish I had known their story then. I might have been even more interested in the parents than I was in their charming daughter.

CHAPTER SEVENTEEN

My Dad

I believe Dad had the best disposition I have ever encountered. He was no pushover; he was courageous; he was the most truly courteous man I have known; and his temperament was extraordinarily even.

Although no one who knew him as an adult would have guessed it, when Dad was a 13-year-old New York City kid, he was frail. His hero was Theodore Roosevelt, who stoutly maintained that the Wild West had metamorphosed him from a puny New York City kid into a rugged he-man. Dad desperately wanted to be a rugged he-man. He begged the grandfather I never knew to take him West.

His father either had not the time or had not the inclination; but he did have a friend with a boy Dad's age, a friend whom he propositioned with something like the following:

"If you will take the two boys out to Yellowstone Park, I will foot the bills."

He did, and he did.

In 1898, the man and the two boys toured the Park by stagecoach. You may recall from Chapter Four that Dad first saw the Tetons from a rise in Yellowstone Park.

You have read of the handshake with Eliza Seaton that sealed the purchase of her property by Dad in 1925. He was 39 years old at the time. As agreed, we all arrived the following Summer. Records show that the deed was recorded in the Lincoln County Court House in Kemmerer on December 8, 1926.

Coming west from Greenwich, Connecticut, we arrived in Victor, Idaho, on the railroad car shunted off the train to West Yellowstone; but we were met by the Amoss family, friends who were leaving the day we arrived and who had driven to Victor a Chevrolet touring car that Dad had bought from the Chevy dealer while still in the East. Jack Neal was there, too, in an identical Chevy touring car. On the recommendation of Harry Harrison, by mail Dad had hired Jack and Bernice to teach us how things were done in the West.

Duffel bags were piled on a baggage wagon beside the Victor depot. Dad climbed up on the wagon to throw ours down. The duffels under him rolled; he fell to the platform; his right forearm snapped. Fortunately, the train had not yet departed. Even more fortunately, Harold Amoss was a doctor, indeed, our family doctor from Greenwich. "Uncle Harold" splinted and wrapped Dad's arm.

Jack Neal, Coulter, Gwyn, and Mother must have had the duffel bags sorted out by then and piled into the second car. I was seven and of no help to anyone. Someone must have arranged to have our trunks freighted "over the hill" (Teton Pass). There must have been trunks. After all, we were moving into a new family home; so there must have been trunks of blankets, sheets, bedspreads, towels—Mother never traveled light. I suppose pots and pans and some china and tableware would have been ordered from a mail-order house, for although those things could be obtained in Jackson, we needed some utensils for the first day or two.

At any rate, finally Coulter got into the car with Jack Neal and the luggage while the rest of us piled into the other. Mother and Dad put the car in gear, and we started for the Pass. "Mother and Dad put the car in gear" because Dad insisted upon driving, even though he had only one useful arm; so Mother had to shift gears when he threw the clutch. Of course, Mother should have driven; she was a fine driver, but this whole western experience was his idea, and he wanted to show it to her.

The road across the Pass was not an engineered grade at that time. In fact, it was little more than a wagon track. There were three or four wide places on the west side and a similar number on the east, where it was safe for two vehicles to pass, two cars, two wagons, or a car and a wagon. Everyone kept a lookout for an approaching vehicle. It was the duty of the downhill driver to stop in the first turnout he came to and wait for the uphill driver to pass him. Uphill always had the right of way. There was a big figure-8 switchback on the western side of the summit, and there were eight switchbacks on the eastern slope.

I recall in the old days crossing the Pass when the road was muddy. Dad had us passengers stand on the running board on the uphill side to give those wheels better traction, and just in case . . . The pitch of today's highway over the Pass is 10 percent. I cannot guess what it must have been on that old road—15 percent?

It was 1938 before I heard of a motor vehicle crossing Teton Pass without boiling over, and that was a 1938 Dodge pickup.

I don't recall that we met another vehicle of any sort that July day in 1926, but we may have. Crossing the Pass driving one-handed before power steering and "neckers' knobs" was no mean feat.

I fought a war. I was awarded a couple of medals, yet the most courageous thing I have ever done in my life was to come with my family to Wyoming that Summer of 1926. My brother, Coulter, was almost nine years older than I; and he had delighted in telling me horror stories of how wild the Wild West would be. I suppose he had read tales of troikas and Siberian wolves. At any rate, I can still see the mental image I had then:

We would get off the train in some little town in the middle of the prairie and pile into an open car, which would then speed across the wide open spaces until and after the wolves saw us. Those wolves would pursue us with slavering jaws. They could outrun the car. As they closed in on us, someone would shoot the lead wolf. The rest of the pack would stop to devour him, and we would gain a little distance before the cycle repeated itself. I really believed that. It's terrible what a kid can do to a younger kid. Why didn't I tell Mother or Dad, who would have straightened things out? I don't know. Kids sometimes keep things to themselves when they shouldn't.

So I was terrified to come West. Of course, I was even more terrified by the thought of staying home alone; so I came. Not that I would have had any choice, but I felt it was my decision.

On that first trip over Teton Pass, I kept a sharp lookout for wolves.

We arrived at "our ranch" to a warm greeting from Bernice Neal and Stub, Jack Neal's beautifully trained stock dog. There were two homestead cabins; one consisted of two rooms and a loft; the other was a sod-roofed shop with dirt floor. In addition, the Neals had erected frame tents. We moved in. I was put into one of those tents to sleep, which was hardly comforting. Couldn't a wolf break right through the canvas? I wished fervently to be upstairs in the loft.

I have no recollection of that first supper which Bernice had prepared; it was probably delicious. I was looking for wolves.

At home we had a German Shepherd and cocker spaniels; so I wasn't afraid of Stub. Within a few minutes I considered him an ally in my search—and in any confrontation to come. That night, every night for a week, and sporadically for a year or two, there was such a confrontation; and Stub did not help me.

In my dream, I lay down at the edge of a mountain stream to drink. Pausing for a breath, I looked up. There, right across from me, perhaps 15 feet away, was a huge wolf also drinking. He never made a move toward me, but both his gleaming yellow-brown eyes were unwaveringly on me as his pink tongue lapped. At that point, I always woke up.

The first morning on the ranch dawned bright and sunny. Stepping outdoors to look around, Dad noticed a fresh bear print on the trunk of an aspen. "This is the Bear Paw Ranch," he declared. And that is how the Seaton homestead acquired its new name. The area is still known as Bear Paw Meadow.

I come by my love of gadgets naturally. Dad loved them. In the mid-thirties, when I was a teenager and about the time that the Bear Paw had become a dude ranch, he brought back from a trip East something new, something so taken for granted nowadays that it is difficult to imagine that they were ever new: reflectors. They are ubiquitous today in all developed nations as well as in many Third World nations; but none of us on the Bear Paw had ever seen or heard of a reflector.

Dad had brought a handful of one-inch, yellow-green reflectors. He enlisted Jack Neal as fellow conspirator, and they screwed a pair of reflectors a couple of inches apart about three feet above the ground into the trunk of a large aspen tree in the vicinity of the garbage cans.

In those days if a bear was troublesome, a rancher just shot and ate it. Bear meat is delicious.

That night after the kitchen gals had finished up, turned off the lights, and left, several of us were sitting around the main cabin reading or chatting when Jack Neal came quietly into the room, walked to the rifle rack left of the fireplace, grabbed five rounds of ammunition from a box, took down a rifle and began loading it.

"What's up, Jack?" inquired Dad, the straight man.

"That old bear that's been eating the garbage has got to where she just tears everything up, and I'm goin' to kill 'er."

"Jack Huyler, let's go with him."

Jack Neal finished loading the rifle; Dad picked up a flashlight; and the three of us tiptoed quietly in total darkness into and through the kitchen and out onto the back stoop. Just beyond the stoop was a noisy irrigation ditch, over which was a plank bridge. On the bridge, the rifleman stopped. Dad whispered to him, "Jack Neal, you've shot lots of bears. Let Jack Huyler shoot this one."

You don't stand and argue in the dark with a bear nearby. Jack handed me the rifle. As I checked the safety. Dad whispered, "I'll switch on my light and swing it left to right. When you see the bear's eyes in the beam, let him have it. Ready?"

I released the safety. "Yes."

Dad turned on his light and swung the beam left to right. I saw the eyes and fired. They didn't even blink. I had emptied the rifle before I could hear Dad and Jack laughing. They showed me the reflectors.

Over the years until the Bear Paw was sold, that ruse was repeated many times—always successfully.

The secret of its invariable success was that either Jack Neal or I would come in, go straight to the gun rack and begin loading without comment. Then Dad, always the straight man of this particular prank, would look up from his book and come in with his "What's up, Jack?" The pattern was identical. It never failed. We tricked greenhorn hunters and experts. The difference between the two was the number of shots fired.

Powder River Jack Lee had ridden and sung cowboy songs in Buffalo Bill's Wild West Show. By the nineteen-twenties and thirties he made his living as a cowboy singer. He had a truly fine baritone and a fund of songs. We would not know that he was coming until—shortly before lunchtime—we would hear his voice over the PA system that he had mounted on his car. "Howdy, friends and neighbors! Here come Powder River Jack and Pretty Kitty Lee." Always it was before lunch, and always Dad and Mother invited them to join us.

Photo by Harrison R. Crandall. Collection of the Huyler Family.

Powder River Jack Lee on C. D. Huyler's Silver King, c. 1940.

On a dude ranch two more for lunch were no problem. They would spend the afternoon on the ranch visiting with family and guests and would sing after supper for a stipend.

They arrived one year shortly after Dad had introduced us to reflectors; so we tried the bear trick on him. We set it up exactly the same way: Jack Neal got the rifle; we tiptoed through the dark kitchen and out onto the plank across the babbling irrigation ditch. A variation on the same pitch, "Jack Neal, I'll bet it's been a long time since Powder River has a shot a bear. Let him kill her." The switch of the rifle to Powder River; then the comment about the bear's eyes in the beam of Dad's flashlight.

The snow-haired old man fired one shot. When the eyes didn't move, he knew something was amiss. The laugh was on us. A tenderfoot would have emptied the rifle.

Dad was wonderful with people. You will recall his handling of the Old Man in Chapter One and of Mrs. Seaton in Chapter Four. Generally, he respected other people's standards. One time he slipped. There were three long tables in the Bear Paw dining room. Two places had been added to Mother and Dad's table. Kitty was seated at Dad's right hand; Powder River at Mother's. Lamb chops were the entrée. When the platter came to him, Powder River inquired of Mother, "Margaret, is this sheep?"

"Yes, Powder River," she replied, "it is."

"I hope you and Coulter will pardon me, but I don't eat sheep."

"Of course."

The devil must have been prodding Dad, for he turned to the waitress. "Marge, are any of those bear chops left from the other evening?"

Marguerite was no dummy; she caught on immediately. "I believe so, Mr. Huyler."

"Then ask Alice to throw a couple on for Powder River, please."

In the kitchen Alice Johnson took two shoulder lamb chops from Marge's platter, peppered them beyond flavor, and threw them onto the stove.

Powder River ate them without complaint; however, I regretted Dad's atypical guile. Was Powder River fooled, or was he just unwilling to embarrass his friend Coulter Huyler by calling him on his skullduggery? I have often wondered. Bear meat, like pork, is rich and greasy. Lamb is not. Powder River Jack, as a good old-time cowboy, might never have eaten lamb; but he had surely eaten bear more than once.

Powder River Jack and Pretty Kitty Lee were quite a pair! They were clearly lovers still. Time had not dimmed their affection. Many years before we met them, Jack had cowboyed a trail herd north from Texas to the railroad. Being a youngster, he was riding drag, the dustiest of all dusty trail jobs. Of course, he wore his bandanna over his mouth and nose, bandit style. That's why cowboys wore bandannas; they were dust filters.

Off to the side on the horizon one day, Jack spotted a homestead. Lifting his cowpony into a lope, he rode to it. A pretty lass came out to meet him. He asked for a drink of water. She drew it from the well and handed him a full dipper. The water was cool and delicious, and she was very pretty. He thanked her and added, "Ma'am, when I finish this cattle drive, I'm gonna come back here and marry you."

Although he galloped back to the herd, Jack had been smitten. When he drew his wages at the end of the line, he kept his promise to the pretty young girl who had drawn the water for him: He rode back to the homestead, found a job on a nearby spread, and successfully courted Kitty, who soon became Pretty Kitty Lee.

Between 1867, when the first trail herd was shipped out of Abilene, and 1895, Armour's Livestock Bureau reported an astounding 98,350,000 cattle and 10,300,000 horses railroaded east after being herded north from Texas. They sold for $243,000,000. My calculator tells me that comes to $2.47 per head.

One of God's few mistakes is that the older we get, the homelier we become. With all due respect, He should have made us so that as we grow old and lose our physical prowess, to compensate for that loss, we become ever more attractive until we die beautiful.

I'm sure that Kitty Lee was once beautiful, but no trace of that beauty remained except in her spirit—and in their devotion to each other. She had totally lost her singing voice, if, indeed, she ever had one; but as Powder River (we all called him Powder River) sang, she would from time to time squeak out a high pitched "Yippee!" Those interjections he never ignored, but, continuing to strum the guitar that President Herbert Hoover had given him, would stop his singing and remark to the gathering, "There's lots of kick left in Kitty!" Always the same remark, always with obvious love.

Kitty died early in the war years. As I heard it, soon thereafter Powder River Jack was driving too fast, as was his wont, a road in the Pennsylvania hills. He crested a hill while driving the center line and was sent instantly to the Happy Hunting Grounds by an 18-wheeler, whose driver was unhurt. Not a bad end for the last of Buffalo Bill's riders. He "died with his boots on," of that you may rest assured.

Dad introduced the first registered Kentucky Thoroughbred stallion to Jackson's Hole in 1929 from Front Royal, Virginia. Old-timers in Jackson's Hole predicted that the horse would "Winter kill."

Dad had been a horseman all his life. He rode beautifully. He qualified as a horseman by his own definition: "A horseman is someone who improves every horse he rides."

His childhood had been lived, of course, in "the horse and buggy days." Even though he lived in New York City, as a child he had a pony. He told of riding uptown on Fifth Avenue to Central Park. At 57th Street he could lift his pony into a canter because at that point Fifth Avenue became dirt; but he had to watch out for chickens and pigs.

Later, before coming West, he played polo and was good enough to earn a national handicap. He knew and loved good horseflesh; and having bought land in Wyoming, decided to raise good horses. The Lower Ranch, the Rocking H, would be ideal. First he needed broodmares; then a stallion. Meanwhile, he and Jack Neal were busy getting more sagebrush converted into hay fields and pasture; and Mel Annis was building our barn with a stallion's box stall and convertible stalls for broodmares.

Dad designed each of those box stalls so that when its door and the door of the opposite stall were swung open, each latched into the opposite stall, thereby creating a triple stall for mare and foal.

In 1928 he grubstaked Ed Nichols, who had located a herd of wild horses in Montana. One of the most dramatic days of my life was spent on the top rail of one of our new corrals behind our new barn as Dad and Ed split the herd. I was pretty small; I am not sure how many horses were in the big corral. I think about a hundred: stallion, mares, foals, yearlings. I know that Dad came out of the grubstake with about 40 mares plus their foals. Two mounted cowboys with ropes were in with the herd. Ed was on the fence with us.

As grubstaker, Dad had first choice. To everyone's surprise his first choice was the big buckskin stallion, who was milling about snorting, unable to figure out what was happening to him and his brood. We all knew about the thoroughbred stallion scheduled to arrive the following Spring from Virginia. Why the big buckskin? What we did not know was that Dad already envisioned a certain handsome buckskin gelding as his personal saddle horse.

Someone opened the gate to the side corral that was designated for Dad's selections; and the two cowboys cut the stallion into it before he realized what was happening.

Then Ed chose a long yearling, which the cowboys cut into his corral.

And so it went: Dad chose one, which joined the buckskin. Ed chose one. Dad another; then Ed until all were in the side corrals and only the two mounted cowboys were left in the big corral.

There had been little conflict in the division of that herd, for Ed wanted the long yearlings and the "canners," while Dad wanted the mares young enough to be good broodmares for the stallion to come.

Ed was a highly regarded "bronc stomper." Dad turned to him, "Ed, how about putting a first ride on that buckskin stallion for me?"

"Why sure"; and Ed went to get his saddle, which he stacked on its nose, with his saddle blanket on top, in the main corral next to the snubbing post. Ed stood next to it holding a hackamore. "Okay. Cut that stud in here."

It was a good thing that Ed was a small man and that he was quick, for when that stallion was cut into that corral away from his harem, he felt he had been abused, and he was looking for trouble. Spotting Ed, he pinned back his ears and went for him. Ed skinned out through the rails barely ahead of those teeth. Seeing nobody he could reach since we had quickly evacuated our seats on the top rail, the big stallion circled the corral once before spotting Ed's saddle. With bared teeth he dived at it, picking it up by the horn and shaking it until the stirrups stood out straight. That was a heavy bull moose saddle. It weighed 44 pounds. I know because in due course it became mine. I rode it for years until, during World War II, it, my chaps, Garcia bit, and spurs disappeared.

Had I been Ed that would have been the end of it until that stallion had been gelded; Ed, however, was not flustered. He instructed the two mounted cowboys to rope the stud, and choke him down. That they did, getting their loops on him at the same time and stretching him out between them. When the horse was standing there spraddle-legged fighting for breath, Ed moved up, slipped hackamore and blindfold on him, and told the boys to ease off. Recovering his breath a bit, the big buckskin struck out a time or two, but since he could not see, hit nothing. Then he stood confused in his darkness as Ed saddled him and eased aboard. Taking a deep seat with feet shoved to the heels into his oxbow stirrups, Ed leaned forward and lifted the blindfold. The horse did his best to unseat him, but the Main Event was less spectacular than the Preliminary Bout.

Ed rode him, and it's a good thing that he did, because we learned later that had he been thrown, he would probably have been killed. "Mustang" is derived from the Spanish word "mesteña" meaning "wild one." Teton certainly was that!

The sixteen-hand buckskin, whom Dad named Teton, was gelded and trained. For years he was Dad's top saddle horse. He was not mean, but he did have one disconcerting habit: he would strike anything that fell past his shoulders. I rode him many times in his later years, and it was fun to demonstrate this trait to others. If I dropped my bandanna as I rode along, he would nail it to the ground with the nearest front hoof. Why?

He had a series of black scars on his withers, longer on the near side than on the off. Before being brought to Jackson's Hole, he had lived in mountain lion country. Jack Neal and Dad surmised that at one time a lion had sprung on him from a boulder or a tree, something sufficiently high that he had landed on Teton's withers, digging in with his claws. Clearly, the stallion had shaken him off, but he had left those scars as his signature. It was probably as a result of that trauma that the stallion struck anything which came down past those withers. He became a gentle horse, but he never got over that habit. Had Ed been thrown on that first ride, one of those hooves would have nailed him to the ground with 1,200 pounds of muscle and fury behind it.

As a matter of fact, no one ever fell off Teton. Knowing his reflex and his lightning speed at executing it, we made sure of that.

Teton lived a long and useful life. He was a good horse in every sense of the word; but I never walked up to him in a corral—and I caught him many times to saddle for Dad—without feeling insignificant. He never stood sideways nor with his rump to anyone approaching him. He faced me; and although he never attempted to get away, he drew himself up to his full height and looked down at me. As he grew taller, I shrank.

Teton and Dad were trail and pack trip companions for several years. They got along well except for one set difference of opinion: Dad loved automobiles; Teton abhorred them. Why were cars so abhorrent to Teton? He would not admit that he was afraid of anything. He rarely shied; but he detested horseless buggies. Dad had frequent need to ride up to cars: to welcome arriving guests, or to respond to strangers' requests for directions. Those requirements of Dad's inevitably led to showdowns with Teton.

Dad loved to blaze trails and to trim the branches on them that would hit riders. For that purpose he carried a hatchet in a scabbard. I can hear now in memory the sound of a tom-tom. The tom-tom was Teton's ribs reverberating to the flat of the hatchet as Dad forced him to approach an automobile. Would I might see and hear them today.

Five years later, in 1933, Ed Nichols met an untimely and violent death in our barn, shot by Vick Henrie. The plea was temporary insanity; the cause was cabin fever.

Margaret and I look forward to Winters in Jackson Hole nowadays; we are glad when the tourists have gone and we see our friends on the streets of town; however, on a ranch Winters were not much fun prior to World War II. Television had not been invented; the R.E.A. (Rural Electrification Administration) had not reached the ranches with rural electricity; there were few radios, no four-wheel drives, no good snowplows, no mail delivery, and there was no lightweight Winter clothing. People wore sheepskin coats, which sometimes seemed to weigh as much as a sheep. Neighbors were far between. The men left their cabins shortly after daybreak to feed the livestock, and chores kept them out until dark except for a short break for lunch. Children of school age had to be boarded in town. When telephone lines came to connect the ranches to each other and to town, they were a godsend not only for emergencies, but for chatting.

We had a dog team, which was used to fetch mail and supplies from Wilson, a 17-mile round trip. Only in the movies do dog mushers stand on the runners doing nothing more than shouting, "Mush!" and "Gee!" and "Haw!" In actuality, in order to lighten the load and ease the dogs, the musher runs behind the sled, holding onto the handlebars to keep from losing it and jumping onto the runners to catch his breath or to ride a downhill. There is no significant slope between the Rocking H and Wilson. The women stayed on the ranch while a man took the team to get the supplies.

A couple of times each Winter when they could stand the solitude no longer, and it seemed as if something would snap if they did not get a change,

Collection of the Jackson Hole Historical Society and Museum.

Winter feeding, c. 1930s.

ranch people went to town. The men would hitch two teams to a big sleigh—a hay rack upon which they had erected a shelter—and would drive the women and children to Jackson. In the earliest days of our ranch, the shelter was a tent; later it was a small Quonset hut. The important thing was that whichever it might be, it contained a stove and a supply of stove wood.

Arriving in Jackson, the couples would leave the kids with friends who had kids the same ages; then they would dance and visit and drink for 48 hours or so. Dancing seemed to be most important as it expended pent-up frustrations. They would dance, visit, and drink until exhausted physically and emotionally.

Meanwhile the ranch kids were enjoying friends and such sports as sledding on Bean's Hill. Most readers of this book have driven up and down Bean's Hill without being aware of its existence. It is the little hill on Pearl Street running downhill from King Street to Willow Street. In Winter, a cable was stretched across that little hill to prevent cars and sleighs from using it, thereby making it safe for kids with sleds or skis. "It was a terrific playground for the younger children," recalls Barbara Vandeburg. The next time you drive up or down that incline, bless Bean's Hill and the happy children who played on it "in the good old days."

For bigger kids and young adults, when there was moonlight, there were nighttime sledding parties on Teton Pass. A large pot of chili at the summit warmed bodies and spirits before the hair-raising descents down the old road, in and out of the shadows and moonwashed stretches—almost pitch black to almost bright as day. What fun! Now *there* was a sledding hill to be reckoned with!

Collection of the Jackson Hole Historical Society and Museum.

"Mush!—I said, Mush!" n.d.

For some years there was even a rope ski tow on Teton Pass from Thanksgiving until Christmas, by which time there was usually enough snow on the more accessible Kelly's Hill.

Kelly's Hill, or Kelly's Bench, gradually made way for the ski area now labeled Snow King. First, trees were felled, stumps pulled and burned so that a rope tow could be installed by a committee of local citizens headed by Doctor Don MacLeod. Next, more trees were removed to make a good run all the way from the top, and to permit Neil Rafferty to open and operate a single-chair lift on the site of the current double chair lift. The name was changed to Snow King as the result of a naming contest in the 1930s.

Although most ranch children would have preferred to stay in town, where there were playmates and Bean's Hill, on the ranches, chores awaited the grownups. The teams must be harnessed and hooked to the sleigh; the kids, if any, must be collected. "See you in the Spring!" would be said; the teams must be driven through town until they were on familiar roads. Then the people could sleep in the shelter near the warm stove while the horses took them home. Whenever the teams stopped, there was something to be coped with—perhaps a gate to be opened, a snowdrift so deep it discouraged the lead team, or a fallen tree to be removed. Reaching home there were hungry cattle and horses to be fed and an aching milk cow to be relieved before they could tumble into bed and begin the cycle over again.

Do you remember Winnie, the woman who left her baby to go to the

Collection of the Huyler Family.

Bert, sire of our work horses, c. 1940.

Jenny Lake Dance Hall with the Indian? She brought about the death of Ed Nichols. She and her second husband, Vick Henrie, spent the Winter on the Rocking H in the same cabin with Ed and his wife, Marguerite of the bear meat story. Winnie was bored. Intending nothing serious, she decided that she would liven things up a bit by telling Vick that Ed had made a pass at her. Anyone who knew them knew how devoted Ed was to his beautiful Marge—and she was beautiful—and Winnie was well aware of her husband's hot temper; but she told him anyway. I suppose she thought her remark might trigger a heated argument or even a fistfight. I am sure she did not expect to happen what did happen, Something in Vick snapped. The heated argument was between Winnie and Marge. They were so involved that they did not notice that when Vick left the cabin he was carrying his six-gun. Blind with rage, Vick shot and killed Ed without more warning or discussion than, "You sonofabitch! Make a pass at my wife, would you?"

Ed was in the barn graining and harnessing Punch and Judy for that day's feeding of horses and cattle, and cleaning their stall. At the moment of Vick's arrival, he was in the first stall, cleaning it. When he heard the doors pushed open he must have looked up and seen Vick and his revolver, for the coroner stated that at the time he was shot, Ed was holding a pitchfork in a defensive position, for the bullet went into the upper quadrant of his chest and exited his back lower down.

The deed done, I suppose Vick must have pulled Ed's corpse clear of the stall, or the frightened team would most certainly have trampled him. Or perhaps Ed had stepped clear of the stall with his pitchfork. At any rate, Vick returned to the cabin and to the two women who, arguing heatedly over what Winnie had done, had not identified the single shot. Putting on his sheepskin coat without comment, he returned to the barn, saddled his horse, rode across Snake River, low at that time of year, to the cabin of his cousin, Howard. Howard told him that he must turn himself in. The following day the two men went into Jackson and told the sheriff what Vick had done.

Although preparations for the murder trial were recorded on June 17 (transcript of the preliminary hearing before the Justice of the Peace, Warrants, Subpoenas, and Criminal Complaint issued by that same Justice of the Peace), the young county's second jury trial did not convene until October 27, 1933, and commenced and closed on the same day.

Wilford W. Neilson, County Attorney, was the prosecuting attorney; William Simpson (father of Milward, who became Governor and U.S. Senator, and grandfather of Senator Alan Simpson) was the Defense Attorney. The jury of 12 good men and true: Fleming Cheney, James De Loney (sic),

John James, J. L. Kneedy, Isadore Wilson, Bert R. Schofield, Charles Wilson, W. C. "Slim" Lawrence, Charley Nelson, Sam Smith, Otto Nelson, and Lewis Wilson wasted no time in bringing in a verdict: "Not Guilty." How could that be? Henrie admitted having killed Nichols. Although I was just a 13-year-old kid at the time of the trial, two of those jurors became my good friends. I wish I could have questioned them about the verdict; however, I did not obtain the names of the jurors until 1999.

Vick's defense was temporary insanity—a good description of cabin fever, yet he had killed a man and, incidentally, a fine man.

Our pitchfork was a tagged bit of evidence in that trial. Some 15 years ago I learned that it was still around, but my informant, though a good friend, would not tell me which of her relatives had it.

Sixty-six years after the trial it was returned to the Rocking H thanks to Bob Lucas and his sister, Jennifer. Attached to it is the faded, original tag:

Defendant's Exhibit One
10/15/33

Beneath are three initials, which appear to be CWE.

That fork now hangs over that first stall in our barn, where Ed Nichols tried to defend himself with it.

Clyde Hinesley, Winnie's young uncle, recalled in late 1999, "I was in high school then, but we didn't pay too much attention to the trial, because all of us kids assumed that Vick would get off, because he was a local boy and the jury were all locals.

"I'll tell you one thing for sure: If Jack (Neal) had been on the ranch at the time, instead of in Wilson, there'd have been no trial; he'd have killed them both: Winnie (his stepdaughter) and Vick."

The horses and cattle stand in the snow all Winter. They are fed, but not sheltered. Those wild Montana mares Ed Nichols brought in may have found more snow in Jackson's Hole than they were used to, but they were fed, to which they were unused. Of course, when they were captured, every mare was pregnant and had a foal by her side. It was the following Summer before the mares could use the services of Adanor, the Thoroughbred stallion from Front Royal, Virginia.

Dad had visited the Army Remount Service Stud at Front Royal, where he had examined every stallion that might be available, and had selected Adanor, who arrived from Virginia, the handsomest horse we had ever seen. He was chestnut sorrel with a thin strip of white down his face; he had a marvelous disposition; he was beautifully trained and schooled. As a kid, I could ride him out bareback to wrangle his wives and the geldings. Adanor was a real gentleman. We were lucky to get him

Those were the days of the Army Remount Service, whose duty it was to obtain horses (remounts) for the cavalry and the horse and pack artillery. They required mounts that were at least half Kentucky Thoroughbred and at least green-broken. To insure a steady supply of the kinds of horses they wanted, they raised or bought fine Thoroughbred stallions, which they spread about the nation. Getting a Remount stallion on long-term loan was a bit like adopting a child from an adoption agency. One applied; and if the paperwork submitted was satisfactory, an inspector from the Remount Service came to look over the ranch or farm. If the place passed muster, the owner must agree to breed the stallion to at least 40 mares each year. Whether they were his own or the mares of neighbors did not matter, but guaranteed access to a minimum of 40 was requisite. Nor need the adopter promise to give the Remount Service first choice of the foals. If enough good colts were foaled across the land, enough good prospects would be available for the government.

All requirements met and the papers signed in triplicate, the stallion was insured and shipped. Adanor was insured for $30,000 at a time when

Collection of the Huyler Family.

Dad on Adanor, 1930.

$10,000 was the cost of a good home and $1,000 the price of a good car.

The prophets of doom were mistaken: Not only did the gentleman from Virginia not Winter kill, he thrived. Nature is truly remarkable in so many ways, one of which is that a horse from a warm climate will in the first Winter grow a coat as long and shaggy as those of the native horses.

In the years before the demise of the U.S. Remount Service during World War II, Adanor sired many fine foals for us. The best we sold as polo or roping prospects or kept for the Bear Paw. The Army would take most of the rest at $150 for a half-thoroughbred and $165 for a three-quarter. Doesn't sound like much money nowadays, but it did then, when we could purchase ex-rodeo horses as pack horses for $15 each.

If a horse was four years old or better, had the breeding Remount Service required, and was sound, a Remount Inspector would buy him. Remount Inspectors roamed the nation examining and buying. It gave a reliable bottom to the horse market at a time when a top horse could be purchased for $300.

I dislike the term *horse breaking,* for a good horse is not broken in other senses of that word. He is taught, *gentled;* yet the word persists, and there is no satisfactory synonym for it. *Training* comes later. The 27th definition of *to break* in the *American Heritage Dictionary* is, "To train to obey." The 16th is, "To put an end to by force or strong opposition, especially to end (a strike) by means other than negotiation." I regret to confess that there was too much of the latter in our horse breaking in the early days. The old-time cowboy believed that every horse would buck sooner or later and that the sooner you "got the buck out of them,"

Collection of the Huyler Family.

Slats and Baldy, c. 1936.

the better. The truth is that method rarely took the buck out of one; it merely taught him how to buck. The old Remington and Russell paintings illustrate that clearly.

In the eastern states and western Europe horses were "broken" over a period of months, first learning to carry an empty saddle and to wear a bridle while being led; then carrying a man while still being led.

Yet why is it that today I see so few hunter/jumpers who have good stable manners? The "western" horse stands back, accepting his rider as the alpha animal in the relationship, while the "eastern" horse so often walks over, pushes, and rubs against his rider. The well-trained "western" horse stands quietly while his rider brushes, curries, and saddles. His "eastern" counterpart usually must be cross-tied. Why? "My horse has more spirit," quoth the English rider. Baloney! Ride them side-by-side and let's see.

Horses schooled by the justly famed Jimmy Williams were mannerly. He wouldn't tolerate equine ascendancy. Every stallion he accepted into his training program was at the beginning penned with a rubber-shod gelding who refused to be dominated. Those stallions came out of that first encounter ready to accept man as the alpha member of the herd.

I wish I knew who schooled Adanor. One could drop his lead shank while brushing and saddling him and he would stand. If he nickered at one of his harem, all that was needed was, "Quit!" and he did. Of course, he was a stallion; one could not walk away and leave him "ground tied."

With 40 colts to break in four months every year, we had neither the time nor the inclination to try the "Eastern Method." We did it all pretty much at once. Each of four of us had a string of roughly ten to break. We rode each colt every other day. We didn't exactly make them buck as had our predecessors in the West; neither did we actively discourage it. If the horse bucked, he was spurred and/or quirted until he stopped or the rider was thrown. It wasn't until Slats Helm signed on at the Rocking H that we learned a better way. You may recall that day and Slats's dealing with Baldy in Chapter Three.

Slats worked for the Bear Paw and Rocking H for 13 years, by the end of which period we had sold the Bear Paw and were raising few colts. He was the best horseman I had ever seen until I met Jesse W. Kahle in 1949. They would have been a pair had they known each other. Their methods were much alike. Each of them could keep nine out of ten colts from bucking. I only saw Slats bucked off once.

He was breaking a filly named Calamity Jane. I was riding a pinto colt called Flash. For both it was the second saddling. Slats had finished working in the round corral; and in his usual relaxed style was sitting on the young mare with a knee hooked over the horn while he rolled a cigarette. I asked young Friday to open the gate and let me try Flash outside. As we came through the open gate, something spooked my pinto and he bucked a couple of jumps in surprise. Slats guffawed and slapped his knee. I have never seen a man thrown higher.

I learned a great deal from Slats and Jess and more from Monte Foreman in the late 1960s, the '70s, and the '80s. Now I am learning from Ray Hunt and Cam Schryver. I like to think I am a horseman. No horseman ever stops learning horsemanship.

Horse breaking in the West is nothing like it used to be, I am glad to say.

Until rheumatoid arthritis devastated him in the late 1930s, Dad was one of the most powerful men I ever saw. One time Jack Neal, in need of an extra-heavy anvil for some iron work, had borrowed such an anvil from Charley Brown, the town blacksmith. When finished with it, Jack had carried it to the car in the usual fashion for moving large anvils: the horn and the butt cradled in his elbows. In Jackson an hour later, without thinking about it, Dad opened the trunk, seized the anvil by its horn, and carried it into the blacksmith shop dangling from that one hand. Even Brown was impressed and said so.

Once in the early days as we went to leave the rodeo, we found a drunk sitting on a fender of our car. Dad asked/told the man to get off. Coulter was at the wheel and had to back out through other parked cars. Dad stood in front of the car to guide him. The drunk, being drunk, took offense at having

Collection of the Huyler Family.

Dad in camp, 1928.

lost his seat and, without warning, hit Dad alongside the head with his fist. Barely pausing in his guiding of Coulter, Dad turned and, with no preliminary squaring off, knocked the man down just as simply as that. Furthermore, he had sufficient confidence in his one blow to turn his back on the man and continue with his directing.

Yet, by 1938, that same man could not pick up a pair of shoes without putting one hand into each shoe. I recall coming quietly into his and Mother's room one time on who knows what mission and catching sight of him through the open bathroom door. He was standing in front of the mirror tying a necktie. Tears were rolling down his cheeks—tears of pain and frustration. I tiptoed silently away, returning noisily a few moments later in the hope that I might tie his tie for him. I was too late: The tie had been tied and the tears had been wiped.

His arthritis prevented his and Mother's living in Jackson Hole year-round. By sometime each November the cold would have practically immobilized him, and they would seek a warm climate, not to return to the valley they loved until late April.

It was Dad's tragedy that, as he put it, "My grandchildren will only remember me as an old crock." That really troubled him. Who said life is fair?

I want his grandchildren and great grandchildren to know the man he was. He was a great raconteur, a gregarious, merry, fun-loving man of adventurous disposition. He was inventive: During World War II, when gasoline was strictly rationed, but kerosene was not, it occurred to Dad that his De Soto might function on a mixture of kerosene and gasoline. And so it did, as a result of which my crippled father drove his car many more miles than he could have otherwise.

Dad would usually take a dare. Mother was not above issuing one.

Once when they were young, they spent a Winter weekend at Lake Placid, New York. Pulling a toboggan, they were above the Olympic ski jump when Mother dared him to ride the toboggan off the jump. Dad was no skier, but knowing that men and women went off that jump on skis led him to believe that he would not break his neck. He was right; he broke both wrists. He knew enough to lie down on the toboggan and to hang on. He didn't fall off in midair as he had feared, but his landing broke the wrists.

There is an old family movie taken about 1924, when Dad and Mum were in their thirties. Mother was taking the pictures as they paddled up next to a large buck deer swimming across a lake in Maine. She dared him to ride the deer. The filming stops just after he has leapt from the canoe onto the deer and they have both disappeared under the surface. Just for a few seconds Mum must have been worried: Deer have very sharp hooves as every hunter well knows.

Dad swam the sidestroke, and he waded into the water up to his waist and then lunged. We kids loved to watch him prepare for a swim. His generation wore bathing tops as well as bathing trunks. As he changed into them, off would come boots, socks, Levis, and shirt; then he would remove his Stetson long enough to take off his undershirt. Then back onto his head it would go. An extremely modest man, his undershorts would come off last and be quickly replaced by swimming trunks. Then, once again, off would come the Stetson while he pulled on the top of his bathing suit. If all went well for us kids, he would absent-mindedly put the Stetson back on his head before walking to the water's edge. Would we remind him of his hat? What do you think? And once Mother learned what joy it gave us, she would hold her tongue also.

Out into the water he would wade; and our day would be made if when he lunged into the pool or river his hat floated away. We knew no greater joy than that. I once chased his big white Stetson 200 yards down Snake River until I caught it.

Was he so absent-minded that he always forgot that he was wearing his hat? Or did he sometimes do it just to delight us kids? That possibility didn't occur to me until I had kids of my own. By the time it did, he was gone and I couldn't ask him.

When Dad had his first heart attack in 1950, he was bedridden for a month. He said he passed his time by taking imaginary trail rides from the Bear Paw. I have tried it, but cannot. He, however, would, of a morning, decide what trail he wished to ride, would then start at the corral and go for his ride mentally, trying to visualize every scene and every turn.

That afternoon, he would take a different trip.

That imaginative ability of his may have saved the life of one of his friends.

A couple of years prior his heart attack Dad had heard that his great friend, Sam Bingham of Tryon, North Carolina, and the Bear Paw, was hospitalized with the hiccups. Imagine how horrible that would be: hiccuping every few seconds for two weeks! He couldn't eat; he couldn't drink. Despite the intravenous feeding, he was weakening. The doctors said that his hiccuping might kill him. [The March 28, 1996, edition of *USA Today* reported a death from hiccups.]

Dad went to Tryon to see Sam Bingham. When he walked into "Uncle Sam's" hospital room, he was shocked; but he sat down and began talking about the Bear Paw, about the trails they had ridden, about the good times they had had together. Suddenly, both men realized that the hiccuping had stopped. Sam Bingham's concentration on their memories had broken the recurring spasms of his diaphragm. Uncle Sam was saved. The hiccups never recurred, though for the few years remaining to him, he must have been close to panic whenever a normal hiccup hit him.

Writing of Dad's recollections of trail rides reminds me of one that was typical of him. Alone, he was trimming trails up the mountainside we called "Middle Lookout." That day he was riding a mule. Suddenly, they startled a yearling black bear. Dad's first thought was that the young bear would make a good pet (Shades of Harry Harrison's Ming in Chapter Two). The mule's first thought was that he wanted no part of that bear no matter how young it might be. He refused to follow. The flat of Dad's hatchet on that mule did not produce the desired results. Frustrated, Dad removed his jacket and with it blindfolded that mule. Advantage Huyler! Urging his blinded mount forward, Dad followed the bear, which shortly climbed a tree as is the wont of black bears when pursued. At the foot of the tree Dad sat in thought. No one else was likely to come that way that morning; so he must ride to the ranch for help.

Hoping that it would keep the cub up the tree, Dad removed his jacket from the mule and tied its arms around the tree. The mule, confused and glad for vision once again, stood during the transfer; however, a noise from above caught his attention.

Despite their record-setting return to the Bear Paw, by the time Dad returned to the tree with a rope-bearing posse, the bear had departed. The Bear Paw Ranch never had a pet bear, which was probably just as well. I know who would have been given the job of taming and feeding it.

As I remarked at the beginning, of all the people I have known, I believe Dad was the most truly courteous, yet he disliked lack of courtesy in others, and resented being put upon.

Around 1933, he and I were fishing that stretch of the Lewis River in Yellowstone Park that runs quietly alongside the road and has a grassy east bank. We had waded out until we could cast against that grassy bank. That has always been good fishing.

Suddenly, we heard a peremptory blast from a car horn. We looked around. A uniformed Park Ranger was standing by his pickup truck. "Come over here!" he demanded.

"Ignore him, son, " instructed Dad, retrieving his fly and making another cast.

Again the horn. Although Dad ignored it, I could not refrain from looking around. "Come on over here!"

"Just keep on fishing, son."

A few more blasts and a few more shouts, and the Ranger waded into the river and across to Dad. "Let's see your license!" he demanded angrily. Calmly Dad tucked his rod under his arm, removed his Stetson, removed the license from the sweat band, and handed it to him.

"If you had a license, why didn't you come when I called you?"

"I never come to anyone who calls me that way."

Dad returned to his fishing. I couldn't resist turning all the way around to watch that Ranger as he waded back to his truck, poured the water out of each of his black Oxford shoes, wrung out the bottom of his twill uniform trousers, and drove off.

I'd bet that the next time he hailed anybody, he was courteous.

About 15 months later, Slim Pendergraft drove into the Bear Paw and asked for Dad. At that time, Slim was a game warden; so we wondered what he was up to.

"Mr. Huyler, I'm sorry, but I have a warrant here for your arrest."

"What did I do, Slim?"

"You killed a sheep [mountain sheep] without a license."

"Did I, Slim?"

"Yessir, either you or somebody in your camp; an' I'm afraid I'll have to see you in court Monday morning."

"I'll be there."

"Sorry about this, but it's my job."

Monday morning we all went with Dad to court to see if he'd be hung, or what.

Dad chose to represent himself. In 1907-08 he had spent a year in Columbia Law School; I'll bet he relished this opportunity.

The Clerk read the charge: the whole world (county, state, and federal government) vs. Coulter D. Huyler on the matter of a Bighorn Sheep shot illegally in the Lower Granite Creek Basin. (Sounded to me as if Dad was going to be hung for sure.) "How does the defendant plead?"

"Not guilty, your honor."

Slim took the stand and outlined how, it being hunting season, he had been riding the back country in line of duty. In Lower Granite Creek he had noted an abandoned campsite. Riding over to it, he had discovered where something had been buried. In line of duty, he had dug around and exposed the remains of a sheep.

Returning to town a couple of days later, he had asked around and learned that the Bear Paw had recently had a hunting camp on Lower Granite Creek.

In line of duty, Slim had gone to the records of the Game and Fish Department and found that no sheep license had been issued to anyone from the Bear Paw.

So, sorry as he was, in line of duty he had served a warrant upon his friend, Mr. Huyler now seated before him in the courtroom.

The judge asked the defendant if he had anything to say.

Dad arose and asked one question: "Where is the evidence?"

All eyes swung to Slim, who responded that he had buried the remains where he had found them.

"Well," declared Dad, "without evidence you most certainly are not going to convict me of anything."

"Do you mean that you want Slim to ride back down to Lower Granite Creek and dig up the remains of that sheep?" asked the County Attorney.

(That is when I learned the meaning of the word *immaterial.*)

"It's immaterial to me whether he does or doesn't, but you most certainly aren't going to convict me without it."

The County Attorney, the Judge, and Slim put their heads together. Court was recessed until Thursday.

Meanwhile, Slim had to load his horse in his pickup (few owned trailers in those days), drive down to Battle Mountain, unload the horse, ride to Slim Bassett's ranch, borrow a pack horse, saddle, panniers, and lash rope, ride up Granite Creek, dig up enough of that stinking sheep for evidence, pack it on an unwilling pack animal—which he then led back to the highway with its noxious load—unpack the evidence, lead the pack horse back to Bassett's, ride back to his truck, load his saddle horse, and drive back to town. The remains he must have taken into the cab with him. No horse would have loaded with those stinking remnants in back. Can't you picture the pleasures of that drive back to town?

In court Thursday morning it was once again the whole world against

Coulter Huyler. This time, however, there on a gunny sack on a table were a few pieces of sheep, the hooves and the bit of hide which had been cut off with them.

Again the defendant was asked if he had anything to say.

"Your honor, I have just one question to ask of Slim: Does a mountain sheep have hair or wool?"

"Why, hair, of course."

Without another word, Dad turned, pushed open the swinging gates in the rail, and walked out of the courtroom. I fully expected him to be shot in the back.

Judge, attorney, clerk, and game warden gathered around the redolent remains. Wool!

It hadn't occurred to those men of Jackson Hole that their friend Coulter Huyler would stoop so low as to eat sheep. Bighorn, yes; but wooly, no.

The truth of the matter was that all Huylers love lamb, and that a sheep had been taken to Lower Granite Creek as camp meat until an elk, deer, or bear would be shot.

Nope, Dad did not like to be put upon. Had Slim asked him, instead of accusing him, Dad would have explained.

Sheep, yes; sheep also.

Dad loved to hunt and did so in Maine, Newfoundland, Montana, and Wyoming: moose, elk, deer, antelope, bear, grouse, duck, pheasant.

Every Fall in Jackson's Hole, until he was decimated by rheumatoid arthritis, Dad bagged his elk—one year more than one.

We were hunting near Colbron Creek in the south end of the Valley. Dad sought a spike for good meat rather than a trophy bull. Suddenly he saw one and, dropping to a sitting position, fired as the young bull entered an aspen grove. Although he was a fine shot with pistol, rifle, or shotgun, he missed. A moment later we spotted the young bull in the middle of the grove. As he passed a gap in the trees, Dad fired again; yet a moment later, we saw the young bull burst out of the aspens. This time Dad dropped him.

As we moved in to dress out the elk, Jack Neal and I were teasing the rifleman for needing three shots to drop one elk.

Arriving on the site we discovered not one dead elk, but three. Dad had dropped the first as it entered the trees. That had startled a second young bull, who sprang up and momentarily appeared in the gap. His fall had startled a third, who had broken cover into the open. Three elk with three shots! Not bad at, perhaps, 350 yards!

Fortunately, those were the first kills of the season for any of us; so we had enough tags to account for them. In those days the law did not require that each licensee bag his or her own game. One member of any household could hunt for any family member with a license. Not so today.

Some years later, after Dad had been crippled by arthritis and could no longer hunt or fish, he and I were driving through the Rocking H. As we approached our Lake Creek bridge, we saw an unknown auto, and three or four people ran off into the trees. Fishermen, no doubt. We usually let people fish if they asked permission, but ran them off if they hadn't been polite enough to do that.

Dad blew the car horn. He stopped the car and blew again. No response from the trees. "Give them a shout, son." My shout can be heard for miles. I stepped out of the car and called them to "Come on out an' talk." No response. I repeated my shouted invitation. Silence still, yet we knew that they could not be more than a hundred yards away.

I turned for further instructions. Dad was writing a note. "Put this under their windshield wiper and let the air out of all four tires."

In Dad's beautiful penmanship, the note read, "The next time you are on someone's property and he wants to talk to you, I suggest that you talk."

With pleasure I put the note under the wiper. With mixed feelings I let the air out of all four tires.

Over the years since, I have frequently wondered how those men coped with the four flat tires. In those days, they probably had a tire pump in their trunk; but pumping up four tires was no mean task.

Surely, under the circumstances, they did not dare bring in another auto. They could jack up only one wheel at a time, removing that tire and rolling it to the gate, a half-mile away. Then by car, they had to take it to Wilson for air. There was no Teton Village in those days.

Four round-trips from car to gate to Wilson and return. My bet is on the pump. In either case, I'd bet their poaching days were over.

Yet, I maintain that Dad was the most courteous person I have ever known. It was impossible to do anything for him, no matter how insignificant, without getting a sincere thank you. Every night at bedtime when his grandchildren kissed him good night, he thanked each by name. When our turn came and Margaret kissed him good night, he always gave her a quiet, heartfelt, "Thank you, Margaret." His last words to me were thank you.

When his final heart attack hit him in September 1955, we carried him to his station wagon on his mattress and drove him to the old St. John's Hospital, the log one. He was conscious and thanked the four of us who carried him.

He was in that hospital for a week. Mother sat with him all day; I, all night. Coulter was coming from Paris, where he was stationed by the State Department. I had a comfortable cushioned chair to sit upon and another chair for my feet. Dad had sunk into a coma shortly after reaching the hospital, but Dr. MacLeod was keeping him alive with oxygen and with injections of nicotine until Coulter should arrive. The irony of nicotine for a man who never smoked!

In those days patients on oxygen were kept in oxygen tents, clear, plastic hoods which, without touching them, tented head, shoulders, and chest.

About two o'clock one morning he was very restless as if he were having a bad dream. I felt so sorry for him. Why that on top of his other troubles? All alone with him there in that darkened hospital room, I said quietly, "I love you, Dad." He hadn't spoken in days, but immediately the response came, "Thank you, son." I wept then and I weep now.

The nicotine, oxygen, and intravenous feeding kept Dad alive until Coulter arrived from Paris. I had doubted the wisdom of keeping him hanging on. After all, he was in a coma.

Collection of the Huyler Family.

Margaret Porter Huyler, c. 1938.

I understand now, however.

When Coulter walked into Dad's hospital room, Mother said to her comatose husband, "Coulter, Coulter is here!" Dad sat bolt upright carrying his oxygen tent with him.

"Oh, Son!"

He smiled and dropped back on his pillows, never to speak again.

I guess I shall never understand the modern concept of the inevitability and propriety of serious conflict between father and son. We never had one of which I am aware. Disagreements over small things? Yes, many of them. But I admired the man and his values. It never occurred to me to revolt against either, God bless him. I loved him then; I love him now; I shall always love and revere him. What a great Dad he was! How lucky am I to have had him as long as I did! Would I had had him longer.

Dad lies buried in the Wilson Cemetery next to Mother and my sister, Margaret.

On September 8, 1955, when Mother, my Margaret, and I went to our plot with Dad's friends the Schofield brothers, who were not only to be pallbearers, but had volunteered to dig the grave, Mother decided the grave should lie north-south. Immediate and determined were the protests of the brothers:

"Oh, no! He must lie on his back with his feet to the east so that when Gabriel blows his horn on Judgment Day, he will arise facing the rising sun." So that is the way he; my sister, Margaret; and Mother lie awaiting Gabriel's summons.

To Dad Jackson Hole was definitely the most beautiful and wondrous place on Earth.

CHAPTER EIGHTEEN

"A Wheel Hoss, a Regular Wheel Hoss"

You don't put a Model A Ford station wagon into cruise control and just sit there steering. I never truly appreciated what my mother had done in 1929 until I bought a 1929 Model A in 1988. The driver is busy every minute—no, every second: steering, shifting gears, adjusting the spark, watching the radiator heat gauge on the radiator cap. It is not relaxed driving. Add to that five kids, Summer heat, and the drought of 1929, the Dust Bowl. The intrepid, tiny lady handled it all with aplomb, and with good nature so long as we kids behaved.

Not only was there no air conditioning, there were no windows; but that made no difference unless it rained, which it didn't in the Summer of 1929. Had we put up the side curtains, we'd have suffocated.

Mum was driving Coulter, Clyde Hinesley, Stanley Resor, Jr., Swift Tarbell, and me from Greenwich, Connecticut, to Jackson's Hole. Where was Dad? Wisely, he was working in New York. Before he and Mum moved West to stay, he worked in the big city until some time in July. I am not sure that I know of any other woman who would have tackled that drive under those circumstances. It wasn't really necessary; it was a vacation trip to the ranch. But then . . .

Mother had enough gall to be divided into a hundred parts. She was a tiny woman, five feet three inches tall even before she began to shrink with age as we all do. She was so large in her attitudes and accomplishments that I never realized that she was truly petite until I looked at a movie of her riding her grandson John's motorcycle with him when she was 84. When I helped her dismount at the end of the ride, she stood between John and me, and I saw that she was in fact tiny. She was a little giant who feared nothing on this Earth. Thank God, she feared God!

I was a disappointment to her. She always wanted me to address her as

"Mother." I rarely did; she was "Mum" to me.

She was born a North Carolina Tar Heel, and so it was rather improbable that she would marry a New York Yankee. What made it even more improbable was the fact that her father had fought in the Confederate Army, while Dad's father wore the navy blue of the North. The two men had, some 35 years later, become fast friends and their children, sweethearts, who married in 1907.

Mum was an enthusiast. She was a faddist. We, her children, were guinea pigs for most of her fads.

When I was very small, she read about a French psychologist, a Dr. Coué of unlamented memory, who maintained that one could actually improve oneself by the simple expedient of repeating over and over until sleep, "Every day in every way I'm getting better and better." Self-hypnosis, osmosis, or just the power of repeated suggestion? Whatever the explanation, I was required to repeat that every night after I went to bed. A little boy repeating over and over, "Every day in every way I'm getting better and better. Every day in every way I'm getting better and better. Ever-y d-a-y I'm g-e-t . . ." Obviously, it didn't work.

And then there was head standing. Brains need blood. Brains have been shortchanged since men stopped traveling on all fours. If one stood on his head for a few minutes each day, it might help. It might. Anyway, Mum and her sons stood on their heads every day. On her 70th birthday, she stood on her head on the buffalo robe in the Main Cabin of the Rocking H for a clocked five minutes just to prove she could still do it. Whatever the reason, there was no lack of circulation to or within Mum's brain.

Last Summer, at 79, I recalled that feat, and decided to attempt it myself. I still have a stiff neck four months later.

Mum's enthusiasms included special forms of Christianity. She was a devoted member of the Oxford Group, and she foisted it upon all of us. She didn't quite succeed in implanting their Quiet Time into our morning schedules—a pity, as meditation is probably beneficial to everyone. But she did for awhile insist that all kids on the Bear Paw who were her responsibility (a few teenagers were permitted to come without their parents) gather at Prayer Rock for 15 minutes each morning before breakfast. Although I could always find the need to be with the horses at that time, I sometimes joined them because of the pretty teenage girls. At Prayer Rock she would read from the Bible and pray aloud, a prayer in which all were invited to participate.

Every morning as long as she lived, before arising, Mum read her

Bible, had her Quiet Time, and read a newspaper from cover to cover if one was available.

She was feisty. I only witnessed two occasions in her life when Mother was rendered speechless. On the first occasion, the Old Man had walked down with Honey when she came to deliver the milk. They had stayed for supper. It was that first Summer; we ate in a wall tent while the cabin was being built. We gobbled our food. The Old Man may have been lightning with his gun, but he was slow with a fork. He ate deliberately. Mother was up scraping our plates into the zinc washtub when she noticed that he was just well into his meal. "I'm so sorry," she said, "that we eat so fast. Please don't let us hurry you."

"Nobody ever hurries me, Ma'am," was his soft rejoinder. His record with a gun would suggest otherwise.

The other stymie occurred at her own dinner table. Jerry Vogt, a tough German and foreman of the Rocking H at the time, and his wife, Joyce, were eating supper with us. In her hot-blooded way, Mum was "sassing" Dad about something. She often did. Jerry turned to Dad and remarked, "Mr. Huyler, if my wife ever spoke to me like that, I'd drive her into the floor like a nail."

He just might have, too. In addition to having seen him carry a refrigerator and place a huge beam atop the gateposts, I saw him knock a young mare down with his bare fist when she tried to bolt through a gate he was closing.

After the Vogts had returned to their cabin and we were kidding Mother about Jerry's comment, she said, "I'd just like to see him try!" But at the time, she had nothing to say.

I wonder what might have happened if the prank involving Mum and "Ma" Reed had not been aborted at the critical moment.

In the early days of the valley, "Ma" Reed was proprietress of Reed's Hotel, which you may recall from the account of the Wingers' and Kellys' arrival in 1913. "Ma" was small like Mother. She, too, was feisty. In her apron pocket she carried a set of brass knuckles with which she brought rambunctious cowboys into line. As she supervised the serving of dinner, she would ease herself behind the culprit's chair, slip her hand into her "knucks," step up on the rung of his chair to gain altitude, and give him such a crack on the skull as he would never forget.

Reed's hotel became the Crabtree Hotel in 1917, and is now metamorphosed into part of Crabtree Corner. "Ma" left the valley for a time in the late teens, returning some years later to open a dining room east of the Crabtree Hotel and across Broadway from the Van Vleck House (now Jedadiah's House of Sourdough).

"Ma" Reed's dining room was one of the best spots in town to eat dinner. Around 1927 our family and the Neals had dinner there after the rodeo. I was a small boy. I cannot imagine the lie which Jack Neal must have drummed up to direct "Ma's" ire against Mum. I believe Dad was party to it. I do recall the laughter when the hoax was exposed, and that Mum's and "Ma's" laughter was a bit forced.

Whatever the lie, they convinced "Ma" that Mother had said something scurrilous about her or her establishment. She moved in behind Mother's chair; her hand went into her pocket; her toe went up on the rung of the chair—and Jack Neal intervened before anything really happened. He and Dad thought it was funny; but I have wondered ever since what would have happened had she really hit Mum. Of only one thing am I truly certain: There would, indeed, have been Hell to pay.

When we set out in that boxy little station wagon in 1929, Mum probably had as much driving experience as any other woman in the United States. Even before she and Dad were married, she had been called upon from time to time to steer and to operate clutch and gears on an old chain-drive C.G.V. French touring car while the men pushed it up a steep hill, or out of a mud hole. Photos of early automobiles show either small buggy-like vehicles or monsters. That car, owned by Grandpa Huyler, was a monster; but it never daunted her. Nothing did. Recall the 1929 trip from Connecticut to Wyoming in the Model A Ford.

The next time you see a Model A Ford station wagon, please take a good long look for Mum's sake. How would you like to drive such a vehicle across the country even on today's good roads? I would not. I was unwilling even to drive my Model A from Wyoming to California. I trailered it; however, as has been stated already, this little lady thought nothing of setting out in such a vehicle with five kids. Granted, Coulter at 17 was large enough, strong enough, and sufficiently knowledgeable to change and repair the frequent flat tires, to refill the radiator, gas tank, or crankcase from the red, white, and blue cans fastened to the running board, and even to drive some, I suppose, though I don't remember his driving.

West of Chicago, the roads were dirt except within city limits. Although Mother and Coulter were protected by the windshield, all of us in back wore goggles. By nightfall each of us had three clean spots: a circle around each eye and as far around our mouths as our tongues would reach. As a treat, a reward for appropriate behavior, and a break during each day's drive, she gave each of us a chocolate soda every afternoon. In those days every town had a soda fountain, and every highway went right through the middle of every town along the way, right down Main Street. The concept of bypasses was unheard of. The businesses wanted the cars, and the people in the cars wanted to see the businesses. In the heart of a town, Mum would stop the car and we would pile out noisily and eagerly head for the nearest drug store. Six chocolate ice cream sodas would be ordered. When all were on the counter, Mum would take from her purse a small bottle from which she would put four drops into each soda. I suppose some of the soda jerks (yes, that's what they were called and what they called themselves) thought it was some kind of narcotic; but we knew that it was essence of peppermint. Each soda had now been transformed into a chocolate mint soda. Yummy!

Until she was put into a nursing home a few months before she died at 89 in 1973, Mum carried such a little bottle. After she was interred in the Wilson cemetery with Dad and my older sister, Margaret, family who were there (Margaret, Coulter, Mother's brother Steve, our son John, and I) adjourned to Porter's Drug Store (Jackson Drug) to have chocolate ice cream sodas. John had an inspiration. Going to the pharmacist, he obtained a small bottle of essence of peppermint with a medicine dropper cap. Onto the bottle he affixed a label, which declares: *Margaret P. Huyler Memorial Soda.* To this day anyone who sits down at Jackson's only soda fountain, and requests "A Margaret P. Huyler Memorial Soda" is handed that little brown bottle. Anyone who doesn't know the name is not supposed to get the bottle. Go in and have one while Jackson still has a soda fountain. Your patronage just may help the community to keep it. Few towns have one nowadays.

Remember. Four drops are just right.

The Snake River Ranch, one of the few real cattle ranches remaining in Jackson Hole, is a direct offshoot of Mother's 1929 drive. One of the kids in back was red-headed Stanley Resor, Jr. Stan took to Jackson's Hole immediately, as who doesn't?

1929 was before the party telephone line came to the Bear Paw. On Saturday afternoons, Mother or Dad would drive us to Jackson so that Stan could phone home from one of the phone booths outside the Bell Telephone Office. Of course, if one kid goes somewhere, all do. We would sit in the Model A with Dad or Mother while Stan entered the booth and made his call.

One such afternoon, Stan left the receiver dangling, came out, and said to Dad, "Mr. Huyler, Dad would like to talk to you."

"Yes, Stanley?"

"Coulter, I understand that you have a ranch for sale."

"I do."

"How large is it?"

"Four hundred and eight acres."

"Stan thinks I ought to buy it."

"Well, Stanley, I'd love to sell it to you. Why don't you come out to see it?"

"I can't at this point, Coulter; but I gather that you think it a good value at the asking price and a good investment as well."

"I do. Property in Jackson's Hole is increasingly in demand."

"Then, I'll take it."

"Stanley, I'm not going to sell you a property you haven't seen."

"Stan says I'll like it." (Stan was 12 years old.)

"Stanley, unless memory fails, not only have you not seen this property, you have not seen Jackson's Hole or even Wyoming. As I recall you stopped off the train twice in Denver on business en route to the West Coast, and those are your only visits to the Rocky Mountain area."

"True, but Stan loves the place; you say it's a good value; and I want to

Collection of the Huyler Family.

Mum at Phelps Lake, c. 1938.

buy it."

Dad's brain must have been racing.

"Stanley, I'll tell you what I'll do. I'll sell you an option on the property. Next Summer you bring your family out. There's a farmhouse on it that you and Helen and the children can sleep in. I'll hire a couple for you to show you the ropes and handle horses, which we can lend you. If you like the place, it's yours; if you don't, I keep the option money and nobody's hurt."

"Done."

And that is how the Resors came to Jackson's Hole and the nucleus of one of its finest ranches came into being.

The five Resors came the next Summer, and four of them fell in love with the place. No ranch was Mrs. Resor's cup of tea, but she was a good sport about it and pleased that her four were happy; so she continued to come every Summer as long as she lived.

As for Mr. Resor, I believe it was love at first sight. And he loved to work on his ranch. It is contiguous to our Rocking H, and both had received more than their fair share of river rocks in the Kelly Flood of 1927. Despite a bad sacroiliac, Mr. Resor picked rocks and piled them. He seemed to enjoy it, whereas everyone else I have known has, after the first very few minutes, despised picking rocks. Despite his bad back, he painted gates. With one hand on that aching sacroiliac, he painted. Every gate on the Snake River Ranch gleamed; ours remained unpainted.

It wasn't long before Mr. Resor decided to expand his acreage and go into the cattle business. Although he knew almost everything there was to know about advertising, he not only knew nothing about the cattle business, he knew that he didn't know. He wanted someone who did. Who? Where? The University of Wyoming seemed a logical resource.

Going over to Laramie, Mr. Resor inquired the name of the Head of the Cattle Division: Mr. Oldroyd.

Shortly thereafter, he was sitting across from the man. The conversation must have gone something like this:

"Mr. Oldroyd, have you ever seen a cattle ranch which was run exactly as you thought it should be run?"

"No, Mr. Resor, I haven't."

"Well, Mr. Oldroyd, I am giving you that opportunity. I know that I do not know the cattle business, and I know that you do. I shall defer to your judgment and experience in matters pertaining to the cattle."

"And how many cattle do you have, Mr. Resor?"

"None yet. That's where you come in. If you'll take the job, I will pay you a thousand dollars more per year than the University pays you."

"Mr. Resor, this sounds like the opportunity of a lifetime; but I must give notice to the University."

"Mr. Oldroyd, I wouldn't want you if you didn't."

Subsequent issues must have centered around how many cattle were required to create an operation that would be self-sustaining. How many tons of hay were required per horse and cow to sustain it through a severe Jackson's Hole Winter? (We always allowed a ton and a half per cow and two and a half per horse.) How many acres were needed to produce that much hay?

Mr. Resor purchased acreage contiguous to the nucleus he already owned. With his approval, Oldroyd purchased not only the requisite, but the optimum, machinery; put in ditches and crops; and bought cattle. Because of Mr. Oldroyd's knowledge and experience and Mr. Resor's intelligence and resources, they could and did buy bulldozer and drag line (backhoes were yet to be invented) with which to put in and to improve hay lands. From the beginning theirs was an efficient operation. Most ranchers, like us, had to get along with what they could. Almost from the beginning the Snake River Ranch was an operation jealously admired by the Rocking H next door as well as by others.

Now the third generation is in charge of the Snake River Ranch, and there is a fourth generation in the wings who already love their ranch and Jackson Hole.

Never underestimate the power of a 12-year-old boy or of a little woman behind the wheel of a car.

Mother was an outdoorswoman; she loved to ride, had ridden all her life, and was good at it. What she loved most were picnics and pack trips. Even before the Bear Paw became a dude ranch, there was never a Summer when we did not take a couple of pack trips. She was a skilled camper and camp cook. She didn't mind the weather or rough terrain.

She celebrated her 80th and 82nd birthdays by galloping across the hayfields with three of her grandchildren, jumping the irrigation ditches as they came. We have that on film. She was riding her old mare, Blondie, by horse standards as old as she was. It occurred to me that the old mare might stumble and fall, breaking both their necks. "Not a bad end for a great sportswoman," I concluded, glad, nonetheless, that it did not occur.

That Summer of her 80th birthday, 1964, Coulter and his family were on the ranch to help her celebrate. One day, the whole gang of us mounted up to ride to Open Canyon to see the wildflowers, a ride of some six hours round trip. It was a beautiful day when we left the ranch; but as will happen in the mountains, thunder clouds gathered as we rode. On the ridge above Kaufman Creek, it started to hail. We adults held a council. We had five children and an old lady with us. Each had a jacket of sorts, but we had not prepared as we should have. We decided to go home. That is all but Mother decided to go home. Her opinion voiced firmly was, "I've never turned back from a trip because of the weather in my life! And I'm too old to start now!"

"Well, we're going back, Mum,"

"Well, one of us isn't!" And she started her old mare up the mountain.

As we started downhill, I should have known that she had no bluff to call. She kept going up; I turned my horse and caught up with her. "Mum," I said, "You can't do this to us! We have little kids to consider." I was prepared to lead her if necessary. That would have created some scene!

"All right," she conceded; but all the way down the mountain she grumbled, "What's the world coming to in the hands of these softies?"

Do I paint an intrepid woman? I hope so. Spunky? The word may have been coined to describe her.

Photo by Olie Riniker. Collection of the Jackson Hole Historical Society and Museum.

Helen Lang, 1979.

Because of her daredevil attitude, Mum occasionally had a serious accident. It must have been the Fall of 1932 that she rode her horse up to the spot on the Bar Nothing where Coulter was skinning a bear. When the wind blew a strong scent toward him, the horse promptly bucked Mum off and broke her hip.

There was a humorous postscript to that accident. That Fall, when it came time for the family's annual exodus to the East, Mum was in a body cast from her knees to her shoulders. Helen Lang, Head Nurse of St. John's Hospital, agreed to travel East with us to furnish Mum the personal help that she would need. Mum was so modest that she would not have permitted even her husband to do those things for her.

It was a rainy day when we set out across Teton Pass, all riding in a Civilian Conservation Corps ambulance. St. John's Hospital had yet to acquire its first ambulance. Station wagons were forced into service. The CCC had a genuine Army ambulance, and they owed Dr. Huff for having repaired a good many of their accidents. They volunteered their ambulance and driver for the trip.

The second road over Teton Pass was being constructed and was slick and tricky in spots. (Sections of it can still be seen from the present road.) The ambulance slewed back and forth. The patient from the stretcher in back insisted that her husband drive, and the driver let him.

At the depot in Victor, it was discovered that the stretcher could not make it around the bends from the platform to the drawing room that had been reserved. Solution? All of us rode in the baggage car. The rain stopped; a warm Indian Summer sun came out; Dad opened the door of the baggage car to let in some fresh air and to give us all a view.

The train stopped in Blackfoot, where a trainman passing by looked in and saw a clump of people and a nurse in white uniform around a woman on a stretcher. Jumping to the wrong conclusion, he inquired, "Is she violent?"

"Not at the moment," replied Dad.

The next moment she made a liar of him.

In 1939 it was my poor judgment that caused Mother to be bucked off and to break her neck. I was 19. I should have controlled the situation.

It was the first ride of the season for Mum and a bunch of teenagers on the Bear Paw. A mile from home, we decided to lope. Mum was at the head of the group; I, at the tail. Several of the kids did not ride well enough to control their horses and they raced past Mother's horse, who wanted to race, too. When she kept him in check, he bogged his head and, at a gallop, bucked her off. I saw her land on the hard road; and as I bailed off to go to her, I noted that her neck had an odd twist. She was unconscious!

I sent one of the kids racing back to the ranch for a station wagon and a mattress and for help. My cousin Addie Marshall (Donnan) rode to nearby Granite Creek and fetched a hatful of water. There was no ambulance, and there were no paramedics. We could not just leave her there. Realizing that Mum must eventually be moved, and knowing enough to keep a gentle pull on her head, I straightened her neck and with my bandanna and Addie's water began to wipe the gravel from her mouth and then the dirt from her face. With her body, Addie shaded her from the hot, bright sun. Mum groaned. Were we ever glad to hear that sound!

About the time the station wagon arrived with the mattress, Mum regained consciousness and opened her deep blue eyes for a moment. It was obvious that she knew who and where she was. Thanks, God! While I held head and neck steady, caring hands lifted her gently onto the mattress and the mattress into the car.

The drive over those rough roads to St. John's Hospital must have been painful for her; typically, she did not complain.

Dr. MacLeod had her neck x-rayed, put her to bed in traction, and informed us that she had two broken vertebrae.

After a rather long stay in the hospital, Mum returned home sporting a high plaster-of-Paris collar, which supported her chin and head. For her nights there was a traction device of weights and pulleys to be attached to the collar. That she must endure all night, every night. If she ever complained, I never heard it.

It wasn't long before she was on her feet going about her usual activities wearing that collar with a silk scarf tied around it.

She even rode that same horse, and at speed. She would have been furious

Collection of the Huyler Family.

"Back in the Saddle Again," c. 1940s.

had she known that I had put quite a few miles on him between her accident and her next ride.

Of the many spots Mother cherished in Jackson Hole, probably her favorite was the Chapel of the Transfiguration at Moose

The Chapel, financed by Mr. and Mrs. Voorhis of Dubois, Wyoming, and Pasadena, California, had been built in 1925 on land donated by Maud Noble. On August 10, 1925, just two weeks after the first service was held in the Chapel and a week prior to its consecration by the Bishop of Wyoming, young Potter Stewart, destined to become a Justice of the United States Supreme Court 35 years later, was baptized in the new edifice.

One of the carpenters who built the Chapel of the Transfiguration was George Lamb, father of Tom and John. Before he died, George shared a little secret with me: "Inside that altar, where no one but God could see it, I carved my name, hoping that the Lord would see it there when He looked down on the Chapel and would be reminded that I helped build the Chapel in His honor."

For years Mum played the old pump organ there. She played it at the marriage of the first local couple to be married in the Chapel, Jack and Ellen Dornan in 1927.

Before the Summer of her broken neck became Au-

Collection of the Huyler Family.

Mum's favorite view in Jackson's Hole, c. 1930s.

tumn, she played that organ. Wearing a huge neck brace, she could not see the keys, nor could she see the music unless I held it up for her, which I did: an open hymnal on a stack of four others atop the little organ. Head held high voluntarily and involuntarily, she pumped away and played those hymns. Indomitable? Indomitable!

Before, during, and after our dude ranch days, picnics and pack trips with Mum were special fun. She read aloud beautifully and tirelessly. After lunch, she would spread an old World War I Army blanket on the ground. She would sit on it while we lay either on it or on the grass nearby. She read aloud to us Charlie Chan mysteries by Earl Derr Biggers, Agatha Christie mysteries, and *Tish* by Mary Roberts Rhinehart. How we loved the *Tish* stories of three old gals and their adventures! What a shock it was when I was about 50 years old to reread *Tish* and discover that those *old ladies* were younger than I.

She would climb to snow patches with us and throw snowballs with us.

On one pack trip that she and Dad took in 1926 to the Middle Fork of the Salmon River without us kids, she had an adventure. Toward the end of one day, they passed an inviting swimming hole. Mum said, "You men (Dad and Jack Neal) ride on and make camp. I'm going to have a nice swim and sun bath. Coulter, leave your pistol with me."

After a nice dip and washing her hair, she stretched out nude on the grass in the sun and dozed. After awhile, she moved her left hand and heard a "Bzzzzzzsssssssh!"

"If this were not Jackson's Hole," she thought dreamily, "I'd think that was a rattlesnake." She dozed off again.

A few moments later she must have twitched that hand. Again the "Bzzzzzzsssssssh!"

"I do declare! That certainly does sound like a rattlesnake." Her eyes must have widened. "This is *not* Jackson's Hole, and that *is* a rattlesnake."

Recall that she had been raised in the mountains of North Carolina. In those Smoky Mountains there were lots of rattlesnakes. She didn't panic. She never panicked.

Dad's Colt .45 semi-automatic lay near her right hand. Keeping her left hand perfectly still, she felt around until she had the pistol. Cocking it as quietly as possible, she slowly raised her body and the gun until she could see the snake. Of course, it saw her and transferred its attention away from the hand to the bigger object. Drawing a careful bead, Mother killed the rattler with one shot and without hitting her own hand.

Now came a new problem: Hearing the shot, the men would come as fast as possible, and there she was naked as the day she was born. Rapidly she dressed. She heard the drumming of approaching hooves and held up the rattler for the men to admire. That was my mom!

Do you know why in fact, as well as fiction, cowboys shoot the heads off snakes? It's not hard, because the snake follows with his head the nearest threat, and that is usually the gun. With his head directly in line with the barrel and moving as the barrel does, it is not a difficult shot. Mum's steely nerves were demonstrated by the facts that she kept that left hand still while she got the pistol, that she held it there while she fired, and that she did not hit her own hand, close as it was to the snake.

It was mom who, in 1938, invited her goddaughter Margaret Appenzeller to come and spend 18 days on the Bear Paw. Before a week was out, I was hooked and have remained hooked for 61 years now.

It was typical of Mum that after Margaret left for college, she came bustling into my room to see if she might help me with my packing for my college. On my bureau was a letter from me to Margaret or from her to me. Anyway, it was lying open and she couldn't help seeing the affectionate salutation.

She turned on me. "Jack Huyler, you stay away from Margaret Appenzeller. She's too good for you!"

Photo by Sanborn. Collection of the Jackson Hole Historical Society and Museum.

"The Last of the Old West," c. 1937.

That was her position so long as she lived. She never sided with me in any disagreement with Margaret, no matter how insignificant. She was right, you know.

Mother was a member of the Wilson Homemakers. She greatly enjoyed her contacts with those ladies in their homes and hers. She was one of the forces behind the establishment of the ski shelter at the foot of Snow King (formerly Kelly's Hill), of the Library, of the Music Festival. She was a dedicated supporter of St. John's Church and Hospital.

Two compliments she cherished when I reported them to her because she understood the rural uses of the terms:

"Your Ma is real common" *(common* as in having the *common touch).*

"She is a wheel hoss, a regular wheel hoss," Elmer Hepler said to me of my mother.

That she was!

As noted in the previous chapter, Mother and Dad lie together in the Elliott Cemetery on Teton Pass above Wilson. Both loved Jackson Hole and its residents deeply; so does their son.

CHAPTER NINETEEN

Tall Tales, Most of Them True

I have this oral history (alluded to in the beginning of Chapter 13) from the lips of the son of one of three brothers, Al, Benn (sic), and Joe Linn, who arrived in Jackson's Hole in 1905, shortly after the Spanish-American War, close to the beginning of the twentieth century. Benn staked out a homestead on the west bank of Snake River just north of the Jackson-Wilson wagon track and, with the help of his brothers, commenced building a cabin.

Their nearest neighbor, Al Nethercott, had coveted that property for one of his children who would homestead it when he became of age. He resented the brothers' intrusion into his plan and, evidently, decided to scare them off. At least, I trust it was not attempted murder.

Al Nethercott, you will recall, had been one of the Mormons' Avenging Angels. Benn Linn had been a Rough Rider, who had ridden up San Juan Hill with Teddy Roosevelt in 1898. None of the four was likely to back away from any sort of confrontation.

One snowy day as the brothers were working on the square of their cabin, they heard a shot, and one felt his hat move. A neat hole had suddenly appeared through the crown of the hat, which was at the time sitting on his head.

"Riled" as Old-Timers would put it, he strapped on his service revolver, mounted his horse, and, because of the fresh snow, easily tracked the gunman back across the road to his cabin. Arriving there, he circled the cabin several times challenging Al Nethercott to show himself. Fortunately, there was no response, or one or the other might have been killed and their descendants would not today be the friends they are.

Since the hole in the hat failed to deter the brothers, Nethercott tried a different ploy: He owned a big dog. Sometime later, when the brothers were away from home, he put his dog into a corral full of the Linns' calves and sicked him on them. Hearing the commotion, the lady of the house grabbed a rifle and went to investigate. Sizing up the situation, she drew a bead on the dog and issued an ultimatum to Nethercott, who, assessing the situation as no-win, crawled through the fence and forcibly extracted his, by now, excited dog.

Was it that incident or the matter of the white team that finally convinced both sides of the foolishness of their feud?

The brothers owned a team of matching whites. Arising early one morning Nethercott was outraged to see through the falling snow his neighbors' white team in his pasture within rifle shot of the house. Suiting the action to the realization, he fetched his rifle and killed the team.

The deed done, he must have had second thoughts, for he went to investigate and found that the team he had shot was not his neighbors', but his own, which, covered with the falling snow, had appeared to him in the light of dawn to be white. Divine retribution? Whatever the reason, as stated above, realization of the foolishness of the feud and where it might lead without either party's wanting it to, brought it to an end; and although that generation never became real friends, the hatchet was buried forever, and their children became neighbors in fact as well as geography.

Collection of the Jackson Hole Historical Society and Museum.

John Cherry, 1890.

John Cherry, most famous of all Jackson Hole storytellers, many years ago wrote a book that he entitled *John Cherry's Lies*. It was published, and for a short while John Cherry was a proud author; however, because one of his stories seriously offended one of his friends, he soon gathered all the copies he could lay his hands on and burned them. Although I have never seen a copy, I know that a few escaped burning, for I know a few old-timers who have seen the little book. I have a standing offer of $500 for a legible copy. It seemed logical to advertise not only with Jackson and Denver book dealers, but in Philadelphia. I have—to no avail. In these days of photocopying, I would give $250 for just a photocopy.

The most famous of Cherry's stories had to do with his pet trout. This yarn was even quoted by Lowell Thomas on national radio as the best Tall Tale he had heard. It has become a classic, told hither and yon as having happened "just the other day."

John's cabin stood right next to a crick in which cutthroat trout were abundant. Cherry enjoyed fish and fishing; and one evening kept fishing after having caught all he would eat that night. He was angling for a big one that he could see from time to time rolling to the surface to inhale a grasshopper. Patiently John put out his fly; finally the big fellow took it and after a brief battle was landed.

Wanting neither to release it nor eat it for the present, it occurred to Cherry to drop the big trout into the rain barrel next to his kitchen. This he did.

The following day, he fed the cutthroat some bread to keep it from losing weight. He enjoyed watching the big fellow rise to the little chunks he threw in; so he kept it there. After awhile, the trout would rise every time it saw John's shadow on the water. Before long, it would stick its head out of water to take a piece of bread or even meat from John's hand. John, who lived alone, developed the habit of talking to the fish. The fish appeared to listen.

As Summer wore on, the water in the barrel began to evaporate. One day John noticed that the trout's dorsal fin was sticking out of the water, yet the fish seemed content and took its daily handout with relish. John began to wonder and to observe how little water would suffice for his pet. In a week or so, the water level reached only halfway up the trout's sides; the trout was breathing air; still it seemed content; it had adapted. John tossed the food to the far side of the rain barrel and noticed that, although there was not enough water for the trout to swim, it kinda crawled across to the food using its pectoral fins like legs. Fascinated, Cherry lifted the fish gently out of the barrel and set it down on the grass. He put more food about a foot away, and the big trout crawled to it.

After that, although the trout slept in the rain barrel, Cherry let it loose around the place while he did his chores. The trout would even follow him into the kitchen for its supper.

All went well until one day John Cherry forgot that the trout was loose and walked across the foot log to his car. As he stepped off the log, he suddenly remembered the trout and looked behind him. Here it came crawling along the log! However, since it had only pectoral fins with which to grip and progress, its tail was unwieldy and flopped from side to side. Just as John turned around, the tail flopped too far to one side, dragging the poor trout off the log.

"He fell into the crick and drownded before I could get to him," concluded John.

Cherry's "cash crop" were hunters, mostly from the East, whom he guided, who loved his tall tales and liked him. They were used to good horses; Cherry's were cold blooded cayuses. One or two of his clients got together and shipped him a black Morgan stallion and five mares so that they would have better mounts on future hunting trips. These are said to have been the first "blooded" horses to come into the Valley. In addition to breeding the stallion to those mares, John crossed the stallion with his mustang mares. The result of both programs was a great improvement in the quality of Cherry's riding stock. Inbreeding once often brings even greater improvement and, in this case, three-quarter Morgans. When John died, he left his stallion to his friend Mose Giltner (Chapter Fifteen). Mose became famous for his horseflesh and started racing his horses in the rodeos. His jockey was Johnny Ryan, whose son, John Ryan, Jr., is today an outstanding local historian whose assistance I acknowledge at the beginning of this volume.

Collection of the Jackson Hole Historical Society and Museum.

When I blow that horn, you dogs better come! John Cherry c. 1900.

Wouldn't it be great to have a little book full of John Cherry's stories? My offer of $500 stands.

A friend gave John Cherry a cat; so he cut a cat hole in his front door so he wouldn't have to get up every time his cat wanted in or out. Well, it turned out that John's cat was pregnant and in due course gave birth to a litter of four. As soon as the kittens' eyes were open, John bored four more holes in his door.

A friend dropping in to visit and noticing the door, inquired of Cherry why he had so many holes in his door.

John replied, "When I say, 'Scat!', I mean 'SCAT!'"

Velarz "John" Hagen told me this John Cherry story:

John said that one day he was walking along a narrow ledge on a mountain when he saw a grizzly bear coming the other way on the same ledge. What to do? John was unarmed. "I thought real quick and shucking my clothes, I dropped 'em down on a bush growing below the trail; then I got down on all fours and went to meet that grizzly. I sniffed him, and he sniffed me, and we both went our separate ways. After all, he wuz a bear, and I wuz a-bare; so we passed without incident."

John had a pet grizzly bear that he had raised from a cub. He kept him on a chain at his cabin when he was little (Remember Ming in Chapter 2?) and made quite a pet of him. A mature boar grizzly will weigh 900 to 1000 pounds, the weight of a middle-sized horse; so when the cub grew up John "taught him to ride," and they'd really sail around the forest. Well, John liked to hunt and the bear liked to hunt, too; so they made quite a pair. John'd grab his rifle, jump on his bear, and off they'd go.

One day when they were out hunting, they came upon quite a group of grizzlies feeding on grubs and berries. Well, John didn't want his bear getting mixed up with that bunch; so he jumped off and emptied his rifle into the air to scare the others off. For a few minutes there was quite a commotion, with bears going every which a way. When they had all left, John jumped back on his bear and started for home; but they hadn't gone very far when he realized he was on the wrong bear.

As a matter of record, John Cherry was one of the guides for Theodore

Roosevelt on his trip through Yellowstone Park. One night after supper as they were sitting around listening to John tell his famous tall tales, one of the Park bears was hanging around the porch begging for scraps as they were wont to do.

Turning to Cherry, who had just finished his story about his pet grizzly, one of the party said, "Well, I'll give you $100 if you'll ride this one." To the surprise of the bear and everybody else present, John jumped off the porch onto the bear's back. Startled, the bear headed for the woods as fast as it could go, with John holding on with both hands full of fur and his legs wrapped under the bear's stomach. They disappeared, leaving TR and his group both amused and concerned.

A few minutes later there was a call from out the darkness, "Hey! Somebody bring me some clothes. That bear and the brush ripped mine all off."

According to accounts, Cherry, though badly scratched from the thickets through which the bear had run trying to dislodge his tormentor, was not seriously injured. $100 was a lot of money in those days.

Although her first purchase of Valley real estate was the Elbo Ranch on Beaver Creek, which she and Gib Scott ran as a dude ranch, Mrs. Elena Barron Hunt lived most of her years on Fish Creek a couple of miles above Wilson on her HS Ranch, where she and Gib Scott raised thoroughbred racehorses, show cattle, and one trout.

Mrs. Hunt—Madame Gibeau she had been when she first arrived in Jackson's Hole—knew and loved fine horses, especially Thoroughbred horses.

Shortly after Dad imported Adanor and she witnessed that a Kentucky Thoroughbred could, indeed, stand the extreme temperatures of a Jackson Hole Winter, she brought in the Valley's second handsome Remount stallion, this one named Boleni. Mrs. Hunt bought some thoroughbred mares, and began raising racehorses for the local tracks. Boleni was handsome, and his progeny had speed; however, he was one of the worst-natured stallions I have ever seen. When you entered his corral, you carried a pitchfork or a club of some sort that he could see.

At a half-mile or longer, Mose Giltner's Morgans were her chief rivals; at a quarter-mile it was my golden palomino mare, Dreamy, who, in 1929 before she was mine, but with me in the "irons," ran the fastest quarter-mile ever run in Wyoming on a curved track: 24.3 seconds. She was, in fact, featured in one of the very first issues of the *Western Horseman* magazine. By the time that magazine was founded, Dreamy was seven years past her prime and I had grown too large to be a jockey; nonetheless, she was remembered. She and I were proud to be featured in the first national magazine for western horsemen—at least I was. Of that I am certain; I have the photo and article framed and hung in our Projects Room on the Rocking H. When I showed it to her, she seemed unimpressed.

Dreamy was a phenomenon. In a long career, she won all but two of her starts at a quarter mile; and in both those races the fault was mine: The pressure was on us; after all, we had set a state record the previous year. Everybody in the grandstands was wondering if we could do it again. I became nervous; my nervousness was transmitted to the great little mare, and she did not get her usual fast starts. We lost. Those were "lap and tap" starts without a starting gate. On the third day of the race meet, after the two losses, my older brother Coulter kept an eye on what was happening. Observing Dreamy a typically prancing, fussing, and even rearing out at the starting line, he galloped across the infield and informed me forcefully that if I didn't settle down, he would beat the stuffing out of me. He was eight years my senior. He could have done as he assured me he would, and I knew him to be a man of his word. In worrying about what he might do, I forgot my nervousness; Dreamy lost hers; we won the race and every other race she ran over the next four years or so. Tragically, Dreamy was barren. What a foal she

Photo by W. Thomas McGrath. Collection of the Jackson Hole Historical Society and Museum.

Elena Barron Hunt leads the parade at the County Fair, 1942.

would have had by Adanor!

When I first raced Dreamy she belonged to Jack Neal. After our record-setting run, Dad bought her and gave her to me. At the end of Dreamy's racing career, Mrs. Hunt offered to buy her; she informed me that the offer was good as long as Dreamy lived. She said, "I just want to have her in a stall at the end of my barn where I can point her out to my thoroughbreds when they become stuck-up. I just want to be able to say to them, 'You think you're good, do you? Well, just look at that little mare down at the end; she beat your mothers, your uncles, and your elder brothers; and she could have beaten you.'"

Was Dreamy the reason Mrs. Hunt began to collect Quarter Horses, the most famous of whom were Nevada Grubstake and Nevada Nugget?

Elena Hunt was a grand fisherlady, who preferred a four-ounce rod and a #14 or #16 dry fly with a barbless hook.

Down behind her barn on Fish Creek there lived and grew a monster trout. For several years, Mrs. Hunt tried to net that fish with her miniscule fly. It wasn't that she couldn't hook him. She did several times; but she could not get him into her net. He was just too large, she said; but she would keep trying. It became a game that the trout seemed to enjoy, too. As soon as she would bring her net in behind him, get his tail in, and start to lift him out of the water, there would come a bit of slack in that line; the trout could rid itself of that tiny hook and with a supreme effort propel himself out of the net and back into his creek. He seemed to laugh at her. A true sportswoman, she loved the game and would not have considered using an outsize net or a barbed hook.

Elena Hunt never did land that trout, but as soon as the word of her death had spread, less sportsmanlike fishermen descended upon her fishing hole behind the barn and went after him hook, line, and sinker. Unfortunately, but inevitably, they were successful. The fish could handle the sportswoman, but not the "meat fishermen."

My Dad loved the following two tales of a hot tempered redhead:

Lawrence Carlson, Louie Fleming, Arch Kimball, Lige Ward, John Miller, and a man we shall call "B." enjoyed a friendly game of poker for a few dollars. Mrs. B. was red-headed, hot tempered, and disapproved of gambling. B. had to sneak off for a game.

One day when the boys were off in a cabin enjoying a game, she came riding up and demanded to know if her husband was inside.

"Aw, you red-headed bitch, go away and leave us alone!" called a voice from indoors.

That lit her fuse. In no uncertain terms she told those men what she thought of them and their gambling. When B. came home that night she demanded that he go to Sheriff Jim Francis and swear out a complaint against his buddy. B. demurred, but the next morning she was still after him; so in an attempt to restore some semblance of peace at home, he went into town and looked up Jim.

"Jim, I've got to swear out a complaint against Arch."

"Hell, B., what do you want to do that for?"

"He called my wife a red-headed bitch."

The Law of Teton County pulled himself up to his considerable height and spoke.

"Well, B., if your wife ain't a red-headed bitch, I never seen one."

Case closed.

One Winter's day B. had got away and was holed up in a cabin playing poker with those same cronies. One of them happened to look out the window and saw the redhead snow-shoeing up the clearing.

"B., here comes your wife."

"Gosh, fellers, you gotta stall her till I can get a head start for home." He rose hastily, donned his sheepskin coat, sneaked out the back door, and webbed away as fast as he could.

The others stalled his wife until she got suspicious, circled the cabin, and spotted the fresh tracks. She took off in pursuit.

As he fled, B. developed a plan.

When he reached home, he dug out a bottle of strychnine he had for varmints and emptied it down the drain. He located the bottle of peroxide. Now he was ready.

When he saw his wife coming toward home, he could tell by her stride she was still furious. He took a swallow of peroxide into his mouth and held it there while he recapped the bottle and put it back where it belonged. Then he lay down on the floor next to the empty strychnine bottle.

As she stormed in the door, she saw him lying there apparently dead. She forgot her rage and ran to him noting that he was twitching convulsively. B. let a little peroxide foam out of the corner of his mouth. "Didn't take enough," he muttered. "Didn't take enough."

"Oh, Honey," she sobbed, "don't leave me." It had been quite awhile since she had called him Honey.

"Didn't take enough." A little more peroxide.

"Oh, Honey, I'm sorry. If only you won't die, you can play cards if you have to."

A little more peroxide and a flicker of an eyelid.

"Oh, Honey, are you gonna be all right? Come back to me."

One eye opened then the other. B. seemed disoriented, but coming around.

Of course, he recovered—slowly, with groans, moans, and shudders—and for a while he "had it made." He could go play cards with his cronies without sneaking out. Yes, for awhile; but he was so proud of what he had done that he just had to tell his buddies in strictest confidence, one of whom just had to tell his wife in strictest confidence, who felt she had to tell the redhead.

B.'s good life ended and his normal life of henpecked husband resumed.

Charley Beck of Whiskey Basin outside Dubois, Wyoming, told the next two tales at our campfire. Although he later published them in his small volume entitled, *The Damned Elk Et My Broom*, they are so very good that I repeat them here:

Shorty worked on a large cattle spread in the Absaroka Mountains north of Dubois, which Charley invariably referred to as "Dubious."

Once a week one of the cowhands rode into town to pick up the mail, which came up on the "stage" (a bus) from Lander. On one occasion when Shorty was the mail rider, the "stage" was late. Lunchtime arrived. Shorty went into the café and sat down at the counter. "Lulu, I came into town without my 'choppers,' so I'll have to have soup or hash, either one," he commented mournfully, visualizing the steak he was missing.

On the next stool sat a stranger in a business suit. Turning toward Shorty and extracting a set of false teeth from the right-hand pocket of his jacket, the stranger said, "Here. Try these; maybe they'll fit."

"Thanks a lot, mister." And Shorty tried them on.

"Sorry, mister, but thanks anyway," he said sadly, dipping the teeth into his water glass and wiping them with his napkin before returning them to the stranger.

The man reached into the left pocket of his jacket and produced another set, handing them to Shorty.

"Ummm! Them's just right!

"Lulu," he called, "hold the hash, and fry me a steak."

Shorty enjoyed his chicken-fried steak and gravy immensely—all the more because he had thought he would have to eat hash.

He wasted no time on talk until he had finished meat, mashed potatoes, and carrots. Then, slipping off the stool, he went around the far end of the counter to the large sink, where he removed and thoroughly scrubbed the teeth, drying them with the large dish towel before returning them to the business-suited stranger.

"Thanks a lot, mister. I can't imagine how I could have been so lucky as to sit down next to a dentist."

"Oh, I'm not a dentist, my friend. I'm an undertaker."

One year at month's end Shorty rode to town to spend his wages. The bar girl who helped him spend them seemed to Shorty to be an angel in disguise, and he plighted her his everlasting troth. She seemed to love him with equal fervor; and when he had to return to the range, she promised that she would write him weekly.

Back with his buddies and the cattle, Shorty fairly glowed when he spoke of his passion for his angel and of hers for him.

The following Saturday when one of the cowpokes brought the mail from town, sure enough there was a letter for Shorty—a letter in a pink, perfumed envelope. Shorty was beside himself! He went off into the trees for privacy and repeatedly inhaled the perfume as memories of delights danced in his head.

Things were almost perfect—almost, because Shorty could not read. How could he hear the words of love undoubtedly contained on the paper within that envelope? If he asked one of his friends to read it, the whole camp would learn their secrets. What to do?

Inspiration struck. Taking his best friend aside into the trees, Shorty confided his problem. Bill readily agreed to Shorty's plan:

Bill sat on a log, opened the letter and read it aloud while Shorty stood behind him with his fingers firmly shoved into Bill's ears.

Who could forget Mrs. George Lamb's tale of riding a bear or her skill in telling it?

"One sunny Spring day, when I was pregnant with Tom, George came in and told me that he had killed a bear up on the bench behind the house. 'It's such a nice day! Why don't you come with me to get him?'

"'All right. Just wait until I get ready."

"I was huge, and webbing up that bench exhausted me. 'You'll have to wait till I catch my breath.'"

"'Say! Why don't you ride that bear while I tow him down the hill?'

"It sounded like a good idea. George fastened his rope around the bear's neck and rolled it over. I sat down on its stomach, put my feet in its armpits, held on to the front paws, and we started off the bench.

"The snow had a little crust on it, and it was easy to pull that bear downhill. In fact, it was so easy that the bear began gaining on George. 'Hurry, George! We're catching you.'

"It's pretty hard to lengthen your stride very much on snowshoes; but George did. The bear was still gaining on him. 'Faster, George! Faster!' We both got to laughing. George was coming off the mountain in gigantic strides. The bear and the mountainous woman were on his heels. Those were good old days!"

Tom was born when expected; but he laughs a lot.

Charlie Peterson tells of the young couple from the Buffalo Valley who headed out in a sleigh one Winter's day for Driggs, Idaho, which in those days before the creation of Teton County was the nearest spot to obtain a marriage license. They planned to spend the night in Jackson.

A few hours later, as they approached Jackson, the young man slid his hand under the lap robe onto the knee of his intended.

"We're getting married tomorrow," she commented demurely, resting her head upon his shoulder. "You can go a little farther if you'd like to."

So he drove on to Wilson.

Charlie adds, "One time I wanted to do something my wife, Hilda, disapproved of. She told me, "If you do that, you won't see me for three days. I went ahead and did it anyway; but she was right:

"The first day, I didn't see her.

"The second day, I didn't see her.

"The third day, I could barely see her outa the corner of my right eye."

When Charlie, who lived on "Poverty Flats" (now the National Elk Refuge), first went to school, he particularly loved recess, a chance to play with other kids; and he habitually hung around outside until the last minute.

One day as the other kids were going into the schoolhouse, he realized that he had better make a trip to the outhouse before going in. He ran for the privy, shucking his heavy jacket as he ran. Opening the door, he threw his jacket toward the seat. It fell in!

Charlie was trying to figure out how to fish it out when the teacher came looking for him. Charlie told her what had happened.

"Come on inside, Charlie," she said, "and leave it."

"But my sandwich is in the pocket!" protested young Charles.

There is an interesting but important distinction between self-denigration and denigration by another. The folks who lived on Poverty Flats named the area themselves; as did the folks on Rabbit Row, where until a recent fire one could see proudly displayed the sign "Rabbit Row Garage." Heck of a Hill is another example.

Poverty Flats named itself in 1918 and '19, when there was no snow, no water, and no hay as a result of which the "dry farmers"—those who did not have flowing irrigation ditches—had to sell their cattle before they starved to death. Those were desperate times. With wry humor those ranchers proclaimed that they lived on "Poverty Flats."

Of course it's an entirely different situation when the belittling nickname comes from outside.

Mr. Schwabacher must have fished 300 days a year; he would lease fishing rights on any good trout stream. He enjoyed telling about the day he came upon a young fellow from Idaho fishing one of his stretches of Fish Creek.

"I'm sorry, young fellow, but this is private water. You cannot fish here."

"Oh, that's okay. Old Man Schwabacher gave me permission to fish here."

"I am Old Man Schwabacher."

"The Old Man Schwabacher who gave me permission to fish here didn't look like you."

For years those of us in Jackson's Hole who had telephones were on party lines. So far as many people were concerned, listening on the line was no more of an invasion of privacy than would be listening to a message some woman in town was calling across her fence to another.

Particularly for those folks who could not get out of the house much, the party line was radio, television, and newspaper.

Mrs. Mike Yokel, Sr., particularly enjoyed calls to Dr. Huff, for she was interested in her neighbors, and in medicine; and she had a treasury of home remedies. One day when Dr. Huff came out to the Bear Paw to treat Dreamy, he was still laughing. He had been in telephone conversation with a patient whose child was ill. As the doctor stated that he would leave a prescription to be filled at Porter's Drug Store, he heard a snort, and Mrs. Yokel broke in

"Doctor, a mustard plaster will take care of that just as quick as those fancy medicines and a lot cheaper, too."

Yes, Doc Huff would take care of horses or dogs as needed. There was no veterinarian within a hundred miles. Dreamy had somehow sustained a bad puncture wound. We did not have trailers back then; so Doc drove out to the ranch three times to tend her. He was the first person we knew who bought a pair of oversized balloon tires for his Buick. Because of the dirt roads and the speed Doc drove, we could almost tell by the dust cloud when he left town; and we could have the dressing removed and hot water on hand when he arrived.

I cannot recall who told me the following delightful story in the Fall of 1995:

The transplanted Easterner had purchased and moved into a place on the Upper Gros Ventre. He had telephone service, an eight-party line, which rendered his New York business calls anemic, thanks to all the eavesdroppers. One day, when he received a particularly important business call, he could barely hear. Frustrated, he addressed the party line:

"Ladies, this call is very important to me, but I can barely hear. If you will all hang up, I promise to call you back when it's over and tell you all about it."

He was gratified to hear the clicks and resultant increased volume of his line as his neighbors hung up. Yet, when all seemed to have hung up, things still didn't sound quite right.

"Lulu," he demanded, "are you still on the line?"

"No," came the response followed by a click.

John Cherry may have been the most famous of all Jackson Hole story-tellers, but there are a good many of us who have tried to fill his boots.

We had fun with dude kids, spotted tree squeaks, side hill gougers, and water ouzels.

When you ride in a lodgepole pine forest, you often hear a squeaking caused by two pines rubbing together in a gentle breeze.

"There's one of them spotted tree squeaks," Ike or Slats would comment.

"Spotted Tree Squeak? What's that?" some kid would inquire.

"Wal, they're a little reddish brown animal that's near extinct, but we have 'em in these woods. Keep a sharp lookout for one. They're real shy and duck around the back of a tree whenever they see a man. See! There's one now."

"Where? I don't see anything."

"They move real fast. He was right up there where those two trees cross."

Two more pines would rub together in the breeze and squeak. "There's another one. Now watch for him."

"Aw, you're just kiddin' us. There's no such thing."

"Yes, there is. Didn't you just hear two of 'em?"

The greatest fun occurred when some kid convinced himself that he had, indeed, seen one. "Yeah. I saw him, Ike!" But most kids weren't that gullible until shown a water ouzel. The name itself sounds suspect, and the little bird is found only around mountain streams; so most of our guests had never heard of ouzels.

So we would tell the kids about water ouzels, and the skeptics would say, "Sure. Just the way there are spotted tree squeaks."

"You bet. Exactly the same: both are rare, but both can be found in Jackson Hole." And you'd take the kids up Granite Canyon.

A water ouzel, or dipper, is a little brown bird that walks into mountain streams and feeds off the bottom as he washes downstream. After a few yards he surfaces, climbs out on a rock, shakes himself, bobs a couple of times and flies back upstream to begin his search again. They are remarkable little birds not much larger than a wren and completely unflustered by the roiled waters, which must toss them about under there.

In the lower part of Granite Canyon one can usually find ouzels; so we would take the kids up there. After they had seen ouzels for themselves, we'd catch them searching the treetops for spotted tree squeaks.

Then they were ready for side hill gougers, those peculiar little wombat-like creatures which have lived and grazed on the side hills for so many centuries moving always in a clockwise direction in the northern hemisphere, and counterclockwise in the southern, that their right (uphill) legs are considerably shorter than their left (downhill) legs. They are good eating for a desperate man, and are easy to catch. You just hide in some brush till one comes grazing toward you. When he's close, you jump up in front of him. He gets so alarmed that he whirls and starts away from you; but his right legs being so much shorter than his left, he cannot keep his balance going counterclockwise; so he rolls down the hill. If you are quick and on the ball, you can catch him before he gets up. But be sure to stay on the right side of him, so that if he does get up before you get your hands on him, he'll fall again.

Bert Charter, riding his fence line in Spring Gulch, came across a wagon, the team tied to a rear wheel, and a family having a picnic. They were cooking over a small fire. So far, so good; however, as he drew near, Bert noticed that one of his fence posts was missing and was, in fact, the fuel for the fire.

The picnickers said nothing; Bert said nothing. He rode up, dismounted, walked over to their fire, picked up their axe, walked over to the front of their wagon, cut out about four feet of the wagon tongue, sharpened one end of it, walked over to the spot from which his fence post had been removed, drove the piece of wagon tongue into the empty posthole, stapled the three strands of wire to the new post, returned the axe to the fireside, gathered his reins, mounted his horse, and rode on checking his fence.

"I never said a word, an' they didn't say nothin' neither."

It's a good thing they didn't. They did not know that they were dealing with a former member of Butch Cassidy's Wild Bunch.

One day, Bert met his friend "Butch" Lloyd on the street. They stopped to chat. "Butch, I don't like to complain, but that piece of meat you sold me last week was so damned tough I could hardly chew it."

"Hell, Bert, that was my milk cow. You wasn't supposed to *chew* it; you was supposed to *suck* it."

Bert Charter had trained getaway horses for "The Wild Bunch" (Butch Cassidy's gang). Bert maintained that he had never participated directly in a holdup, but always had relays of horses ready for the gang to make their getaway. In later years, Bert was a respected citizen of Jackson's Hole. His ranch was the one in Spring Gulch currently owned by the Cliff Hansen family.

No native of Jackson's Hole believes that Butch and Sundance died in

Central America as depicted in *Butch Cassidy and the Sundance Kid.* Why? Because many of them saw and spoke with Butch in the early 1930s. Butch was terminally ill, but while his strength was still sufficient, he drove his old Ford from point to point visiting old gang members to say good-bye.

In the 1930s, '40s, and '50s, everybody in Jackson Hole knew and respected little Bob Crisp. Bob was one fine cowboy—be it on a ranch or in a rodeo arena. He was one of the best bronc riders of his time. He won a lot of money in the biggest rodeos of the day: Madison Square Garden, Cheyenne, Walla Walla, Pendleton, Denver, Fort Worth. The National Finals Rodeo had not come into being while Bob was young enough to compete.

In rodeo Bob was always either in the money or bucked off, for he was a wild rider who took chances. Many a time I watched him ride broncs; never did I see him play it safe. He sustained many broken bones, but he won quite a bit of money—enough to pay for medical repairs. There was no medical insurance in those days.

Along with the purses he won, came silver-and-gold belt buckles; but Bob Crisp always wore the same buckle of sterling silver surrounding an old silver dollar. "Why," I asked him, "with all those beautiful buckles you've won, do you always wear that silver dollar?"

"'Cause Butch Cassidy give it to me.

"I was just a kid when I heard that Butch was over at Bert Charter's. I wanted to see and meet him; so I rode over there. There was a bunch of older fellers I knew talkin' with a stranger. I eased over to them and listened. The stranger, of course, was Butch.

"The more I listened, the more I wanted to meet the man; next thing, I decided I'd just have to have something that belonged to Butch. What did I, a kid, have that I could swap him? He had a better pocket knife than mine; I had seen that when we was whittlin'. Well, I had a silver dollar in my pocket; so I asked him if he would trade dollars with me. He did. I worked for Harry Harrison on the Circle H, and he set it in this buckle for me. I have never worn any other buckle since that day except as one was presented to me and I felt I had to wear it for a little while."

As the reader might surmise, I decided that I wanted that Butch Cassidy buckle when Bob died. He had no wife or children—only one brother, Claude; and he wasn't a cowboy.

Bob spent his last years in a nursing home in Idaho Falls. When I heard news of his death, I went to Claude and offered to buy that buckle, promising that I would leave it to the Jackson Hole Museum when I was through with it.

"Jack," said Claude, "I don't know what happened to that buckle. You know he wouldn't have parted with it while he was living, but it wasn't in his things when I went over to collect them right after I got the word that he had died."

Bob had probably told once too often his tale of meeting Butch Cassidy and exchanging dollars. I'd bet that one of the male attendants at the Idaho Falls hospital has Butch's dollar.

Margaret and I have a biography of Butch Cassidy written by his sister. On the flyleaf is this inscription in Bob Crisp's hand:

"I knew Butch Cassidy. He was my friend.
Bob Crisp"

"World's Champion Beer Drinker! That's what he was," declared Bob Crisp, who was noted for understatement and never known to exaggerate anything. "He got into a beer drinking contest in the Log Cabin and drank 96 glasses of beer without even gettin' up." There was a multitude of witnesses. The drinker was Wilford Neilson, County Attorney and Editor of the *Jackson's Hole Courier*—and prosecuting attorney in the Vick Henrie Trial of 1933. He did not reach his goal of 100 beers, but can you even imagine

Photo by R. R. Doubleday. Collection of the Jackson Hole Historical Society and Museum.

Bob Crisp hits the dirt, c. 1938.

anyone drinking 96 glasses of anything? True, the glasses were neither masskrugs nor pilsner glasses—just normal bar glasses. But 96!

Of course, Wilford practiced. Frequent practice was required if he were to reach his goal, and those practices altered his boyish figure until he appeared especially constructed for his feat. He was a walking barrel; his belt was longer than he was.

Once a year Wilford entered the Fifty Yard Fat Men's Footrace at the County Fair, and could he run! I think he held his breath for the entire 50 yards, for at the finish line he looked apoplectic and gasped for breath in great, heaving, noisy sobs. I fully expected him to die on the track, but he didn't. He died at home, tragically blind from diabetes.

I suppose his death wasn't as sad as it might seem because, while he could, Wilford enjoyed life: he liked his work as County Attorney; he liked his newspaper; he loved his family; and he loved drinking beer with friends.

Was his a wasted talent? Perhaps at the end. At the beginning, he was a young sheepherder in Star Valley with a lot of time on his hands. To relieve the tedium, he began to study the law via correspondence courses. He was 17 years old.

By the time his 19th birthday came, he felt he was ready for the bar exams; however, he was informed that he was too young, that he must wait a couple of years. Wilford retreated, law books in hand, studied, and challenged the ruling. Neither he nor the authorities could find legal support for their stand. Wilford took the examinations and became at 19 the youngest man ever to pass the Wyoming Bar. Has there been a younger since? Not that I can determine.

Toward the end of his tenure as County Attorney, Wilford remarked to Clifford Hansen that all the other attorneys in town were taking continuing courses in the law in order to keep abreast of things. "But I don't want to go back to sheep herding," quoth Neilson with a grin.

Talents? Lots of them. Wasted? Some of them.

The World's Champion Beer Drinker and the youngest man to pass the Wyoming Bar. One and the same! What had his two claims to fame in common? Bars.

J. D. Kimmel owned the Jenny Lake Store. His clerks were sisters, Anne and Nell. His girth almost challenged that of Wilford. One evening a carload of boys drove up to the store and began playing the nickel slot machine. The problem was that they were using a nickel with a hole in it and through the hole a string with which they retrieved their nickel each time they pulled the handle. Such a device was known as a "hickey." They were having so much fun that they were noisy and drew Nell's attention. She was a large and impressive woman. When she saw what they were doing, she reprimanded them severely as they took off with their ill gotten gains.

Angry, Nell reported the incident to Kimmel, adding that they had departed headed south. J. D. pulled his Colt .45 semi-automatic from the desk drawer where he kept it, and stuck it into the waistband of his trousers, where it was completely hidden by his ample paunch. Hurrying as fast as he could to his Cadillac, at great speed he also headed south. Catching up with the miscreants, J. D. forced their car onto the shoulder of the road and got out of his Caddy. As he walked to their car, he heaved up his paunch and extracted the .45. "Gimme back them nickels!" he demanded.

A true story as recounted with great delight by J. D. Kimmel, himself, with embellishments by Nell.

Joe Singleton of St. Anthony, Idaho, was eight years old the evening he neglected to put up the second rail on the corral and the bull got out.

His father, thinking to impress his son with the seriousness of his neglect, remarked, "Well, Joe, you and carelessness let him out; I guess you'd better go after him first thing in the morning."

The next morning Joe saddled his old cayuse, took the sandwich his mother had made for him, climbed aboard, and set out to track the bull.

When Joe caught up with him, the bull was reluctant to turn back. Evening was approaching. The eight-year-old unsaddled, staked his horse, and rolled up for the night in his jacket and saddle blanket.

The following sunrise, Joe arose hungry, saddled, mounted, and easily picked up the trail of the bull. Catching up with him, he kept turning him as best he could. A kid on a 1,000 pound horse can't just throw a loop on a 1,900 pound bull and drag him home.

Frustrated, Joe was getting desperate when three or four cowboys came by trailing a herd in the right direction. "Where you headed, son?"

Joe told them.

"Throw that bull in this herd. We're going past your place; and when we go by, we'll help you cut him out."

Gladly Joe let the bull gladly join the herd.

"Boy, you look hungry. Have you had anything to eat lately?"

From pockets they produced the best food Joe had tasted in a couple of days.

Several hours later, passing the Singleton homestead, the cowboys helped little Joe cut the reluctant bull into the corral next the barn. Joe thanked them and put all three rails up this time.

He unsaddled his horse, turned him into the pasture, walked into the house, and announced matter-of-factly, but with justifiable pride, "Bull's back."

Can anyone imagine in this day and age a parent permitting a child of that age to go off by himself? The mother was doubtless worried when night fell and her son was not home. The father probably tried to hide his concern behind, "He'll be all right. We've taught him well and that's a good, reliable horse."

When, many years later, Joe told me that story, he was surprised at my astonishment. "Well, I'd let the bull out, hadn't I?" was his comment.

Joe showed the same tenacity many years later. I suppose it was around 1955. I had strongly recommended Joe for the post of Director of the Horse Program at the Ojai Valley School in Ojai, California. He and the school seemed to Margaret and me to be ideally suited to each other. Over a period of ten years or more we were proved correct.

At the time, we had only a two-horse trailer and wanted three horses at the Thacher School (also in Ojai), where I worked in the Winters; so I asked Joe if he would haul old Kim from Wilson to Ojai when he came. He would. He, himself, had a two-horse trailer—and only one horse at that time.

Out in the middle of the Nevada Desert, Joe's trailer blew a tire. Joe unloaded the horses and tied them to the trailer, as there was nothing else around to which to tie. He got out the jack and commenced raising the trailer. Despite being a great kids' horse, Kim was spooky. He did not know Joe, and the action of the jack handle up and down no doubt alarmed him. When Joe straightened up unexpectedly, Kim pulled back hard enough to pull the trailer off the jack. That crash did it: Kim broke the snap on his halter and took off, tail high, for Wyoming. I know what I would have done, and it would not have been constructive; however, Joe, who had trailed that bull so long ago, wasted no time in cursing. He saddled his horse, took down his rope and set off in pursuit of that d—— Kim, who could just be seen on the horizon. Had Joe been on a horse appreciably faster than Kim, one might have foreseen success; but the two horses were pretty evenly matched, and Kim longed for his Wyoming home. How Joe ever got close enough out there in the middle of nowhere to throw his loop over that Roman-nosed head I'll never know; but he did.

Two days later when he delivered Kim safe and sound, Joe told the tale with a glint of humor and without rancor. "Well, I was the one he got away from, wasn't I?" A true, old-time cowboy. No wonder the O.V.S. kids loved him so. No wonder they still kept in touch with him until he died at 96, in his trailer behind his daughter's home in Arizona.

"Little Joe, the Wrangler, he will wrangle never more . . ." begins the old song.

This I saw with my own eyes:

The hay was wet; there would be no haying that day. Edmund White and Austin Blodgett, two unusually powerful men, were hanging around our barn when it occurred to them to wonder which of them was stronger and how to find out. Hundred-pound sacks of oats seemed to be good equipment.

Each grabbed a sack from the grain room. Each took a sack under each arm and walked off with the 200 pounds. What next? Austin fetched another hundred pound sack. He stood that sack up in front of the other two. Then, picking up a sack under each arm, he leaned forward, picked the third sack up with his teeth and began swinging it like a pendulum. To and fro, at first in short arcs, then longer and longer until with a final swing, he heaved it

Collection of the Huyler Family.

Haying on the Rocking H, c. 1940.

over his right shoulder. Still holding it with his teeth, he walked off with the 300 pounds. I was flabbergasted; Edmund was impressed; yet he did the same thing. Still no decision.

Now another contest occurred to Edmund: see which of them could throw a hundred pound sack farther with teeth and neck only. Each would lift his sack and commence the pendulum swing described above. When he had it swinging as fast and hard as he thought possible, he released his bite as the sack approached its apogee. Each man managed to throw his sack a short distance. Any difference in distance was indistinguishable there in that hoof-marked barnyard. They shook hands and called it a draw.

I was about 35 at the time and a hay hand. I could throw a bale up onto the hay wagon and three tiers above—perhaps five feet above my head. I decided to see whether or not I could pick up a sack with my teeth. It felt as if my teeth would fall out, and I surrendered before I even got the sack clear of the ground.

Edmund White was a black man from South Carolina; Austin Blodgett was a redneck from Oregon. They not only respected each other, they were friends.

Some years earlier I had beheld other feats of strength on the Rocking H. Three of us hands on the ranch were happy that Jerry Vogt, Dad's foreman at the time, had not read *Tom Sawyer* and that we had.

Plumbing had come to the Rocking H, and Jerry had set three of us to digging a hole near his cabin for a septic tank. As has been mentioned previously, the Rocking H lies just upstream and across the Snake River from its confluence with the Gros Ventre River. Eons of Spring floods had laid down layers of rock and gravel. Digging by hand on the ranch has always been especially difficult. We three had been at our assigned task for a couple of hours when Jerry came home for lunch.

"Is that all you've got dug all morning?"

We pointed out the heap of gravel next to our hole. Jerry was unimpressed:

"Hell! I coulda dug that much all by myself in less time than you have used."

Suddenly, thoughts of Tom Sawyer flashed through my mind.

"You really think you could? I've got $15 says you can't finish it by the end of the afternoon."

"Why, that's taking candy from babies! You're on!"

Hiding our grins, we climbed out of our hole and washed for lunch. Each of us was delighted to contribute $5 to keep from having to get back into that gravel pit.

I cannot recall what our chores were that afternoon, but I know that we were smiling as we did them. Jerry finished before sunset; we gladly paid, making sure to flatter him profusely about his strength. There would be other unwanted jobs, and we wanted him to show off on each of them. He fairly bloomed under our admiration.

Dad purchased a new refrigerator for the Foreman's Cabin. Jerry went to town in the pickup to fetch it. We didn't lose even a dollar over this one. We merely commented loudly that it was going to be difficult for us to squeeze through the kitchen doorway with it. We removed the door and noisily began measuring doorway and refrigerator as we slid the latter onto the tailgate.

"Aw, Hell! You boys just stand out of the way and let a man get a-hold of that thing." He wrapped the webbing carrying strap around the refrigerator, backed up to the tailgate, and simply walked into the cabin with that big refrigerator on his back. We were truly impressed and made certain that he knew it.

Then there was a new corral gate. We laid out and built a pole gate on the ground. Before erecting it, we removed the old gate, cleaned the postholes, and heaved the new gateposts into position, tamping the dirt and gravel tightly around each. Now came the heavy work: getting the 15-foot, 18-inch-wide log across the top of the entire gateway. Today we'd use a tractor and skip loader. Then, two of us would have to strap the ends of that pole to our shoulders, then simultaneously climb two ladders and set the holes in the ends onto the pins left atop each post.

We decided what it would be worth to us if we could trick Jerry into doing it for us.

"Jerry, we sure were impressed by your carrying that fridge into your cabin. In fact, we got to betting as to whether or not you could walk this log beam up a ladder and set it in place. We really doubt that even you could do it."

"Why sure, I could if you boys would hold the ladder steady."

"We can do that, for sure."

We drove the pickup truck into the gateway and leaned the ladder against the cab. Two of us stood on the bed of the truck, braced our feet against the opposite side. The third stood on the ground to keep the ladder from "walking." It was precarious because the upper end of that ladder leaned only on air. Positions and bracing rehearsed, we descended to lift the log onto

Jerry's shoulders, where we strapped it with the web moving straps he had used on the refrigerator. Quickly leaping back to our bracing positions, we called, "Ready!" Jerry began his slow climb. The ladder trembled and swayed as he mounted. All at once, our idea did not seem so good. Suppose Jerry fell with that big log on top of him. Just suppose! We put all of our combined strengths into the bracing.

Up Jerry inched. A few rungs from the top he was high enough. Slowly he aligned his log with the pins and backed down just enough to settle it properly. We three breathed sighs of awe and relief.

"A strong man can do just about anything, boys. Never underestimate one."

"Yes, sir." I believe we never addressed Jerry Vogt as "Sir" before or again.

Was Jerry stronger than Austin or Edmund? Could either of them have placed that log atop the gateposts? I'll never know.

Do you believe in water witching? I don't know whether I do or not; however, Margaret saw Austin Blodgett witch, and Margaret is a reliable witness if ever there was one.

It had rained that day, and I had driven Dad to Swan Valley to see a new type of baler.

Where had once stood a washhouse, we had had a hand-powered water pump. The washhouse had been moved to the Bear Paw and the pump abandoned and broken off. Once rural electricity arrived on the Rocking H in 1952, it seemed a good idea to run water to the bunkhouse. Rather than drill a new well, why not find the old one, although it had been abandoned some 15 years earlier? Dad had even offered a reward to him or her who found it. I suppose that all of us had unsuccessfully searched the vicinity at one time or another looking for a buried end of a one-inch pipe. In the yard of a working ranch, much is dragged back and forth: logs, sleds, wagons, sleighs; and the hooves of livestock. When Austin decided to search, he cut himself a forked stick from a willow bush, grasped the angles of the Y with reversed hands—little fingers to the front and knuckles up—and commenced to traverse the area.

The others on the ranch had never before seen a "water witch," so they congregated. Suddenly, Austin stopped. Margaret says that the muscles in his arms corded as the willow seemed to pull hard toward a spot on the ground.

Be that as it may, a bit of digging around with boot heels showed that Austin had found the one-inch water pipe. Could he have stumbled across it previously and saved that knowledge until he could put on a show? Possibly; however, none of the witnesses believes that. All were convinced of the genuineness of Austin's accomplishments. Margaret maintains to this day that Austin's forearms strained and that perspiration broke out on his face as he resisted the pull of the willow for all to see.

Yes, Austin just possibly may have been a fraud; but 15-year-old Tom Walden had never been in Wyoming or set foot on the Rocking H until that Summer day in 1958.

The grease trap from the kitchen sink in our cabin had clogged and backed up. We had to find it and unplug it. The sludge backing into Margaret's sink was a stinking mess. Our son John and I had made sporadic and futile attempts to locate the trap under our front yard. The yard looked like a prairie dog village.

The Walden ranch south of Tucson was larger than the State of Rhode Island. Keith Walden flew Bobbie and their two sons, Tom and Dick, in their Cessna from their ranch to the Jackson Airport, where we Huylers met them.

Arriving on the Rocking H, we dropped the boys off at John's cabin, showed the parents the guest room, and suggested that they meet us on the front porch for a drink as soon as they were settled.

When they joined us on the porch, I apologized for the prairie dog village. Keith's response was, "Why don't you get Tom to witch that grease trap for you?"

"Can Tom witch?" (stupid question.)

"Yes, he's been able to do it since he was a little boy. He's brought in several wells on our ranch."

A few minutes later the boys strolled onto the porch.

"Tom, Mr. Huyler has a blocked grease trap out here. Why don't you witch it for him?"

"Sure, Mr. Huyler." Not, "I'll try, Mr. Huyler." Nor, "I'll do it if I can." But, "Sure, Mr. Huyler." Just as if I'd asked him to pass me the cheese and crackers.

"What kind of line is it? Metal?"

"No, it's that terra-cotta stuff that drain pipes are made of."

"Then I'll want metal. Do you have a couple of extra wire coat hangers and a pair of wire cutters?" What home hasn't? They were quickly produced.

Tom cut the hooks and twists off the hangars and shaped each into a long L. Grasping the short ends in his fists, and holding the long shanks parallel to each other and to the ground, he began to walk across our yard. At one point, the long pieces crossed. Tom made a mark in the dirt with his heel and walked briskly to the fence on the other side of the yard. There he turned about and began again his slow walk with the shanks of the L's parallel to each other and to the ground. At the same spot, they crossed once more.

"Here's the line, Mr. Huyler."

John was standing by with a shovel. Within a minute, he had exposed the line. From there it was easy to sight back along the line to the kitchen and in the opposite direction to follow the line and locate the grease trap.

"There are more things in heaven and earth, Horatio, / than are dreamt of in your philosophy," quoth Hamlet to Horatio.

Indeed, there are!

Cecil is a name that sounds a bit as if its owner were British. This Cecil was every inch a cowboy. Big, loud, gregarious, charming, unethical, he was the "bronc stomper" who could ride, but could not break, Baldy.

One Winter word got around that Cecil was selling elk meat. In the first place, it is illegal to sell game even if it is taken legally. In the second place, according to rumor, there seemed to be an endless supply of elk meat. The sheriff drove down to investigate.

As he arrived at the end of the unplowed road leading to Cecil's place, the sheriff met Cecil coming out on snowshoes accompanying his son and daughter to the school bus.

"Cec, I hear you've got quite a stash of elk meat at your place."

"Who, me, sheriff?" Cecil's big face registered shocked dismay; his blue eyes, innocence.

"That's what they tell me, Cec."

"Well, sheriff, help yourself to my webs and go down and look for yourself." I am sure that he counted on that offer to assure the sheriff of his innocence.

"Reckon I'd better, Cec; but I brought my own webs."

The story goes that the sheriff found several carcasses of elk, moose, and deer hanging from the rafters of that barn.

Cecil was, of course, haled into court.

Winters were tough in those days; Cecil was no longer young; a hundred dollars then was worth a thousand now. Cecil was fined $100. Case closed. Pay the Clerk.

Prepared, Cecil pulled a check from his wallet. To the Clerk of Court he declared, "If you'll write me out a receipt and lend me your pen, I'll write you a check."

The Clerk wrote, passed the pen to Cecil, and Cecil wrote; then the exchange took place.

"Hey!" exclaimed the Clerk. " This check is for just one dollar!"

"I've got a receipt here in my hand for '$100 paid in full,'" declared Cecil with his big grin; and he strode out of the courtroom delighted with his knavery.

So astounded were the Clerk and the Judge at his audacity that they laughed until their sides ached. As the word spread, the whole town laughed. "Old Cecil has done it again."

One Fall morning a rancher down toward Hoback Junction missed a few bales in his field. He had not yet stacked; so the fact that some bales were missing was obvious.

The next morning more bales were gone—not a great many, but perhaps 18 or 20. That night before going to bed, the rancher flooded the swale in front of his gate down near the highway.

The following morning there stood Cecil's pickup fully loaded with hay bales and stuck to the hubs in the mud. The rancher had properly surmised that an unloaded truck might make it through the swale, but that fully loaded it would not be able to make it back across.

What did that rancher do to Cecil? The best possible punishment: He ignored him and his truck. He went about his business as if no truck were there. Of course, he had spread the word amongst his neighbors that someone was stealing hay and they should be on guard. All the ranchers in Jackson's Hole knew Cecil. The word got around, probably spread by telephone. At any rate it must have seemed to Cecil that everybody he knew drove past and blew his horn as he unloaded the bales and put them back on dry land. Did he pay for the bale or two that he broke and spread under his tires? What do you think?

Cecil was truly old when he pulled his last. It was the Summer of 1993. He was living "across the Hill" in Idaho at the time. In his mid-eighties he was still riding horseback when Jackson's television channel featured him in a special. It was impressive. The old man put his horse through its paces, talking all the while via a lavalier microphone.

At the end of the interview, Cec stood in his corral and recited a poem that he called, "Take Me Back to Old Idaho."

Take me back to old Idaho,
Where there's plenty room and air,
Where there's cottonwoods and pine trees,
Greasewood and prickly pear,
Where there ain't no pomp nor glitter,
Where a shilling's called a bit,
Where at night the magpies twitter,
Where the Injun fights were fit.

Take me where there ain't no subways,
Nor no forty-story shacks,
Where hosses shies at autos
Dudes, plug hats, and three-rail tracks,
Where that windin' old Snake River
And the muddy Yellowstone
Make green patches in the badlands,
Where old Sittin' Bull was known.

Take me where there's sage a-plenty,
Where there's rattlesnakes and ticks,
Where a ton of hay costs twenty,
And they don't sell gilded bricks.
Where that old sun-tanned prospector
Dreams of wealth and pans his dirt,
And the sleepy nightherd puncher
Sings to steers and swings his quirt.

Take me where there's diamond hitches,
Ropes, brands, and cartridge belts,
Where the boys wear chaps for britches,
Flannel shirts and Stetson felts.
Land of alkali and copper,
Land of sapphire, jade, and gold.
Take me back to Old Idaho
Let me die there when I'm old.

A reader will note that the word Idaho does not quite fit; nonetheless, it was quite moving to me to hear old Cecil recite them because I had heard an old friend sing virtually those same words many times prior to World War II—only he sang "Take Me Back to Old Wyoming," which fits metrically. I knew the tune and most of the words and had wanted to learn the rest; but Guy Sutton had been gone when I returned from the war. Delighted to hear those words again, I got on the phone and reached Cecil.

We chatted awhile. I congratulated him on the TV spot and asked if he would please send me those words.

"Yeah, Jack. I'll mail 'em to you tomorrow." And he did. They arrived shortly. The poem was titled "Take Me Back to South Dakota." South Dakota fitted the metre. Cecil wrote that he and another feller—not Guy—wrote it "in honor and memory of Casey Tibbs." I well knew that Guy Sutton had sung that song around the Hole long before anyone heard of that greatest of all bronc riders, Casey Tibbs. I smelled a fish. Although Guy never claimed to have written it, I rather imagined that he had.

In 1994, while going through one of my old books of folk songs in preparing for my weekly participation in the Hootenanny, I found the words in Guy's longhand on a piece of Slash G stationery (the ranch near Jenny Lake that Guy managed before World War II). So I had written evidence that Cecil had not written the words.

In 1996, somebody (I am sorry my memory fails me) gave me xeroxed pages 630-632 from I. S. Bartlett's *History of Wyoming*. The writer quotes the song and states that the poet is anonymous, but that one Miss Edith Lehman recited it at the Memorial Day service at the Catholic Convent in Cheyenne on May 30, 1918; so Guy did not write it, either. He never claimed he did; however, the documentation is clear evidence that old age did not cure Big Cecil of his wayward way. Nonetheless, I credit Cec, that charming rascal, with teaching me the words.

Jackson's Hole was a colorful valley. People such as Big Cec and the others in this chapter gave it its color. It would have been a less interesting place without them and their contributions to our oral history.

Fox hunting in Jackson Hole? "Tally Ho!" and all that sort of thing? Yes, and for me one of the happiest mornings I have ever spent. It was Skip Wright-Clark, Elena Hunt's grandson, who invited Margaret and me to join the hunt one Fall day. I had a horse, Hobo, who loved to jump and only refused jumps twice in all the years I owned him. The invitation sounded like fun to me. Margaret would come along on Carleeze just to watch. We were to gather at 6:30 A.M. the following Saturday at the elk feeding ground south of the Melody Ranch. "We'll be there."

The specified morning dawned cloudless. Knowing that the fox hunting set wherever they may hunt are a spit-and-polish crowd, Margaret and I were up at dawn to brush, curry, wipe down, and polish Carleeze and Hobo. Into our trailer and truck by 5:45 and on the road. As we drove we wondered would this be a drag or a coyote hunt? It seemed unlikely that even good hounds would unearth a fox. Foxes are unusual in Jackson Hole.

At the feeding ground we found no one. We unloaded our horses and waited. Tired of waiting, we waited some more. Finally, concluding that we had erred in time or place, we loaded our horses and started the pull back to the highway. Halfway there, we met a convoy of trucks and trailers coming in. Our host, Skip Wright-Clark, was in the lead vehicle. When we met and I expressed our concern, his response was, "Oh, we're too laid back to be on time." We wished he had said that when he invited us.

Back at the feed ground a handsome group of horses was tacked up, and we mounted. I was surprised to hear and see no hounds. The Hunt Mistress was there with her horn; a stirrup cup was passed. Surely someone would soon arrive with the hounds.

The stirrup cup having completed its rounds, Skip produced from his pocket a cap in the form of a fox's mask. Donning it, he took off at a gallop. After a suitable interval, the Hunt Mistress blew her horn; and we set out in pursuit. There are many down cottonwoods in that river bottom. Every log the fox jumped the rest of us jumped. When the fox needed a breather, he dropped to a walk; and the rest of us did likewise. Regaining his breath, the fox took off again, and so did the hunters. It was great fun! We jumped some pretty big stuff over a period of perhaps an hour before the fox permitted himself to be encircled, and together we returned to the starting point to cool out our mounts before enjoying a fine "hunt breakfast."

Brave or foolhardy? There is a line between what is courageous and what is foolish. Sometimes that line is clear and distinct; sometimes the line is a very fine one. Was Bernice Neal brave or foolhardy? You decide.

Have you ever seen two stallions fight? It is a violent, noisy, ferocious, unpleasant, unforgettable conflict.

Bernice Hinesley Neal, daughter of "Dad" Hinesley, was the wife of Jack Neal, my Dad's foreman of the Bear Paw and Rocking H Ranches. They spent summers on the Bear Paw with the dude ranch operation and the rest of the year living in the Foreman's Cabin of the Rocking H. I do not know where Jack was when Bernice heard a terrible ruckus coming from the barn, but he was not in the vicinity. Bernice ran to the barn and found that Bert, our 2,000-pound Shire stallion (photo on page 177) had broken down the gate separating him from Silver King, Dad's paint saddle stallion (photo on page 169); and the two stallions were fighting and bellowing. It was the bellowing which she had heard way back at the cabin.

Over the back corral swirled a cloud of dust; in the corral was a black-and-white, brown-and-black whirlwind of bared teeth, iron-shod hooves and rage.

Out in the open, Silver King might have won the battle, since he was surely the faster and quicker; however, in that rectangular pen, he hadn't a chance against that gigantic, muscular draft horse. He would surely have been cornered and killed.

Bernice grabbed a singletree off the wall as she ran through the barn, and shouting at the enraged animals, waded into them with her single-tree, beating them indiscriminately about their heads until they paid her heed and separated. Can you imagine wading into that melee with nothing but a three-foot stick in your hand?

Bernice drove Bert back into his own corral with her singletree and chased Silver King into the barn, where she slammed the doors.

Courtesy of Bob Shervin.

Jack and Bernice Neal, Foreman and Manager of the Bear Paw and Rocking H Ranches, c. 1939.

After a few minutes to catch her breath and count her lucky stars, she began tending the wounds of both horses. A stallion's bite can leave a serious open wound. By now, out of sight of each other, the rage had left their eyes, and they had returned to their usual, tractable selves, allowing her to doctor their injuries. Personally, I'd have been leery still; but not Bernice Hinesley Neal.

Was she brave, foolhardy, or both? Whichever it was, all of us felt that she had saved Silver King's life.

Spry, 98-year-old Tex Little! As we ate lunch, he sat on a chair away from the tables watching us eat.

We were lunching at the Red Rock Ranch, which once upon a time had belonged to Dorothy Redmond's family (Glenn Exum's Dorothy of *The Brawl at the Jenny Lake Dance Hall*). The current owners of the ranch, David and Deborah MacKenzie, had invited as many old timers as they could find who had once lived along the Gros Ventre and those who were familiar with the area. Margaret and I felt honored to be invited to this elite gathering. A dozen of us had sat around chewing over the Old Days, enjoying each other's company and anecdotes while George E. Brown of Denver, an author committed to writing a history of the Gros Ventre, present and past, taped all that was said.

After a couple of hours had fled past, as time does when people are reminiscing, we were invited to sit down to lunch. Every one except Tex moved to the tables. "I never eat away from home," he announced matter of factly.

His Gros Ventre neighbors shook their heads knowingly and whispered that Tex never did eat away from home, that when he and his wife came visiting, they would accept not even a cookie. "We never eat away from home."

Who is this Tex Little, anyway?

Little Tex Little is the only person I ever heard of who conquered emphysema—or rather he and Dr. Donald MacLeod of Jackson's Hole did.

It was 1939. Tex, working in the Texas oilfields, was plagued by shortness of breath and a relentless cough. He went to a company doctor, who advised him that he had better go see one of the company's specialists. That specialist informed Tex that he had contracted emphysema. Tex sought the opinion of another doctor. The verdict was a death sentence: deadly emphysema. Tex was a heavy smoker. In 1939 treatment for emphysema was even less effective than it is now—no portable oxygen, for example. Tex decided that if he was going to die, he wanted to die hunting and fishing; so he came north to Jackson's Hole.

Here, he checked in with Dr. MacLeod, Jackson Hole's only physician at the time, a fine internist and surgeon.

"If you want to take a chance, I've got a treatment I'd like to try on you," declared Don. "I think it might help."

"I was gonna die anyway," says Tex; "So what did I have to lose?"

"Let's try her," he said to MacLeod.

"Once a month for 4 years he injected me with some horse medicine or other with a big syringe in back between my ribs directly into my lungs. I got no idea what it was; can't remember after 57 years, but it burned like tarnation."

It is too bad that Doc MacLeod and Jessie Lundy (Doc's nurse for years) are gone. Janet MacLeod Moore states that she never heard a word about this miracle cure. I wonder what it was. Some kind of horse medicine, as Tex believes? Or, perhaps, a potion which Doctor Don had tried on one of his many horses for strangles or the wheezes? It seems we shall never know, but the proof is running around like a rabbit. I wish I were as spry.

One day Tex set out to drown a bear. He, with a group of fellow fishermen, was camped in an idyllic spot on the edge of a lake—idyllic except for the fact that a black bear kept raiding their camp, spooking the horses, and stealing their grub. They did their best to chase it away: They threw stones at it, banged on pots and pans, yelled. The bear would retreat temporarily, but then return.

Tex decided that the only way to get rid of the raider was to drown it; so he saddled up his good horse, roped the bear and rode right out into the lake, dragging the bear behind him. He got out there until his horse was almost swimming, but the bear was swimming, too. Finally, in exasperation, Tex threw away his end of the rope and turned his horse toward shore. The bear beat him ashore and took off into the trees, where Tex later recovered his lariat not much the worse for wear and wash.

Photo by Angus M. Thuermer, Jr. Courtesy of the *Jackson Hole News*.

"I was gonna die anyway; so what did I have to lose?" (Tex Little), 1995.

Evidently, the bear

decided Tex and his group were more trouble than they were worth and left them untroubled for the rest of their stay.

At 99 years old in 2001, little Tex scurries around at high speed, and you never hear a wheeze or a cough. But in the last year he has mellowed a bit and he occasionally eats lunch at the Senior Center in Jackson with his friends and neighbors.

Louie Leisinger had a real problem: She was big; she was tough; she was ornery; she was black; she was used to having her own way. She hung around the White Grass Dude Ranch. She thought she owned the place. She visited the ranch kitchen every night. She, a big, black, sow bear, wreaked havoc with the garbage can just outside the kitchen of the White Grass Ranch.

Well mannered bears dined down at the ranch's garbage dump; however, this particular bear was a confirmed nonconformist. For her it was the kitchen garbage can every night. Perhaps she preferred her food warm.

Exasperated by the cleanup called for each morning before the cook could settle down to preparing breakfast for the crew and then the dudes, Marion Hammond, owner of the White Grass, asked Louie Leisinger to do something about it.

Louie was equal to the challenge.

First, he got a heavy steel oil drum and cut one end out of it with a welding torch. Next, he removed the garbage can. He set his oil drum where the garbage can usually stood. Then into his drum he piled enough rocks so that it could not easily be tipped over.

A load of tasty garbage was dumped on the rocks.

Photo by George F. Tilford. Collection of the Jackson Hole Historical Society and Museum.

"Western Hospitality. Huh!"

Finally, Louie threw the end of a logging chain over a pine limb directly above the can; and to it, with the help of some baling wire, he fastened a chunk of granite that weighed 60 to 65 pounds He heaved on his chain until he had the rock suspended only a couple of inches directly above the can. He tied it off there, and all hands waited for dusk.

Sure enough, come dark, they heard the old bear snuffling around outside the kitchen, where Louie and some others were hiding quiet as the proverbial mice.

The bear approached the can and shoved the rock aside so she could get her head into the garbage, which was too heavy to tip over. Of course, the rock swung back and tapped her firmly on the head. Annoyed, she gave it a harder shove; but no sooner did she stick her nose into the barrel than here came the rock and gave her a pretty good whack.

Infuriated, she shoved that rock aside as hard as she could; and, satisfied, stuck her head back into her intended meal. This time, having been pushed as hard as only a bear can push, the rock had built up considerable momentum by the time it came swinging back and cracked the sow such a blow on the skull that for 50 yards on her way out she staggered like a drunk.

Never again did that bear bother the White Grass kitchen garbage can; she joined the other bears down at the dump.

Fred Deyo, the Game Warden, was—as were so many of the old timers—a practical joker. When the National Elk Refuge was first opened to hunters, Fred mounted a circular saw blade on four wooden legs, added antlers, and loaded his contraption into the back of his pickup, covering it with a tarpaulin.

Shortly before dawn Fred placed his dummy in an area of the Refuge closed to hunting. Then he hid in a clump of willows and waited for daylight. As dawn crept over the hills, the sound of a gong reverberated across the Refuge, as hunters' bullets hit the big saw blade. Identifying the mystified hunters was not difficult. Fred earned his pay that day.

A good story was mothers' milk to the old timers, who chewed it over, digested it, and stored it away until encountering someone who had not heard it. A good story was passed from home to home until—as with a folk song—variants evolved and became the story. I got the story from Dr. Weldon Richardson, Jr., Jackson dentist and son of the driver of the sleigh.

In a further effort at accuracy I read it to Judy Clayton, who had in hand her notes from an interview with Weldon Richardson Senior, the sleigh driver, himself:

Late one winter in line of duty Fred and Slim Pendergraft, the warden who arrested Dad in the matter of the sheep, were riding the Gros Ventre trying to herd elk away from ranchers' fields down to the National Elk Refuge. Elk that did not winter on the Refuge presented a serious problem to the ranchers. They stole a lot of hay—hay the ranchers needed for their livestock to survive the winter. In self-defense the ranchers were wont to sic their dogs on the elk that invaded their stockyards.

As he came to Ike Powell's spread, Deyo spotted Powell's dog hanging onto an elk's nose. He was latched on with no intention of turning loose.

"Call yer dog off, or I'll shoot him!" declared Fred and fired one shot into the ground to scare it. That shot didn't faze the dog. He fired another and then took after the dog on his horse.

"You kill my dog, and I'll kill you!" responded Powell reaching into his sleigh for his holstered rifle.

Deyo fired a shot which, although it took off Powell's thumb, did not stop him in his reach for his .30 x .30. Fred fired again, this time hitting Powell in the butt as he leaned over. The bullet exited his upper torso next to a nipple no doubt doing considerable damage along the way. Disoriented, Ike staggered to the side of the sleigh and fell.

Collection of the Jackson Hole Historical Society and Museum.

"You shoulda heard that saw blade ring!"
Game Warden Fred Deyo, 1945.

It was then that young Weldon Richardson and Olin Emery arrived on the scene.

"You'd better get Ike off the ground, onto that sleigh, and into town."

Seemed like a good idea; so the kid was dragooned to drive Powell to Jackson to the hospital on the sleigh mentioned above. Olin rode along to keep Powell from falling off the sleigh, which was just a hay rack.

Weldon was 19 years old at the time, and the kid had a tune going round and around in his head as he drove—a tune he kept whistling as they bumped along until, exasperated, the wounded man groaned, "Hey, kid! Can't you whistle something else?"

Slim must have ridden ahead to alert Doc Huff, because they met Huff on the corner below Boucher's Hill.

At the little old log hospital, Doc cleaned and dressed the wound, sewing up and repairing what he could.

Some time later, as he released Ike Powell from the hospital, the doctor instructed him firmly to, "Take it easy for awhile."

That summer Powell was riding a bucking horse in the rodeo, when the wound ruptured, and he bled to death internally.

Vesta Ward Linn, daughter of Abraham Ward, told me that she was baptized in Fish Creek on a brisk morning in April.

Anyone who has wintered in Jackson Hole, even once, knows that there are still spots of snow on north slopes in April, and some ice clings yet to the stream banks.

The Latter Day Saints practice baptism by immersion. The bishop who baptized Vesta was one of her uncles. The water was icy as they waded into the stream, and breathtaking as he held her nose and submerged her.

As she surfaced and grabbed a lungful of air, she exclaimed, "Jesus! That's cold!"

Under she went again—this time held under until she thought she would drown. "I never swore again," she declared to me many years later.

Charlie Petersen tells of going as horse wrangler on a 11-day hunting trip over into Lower Granite Creek and up the west fork of Crystal Creek with "The Countess" (Cissy Patterson), Cal Carrington, and a camp cook. "It was 1928 or '29."

One night most of the horses got away. Cal saddled one of the others and set out in pursuit. He finally caught up with the truants all the way home, at Flat Creek Ranch. When he brought them back to camp, he had all but one: "Said he couldn't catch mine; so I had to walk for the rest of the trip. Packed my saddle on top of one of the packs, and I hoofed it the rest of the trip. I never let those horses get away again."

"Captain Bob," who advocates legalization of marijuana, asked Charlie Peterson if there was more or less drinking in the Valley during Prohibition. Charlie judged there was less. "Fer instance, before Prohibition my dad, Frank, took a nip of whiskey first thing every morning—and that was it for the day. He did that regular until Prohibition; then he stopped cold. Put the bottle away when Prohibition arrived. We never saw it again. I guess he and lots of other folks had respect for the Law, no matter what the law was."

Would Frank have reinstated his morning nip after Prohibition was repealed? Charlie doesn't know, for his father died in 1929.

That same Frank, by the way, was on the first documented ascent of the Grand Teton in 1898. It was their second attempt; they had tried unsuccessfully in 1897. The photo of the group standing on the summit shows three of the four who summited: Jack Shive, Franklin Spaulding, and Frank Peterson. Frank is the one holding the coiled rope. In actuality, the four men made a point of walking the last few yards to the summit together; however, Billy Owen was not in the photo. He was the photographer.

In the late 1930s "Doc" Reno was the only veterinarian for miles around and he lived in Pinedale.

Photo by William O. "Billy" Owen. Collection of the Grand Teton National Park.

On the Summit (left to right: John Shive, Frank Spaulding, and Frank Petersen), August 11, 1898.

Ken Wesley, Betty, and their teenage son and daughter, Charley and Betsy, hailed from the midwest. After a summer on the Square G, where they had been coached by the Gabbys and Bob Kranenberg, they had leased the old, and now-ramshackle Trail Ranch, just north of the Sky Ranch, which is just north of the White Grass Ranch.

The Wesleys had hired Ted Hartgrave to go onto the old place and make things habitable. He had and they arrived in Jackson's Hole for their first summer on their own. They dug into the ranch chores with a will, but not always a way.

Of course, they wanted to ride. That's what Jackson's Hole was all about in the old days. They loved to fish, and Betty was a fine landscape painter. Expeditions for fishing and for painting were on horseback. The Wesleys acquired five horses: Prince for Ken, Lucky for Betty, Monte for Charley, Shorty for Betsy, and Silver as a spare.

Six weeks later those horses needed re-shoeing. Four of the horses were tractable; the fifth, Silver, was absolutely paranoid in that he did not want anyone to pick up his feet. Neither soothing sounds from Betsy as Ken approached with his new shoeing box, nor a firm grip by Charley had any effect upon Silver. He did not want to have his shoes changed—at least, not by the Wesleys. What to do?

Ken Wesley appealed to Ted Hartgrave, who—even with a twitch in hand—found Silver impossible. Hog-tying Silver seemed the only way, and that is awkward shoeing to say the least.

Enter Doc Reno.

Word of the Wesleys' problem not only spread around The Valley, but evidently had reached Pinedale.

The following Sunday afternoon four men in an old sedan made the 200-mile roundtrip from Pinedale to the Trail Ranch.

The Wesleys heard them drive up; all four of them turned out to see who it was and to welcome them.

"Afternoon, Mr. Wesley. My name is Reno. I'm a veterinarian down in Pinedale. I've come to look at that horse of yours that won't be shod. Would you mind bringing him out here so's I can look at him?"

The Wesleys went to catch Silver. While they were gone, Reno filled a large hypodermic syringe from a bottle he had brought for the purpose.

As the Wesleys came around the corner of the barn with the horse, Doc put the hand holding the syringe behind his back. He walked up to Silver, patting him with his free hand and gradually working himself to the side opposite the unsuspecting Wesleys. One quick motion, and the intra-muscular injection was planted. Seconds later Silver's knees buckled. In another moment he was down on his side, groaning the way horses do when laid down.

At that moment, the doors of the sedan flew open; the three men jumped out; Doc opened the trunk to expose four shoeing boxes. As the Wesleys stood agog, each of the men grabbed his shoeing kit; then each a hoof; and they went to work. In a trice four feet had been rasped; four shoes had been nailed on and clinched; four toes had been dubbed; the men had returned their shoeing boxes to the trunk of the sedan, hopped in, and closed the doors.

"So long, Mr Wesley!" called Doc as he stepped on the starter. "He'll come to any minute now. When he can stand, walk him around for awhile until he seems normal." The sedan sped off on its return trip to Pinedale, probably stopping in Jackson at the Log Cabin Bar so that the men could share the fun they had had.

Flabbergasted beyond words at what had transpired so rapidly and unexpectedly, the Wesleys could only wave goodbye; they were speechless.

That may not have been the best shoeing job Silver ever received; however, it was certainly the most unusual and the fastest.

For what he and his friends did for my friends, the Wesleys, Doc Reno will always occupy a warm spot in my memory.

I am also grateful to this little volume for putting me in contact with Betsy Wesley Shirley after 46 years. Cheri Hartgrave sent a copy to Betsy; Betsy wrote to me care of the Historical Society; we got together in August 2001 for the first time since my father's funeral in the Chapel of the

Collection of the Jackson Hole Historical Society and Museum.

A common method of shoeing a wild one before tranquilizers, c. 1930s.

Transfiguration at Moose in September 1955. Some of the details of the story above come from that reunion.

Shad Hobbs's one-room, one-window homestead cabin still stands—thanks to the Rockefeller family and later to Grand Teton National Park—on its original site. The roof is propped up with many poles since Laurance Rockefeller noted some years back that it was in danger of collapse.

Since that cabin now stands in Grand Teton National Park, and the Park has destroyed, among many others, the wonderfully romantic little Fleming homestead cabin in the mouth of Granite Canyon, I am loth to expose its exact location. More than one Park Ranger is, no doubt, aware of its existence and may have joined with me in a tacit conspiracy to preserve it from demolition by their bosses. It is a good thing to have a few old cabins around to suggest to today's riders and hikers how the homesteaders really lived.

In the Wort Hotel there is a well-known painting depicting a mounted cowboy leading a pack string along a ridge. Man and horses are silhouetted against Jackson Lake and Mount Moran. The painting is really a photograph taken and painted by Harrison Crandall, Jackson's Hole's first full-time resident photographer. In the days before color film, Harrison Crandall, who was a painter as well as a photographer and dance hall musician, often added realism to his beautiful photographs by applying oil paints.

The man in this famous photograph is Shad Hobbs.

I have no knowledge of Shad's background, but the centerpiece of his

Photo by Harrison R. Crandall. Collection of the Jackson Hole Historical Society and Museum.

Shad trailing one of the many pack strings he led into the back country, c. 1927.

cabin was a print of six elegantly groomed and leather-haltered horses standing in line on well-groomed grass, ears up, alertly regarding the artist. In front of them stands a German Shepherd dog, also ears up and also looking at the artist. The title of the picture is *Sunday Morning.*

That scene evokes mystery—mystery surrounding the life and background of Shad Hobbs. It is far-removed from his homestead cabin in the Tetons. In that cabin I might have expected a newspaper clipping of a Remington print, or a Russell—or even a "girlie" picture from a calendar. But no. There was this scene of equine elegance in an elegant setting.

Who was Shad Hobbs, really? He came to Jackson's Hole from Montana and to Montana from Texas, a cowboy through and through; but who were his parents? What is his ancestry? Many a young scion of a noble British family moved to the American west as a Remittance Man. A significant number of those settled in Montana. Was one of those noblemen Shad's grandfather? I wish I knew, for that print intrigues me with its introduction of a non-Western theme.

I think I'll take the print that I have of Shad's picture, and invite my friend Greg the locksmith to ride with me to Shad's homestead cabin. There Greg can pick the lock, and I will nail that print back on the wall in his old cabin. I think it belongs there, don't you?

Courtesy of Betsy Wesley Shirley.

Shad's Pinup Picture, c.1935.

Bob Carmichael thought like a trout; in his later years he even looked a bit like a big bull trout. He had a big undershot jaw, and toward the end, when his emphysema became severe, he moved that jaw like a trout gasping for air.

Bob was the best fisherman and fishing guide I ever saw. He and Fran ate trout a couple of times a day during fishing season. The Carmichaels lived on the edge of Snake River just below the bridge at Moose. Fran was Postmistress and storekeeper for Carmichael's Tackle Shop. Frequently, I would arrive with Bear Paw clients shortly after Bob and Fran had finished breakfast. The odor of fried trout wafted our way as we opened the door.

In those days, no one had ever heard of Catch and Release. Perhaps consuming so many trout gave him the ability to think like a trout. Anyway, he did.

When fishermen went out with Bob, he carried a coffee pot; a frying pan; a spatula; an old pot inside of which was a stack of aluminum plates and a bag of utensils; salt and pepper; a head of cabbage; a jar of mayonnaise; a few slices of bacon; and, of course, a sheath knife. On the river when lunchtime arrived, Bob would declare, "Keep on fishing this stretch, and I'll go over there and catch our lunch." Never, "I'll go over there and see if I can catch our lunch" or ". . . try to catch our lunch." He was confident that he could and would, and he did. I never heard of his failing. He thought like a trout: "If I were a trout where would I be lying in this water at this time of this day? What would look tasty to me?" And he'd step across to a side channel and catch enough fish for lunch for himself and his party. He would even start his fire on a gravel bar and snuggle his coffee pot into it before beginning his casting. In those days boiled river water was deemed satisfactory if the river was clear—and why fish when it was roiled?

Driftwood was plentiful on the gravel bars and made a hot, almost smokeless, fire. Trout caught and cleaned, the pan went on and the bacon went into it. While the bacon—and then the trout—fried, the sheath knife was applied to the cabbage in the pot, mayonnaise, salt and pepper mixed in; and, voilà! Lunch of trout and cole slaw.

One would think Bob would get tired of that same meal day after day, but he never seemed to.

Frequently as he fished, Carmichael would see some kid fishing with a grasshopper or spinner. Instead of reprimanding the kid for lack of sportsmanship, Bob would ask him how he was doing and would give him a fly to try as well as a bit of advice on its use. I saw him do that time and again. If the rogue fisherman were adult, Bob would usually pass him by as too set in his ways to proselytize.

I was along as photographer when Margaret Sloan slipped. Almost surely she would have drowned had it not been for Bob Carmichael's skill and resourcefulness.

People drown in the Snake every year because they wade in over the tops of their boots or waders.

Margaret's near fatal accident occurred one day in 1936. Bob was guiding John and Margaret Sloan from Nashville and the Bear Paw. I was along to photograph. To every departing guest, we gave a box of colored slides of him/her/them in action. Those slides were a good investment. Shown to friends and neighbors at home, they were good advertising. My Margaret, Dad, and I carried cameras every day.

That afternoon after the usual lunch of trout, cole slaw, and coffee, Margaret Sloan stepped into a hole above her boot tops and fell. She yelled for help as the current began to move her away. John dropped his rod and sprinted across the gravel bar toward his wife. Bob Carmichael was standing nearby. "Stop!" he shouted to John. "Take off your boots!"

We could hear the screaming of his reel as Bob stripped line and false cast to get distance. Within seconds he dropped his line over Margaret's shoulder on the upstream side so that it would not drift away from her. "Grab my line!" he instructed. She did as he dropped the tip of his bamboo rod until it pointed at her. "Wrap the line around your hand!" She did, and he stopped her drift.

By this time John was out of his boots and into the water, where he gave Margaret his hand and pulled her onto the bar.

Bob Carmichael was a resourceful fisherman! How many other guides would have thought so quickly of an alternative to John's running into the water and possibly compounding the problem by getting swept downstream himself? How many other guides could have laid that line so neatly across her shoulder? How many would have had the presence of mind to lay, not the leader, which would have broken, but the line on her shoulder—and on the upstream side? That required a nine-foot overcast laid down precisely.

Writing of Bob Carmichael's split-bamboo Hardy rod reminds me of his shop, where he sold only fine fly rods, reels, flies, creels, and boots. Graphite rods were yet to be invented; fiberglass rods were not sufficiently sensitive to suit Bob. His favorites were the Hardy rods, and he once showed me why. He touched the tip of his rod to its butt! Try that if you have sufficient faith in your fly rod. I never dared try it with my Phillipson.

In those days we used only gut leaders sunk by running them through a bit of clay, which all of Bob's disciples carried in their vests. Despite the many improvements in nylon leaders, I still prefer gut. It seems to me that they lie straighter and sink more easily; but I cannot find any to buy.

Before becoming Jackson Hole's premier fishing guide, Bob had been a newspaper reporter. He told us about it one night as we were driving back from a fishing trip on Yellowstone Park's Lewis Lake.

We had dropped off one client at the AMK Ranch on Jackson Lake. He had invited us in for a drink after a long day. Colonel Jed Roe of San Antonio had one. As driver, I declined; young "Buzz" Roe was too young to imbibe. Perhaps Bob thought he should compensate for our seeming lack of social grace. He had a couple.

A half hour later as we approached Jenny Lake, Bob was a bit garrulous and maudlin. I think Colonel Roe was a bit embarrassed to have his young son witness his hero in his cups. At any rate, trying to ignore Bob, Jed was looking out the right-hand, rear window at the dark silhouette of the Tetons against the sky.

"Colonel, don't look at those mountains," urged Bob.

The colonel ignored him.

"Colonel, don't look at those mountains!" This time louder.

A third time, almost weeping, "Colonel, don't look at those mountains!"

"Bob, what's the matter with you?"

"Colonel, I had a good newspaper job until I came up here on a fishing trip and looked at those mountains. One good, hard look and I was hooked. Now look at me: I'm just a fishing bum. Colonel, don't look at those mountains!"

It's true: Those mountains have hooked thousands of us, who have never broken free. Chances are that every reader of this book is among the hooked. Certainly, I, my wife, our children, their spouses, and our grandchildren are. Are you?

I wish that just one more time I could hear Bob's voice on the line, "The Gros Ventre is gin-clear, and they're lying in there long as ropes. Let's go fishin."

THE END

Postscript:

When and how did I decide that no matter where I might wander or work, Jackson Hole was my home? I felt it throughout my childhood. Because of my early puniness, the Depression, and Dad's rheumatoid arthritis, we spent Winters here, there, and the other place; but from 1926 we always came back to Jackson Hole for the Summers.

When World War II ended, I was in China. Frankly, I didn't spend much time thinking about home as a spot. Home was wherever Margaret and the son I had never met were. I tried to meet them in Hawaii, where they were living with Margaret's parents. No dice. Most American shipping was still in the Atlantic; so I had to fly back over the Hump and board a ship in Calcutta bound for the Suez Canal and New York City. Frantically, I cabled Margaret, "Go immediately Greenwich!" How she and Johnny got there would make another and interesting book. Thirty-six days after departing Calcutta, the U.S.S. *General Mann* docked on the Jersey side of New York harbor. That night thanks to information from the Red Cross via Addie Donnan, Margaret, Johnny, Dad, Mother, and I were united. What an incredible time! But where was home? I didn't care until one April day in 1946.

In April 1946, with the war just behind us, we drove from the East Coast, where I had been discharged, to Jackson Hole. Passing through Cheyenne, we stopped long enough for me to purchase a Stetson.

As we rounded the curve by the Jackson Hole Hereford Ranch [Porter Ranch], the spot on that road where you first see the Grand Teton, without premeditation, I pulled over and stopped on the shoulder. Getting out of the car, I instinctively removed my hat as I declared to my Margaret, "I'm home!"

Just Passin' Thru

by Howard Ballew

Rode up to Wort's old livery barn;
Steve Callahan was there . . .
Said, "Get down, son; chat awhile.
And give your horse some air.
Might just as well spend the night."
I said, "Thanks, that's what I'll do.
Tomorrow I'll be headin' out,
'Cause I'm just passin' thru."

Well, sixty years have come and gone,
And things are not the same.
What hair I have is snowy white;
Left hip kinda lame.
My campfire coals have glowed and cooled,
Ashes scattered to the wind.
The trail is getting shorter now,
Not too long to the end.

But I love old Wyoming,
And I'm leaving her to you . . .
Enjoy . . . but treat her gently, friend,
'Cause we're all just passin' thru."

INDEX

D

I

X-Y-Z

The Jackson Hole Historical Society and Museum

The Jackson Hole Historical Society and Museum is a not for profit organization devoted to the collection and study of local and regional history. Its mission is history education. In the late 1980s the museum, founded in 1958, and the historical society, begun in 1965, merged to form the organization we have today.

To support its mission, the historical society and museum offers a wide variety of educational programs, from walking tours of historic downtown Jackson, to history excursions and book discussion groups, to customized programs for local and regional students, and wide-ranging historical exhibits. The organization also publishes scholarly works on the history of the region. These activities help local residents and visitors to the area celebrate our western heritage and reflect on the future of our community.

In addition to a permanent artifact collection, the historical society and museum features a research library with archival and biographical data, maps, oral histories, and a photograph archive. The collections showcase material culture from prehistoric times, the story of the fur trade, and the presence of Native Americans. They also explore the people that settled the valley, how they used the land and natural resources, and the traditions and culture that they developed.

The Jackson Hole Historical Society and Museum is a 501(c)(3) charitable organization. For more information about the historical society and museum, please call (307) 733-9605 or visit the website at www.jacksonholehistory.org.